CW01507934

SIDEWAYS...
TO VICTORY!

To Jim. He knows why.

Sideways... to Victory!

ROGER CLARK

in collaboration with

GRAHAM ROBSON

MOTOR RACING PUBLICATIONS

MOTOR RACING PUBLICATIONS LTD
Unit 6 The Pilton Estate, 46 Pitlake, Croydon CR0 3RY

First published 1976
This edition 1998

Copyright © 1976 and 1998 Roger Clark, Graham Robson
and Motor Racing Publications Ltd

All rights reserved. No part of this publication may be reproduced,
stored in a retrieval system, or transmitted, in any form or by any
means, electronic, mechanical, photocopying, recording or otherwise, without prior permission of Motor Racing Publications Ltd

British Library Cataloguing in Publication Data
A catalogue record for this book is available from the British Library

ISBN 1-899870-27-X

Typeset by Zee Creative Ltd, London
Printed in Great Britain by MPG Books Ltd, Bodmin, England

Contents

A *tribute*
by Graham Robson

To signal the passing of Roger Clark, Britain's supreme rally driver, this is a limited reprint of his best-selling autobiography. It is more than 20 years since I helped him shape it, but his words still tell us so much about the man. Roger was in his prime in the 1960s and 1970s – the Golden Age of British rallying. He was so talented, and so important to the period, that I think it absolutely right that we should have changed not a word of what he said in the original edition.

For at least 15 years, Roger Clark set standards by which every other British rally driver had to measure himself. He won the RAC International rally twice, in 1972 and 1976, and until the 1990s he was the only British driver ever to have won a World Championship rally. In his driving style – exuberant, yet with fearless flair and balance – he was a complete natural. Those asking him to analyse his methods were always met with a smile, 'I dunno,' and total indifference; as far as Roger was concerned, he had been born with rallying genius and had never questioned his ability.

The gulf between his own unique approach and that of today's highly-trained drivers was immense. He was a natural indolent, and far happier to share a drink with his friends than carry out further practice runs. Although he was always indulgent with sponsors (he starred in TV adverts for several of them), he was a stranger to physical exercise or to a rigorous sportsman's diet.

It was in a whole variety of Ford Escorts that he became the most successful British rally driver of all time. Starting with victory in the 1968 Circuit of Ireland and ending with a win in Cyprus in 1980, he won events on every continent. Clark and his increasingly fast Escorts were made for each other, and in a car set up to maximise his talents he was always flamboyant, yet always in control. At his peak there was no British driver, and very few Europeans, who could match his pace and versatility.

His public adored him, and they would flock to any of Ford's ubiquitous sporting road shows, quizzes and forums of which he became a resident star. Though naturally taciturn, he could be a relaxed, anarchic and very amusing public speaker. His MBE, awarded in 1979, was no more than he deserved, as a great public entertainer.

Foreword

A FOREWORD should set the scene for a book and, the publisher hopes, grab potential readers with something dogmatic and preferably controversial. How's this for starters:

Roger Clark is the finest rally driver Britain has ever produced.

Perhaps not controversial enough, because although Ian Appleyard, Peter Harper, Paddy Hopkirk, Donald Morley, Pat Moss and others were all great drivers, none dominated his or her British opponents quite so convincingly as Roger.

My first contact with Roger was at a Forum aeons ago when a man who introduced himself as Mr. Clark said that if I had any sense I would immediately sign up his son who had got a bit of talent. Team managers get similar advice all the time so I made appropriately soothing "don't call me I'll call you" noises and promptly forgot all about it. It was one of my biggest mistakes because in order to work with Roger I eventually had to change jobs and join Ford.

But having started by praising Roger, let me add that at times I have found he can be an awkward sod. We have had many arguments, but have always got over them, partly because we have one strong bond — we are both in love with his gorgeous wife Judy. Although we have worked together now for several seasons, it is only in the last couple of years that I really feel I have got to know Roger. It may not be generally known, but early in 1976 he came closer to leaving Ford than ever before, because of a tortuous misunderstanding by several parties. Typical of Roger, he got the warring parties together for a totally frank discussion and sorted things out so that the link is now stronger than ever — and still without a formal legal contract, because Roger is a man of his word. I suspect that he is perhaps more sensitive and shyer than he shows on the outside; he is certainly shrewd and a great tactician, which must drive his opponents mad because they never know how much he has in hand.

Nostalgia is always dangerous, but I feel that the last ten years have been the greatest rallying has ever seen. I have been lucky enough to achieve two of my rally ambitions, Hannu Mikkola being the first European to win the Safari and Timo Makinen taking a hat-trick on the RAC, but I have one more, which is that Roger should stay with Ford until he retires and win the RAC Rally again before doing so. Certainly he has the skill.

Finally, I welcome this book not just because it is about a great driver, but because it is going to save me a lot of letter writing. I get an average of four letters a week from hopefuls asking how they can drive like Roger Clark; now at last there is a book which tells them.

Stuart Turner.

Introduction

I CAN'T PRETEND that settling down to write this book has been easy. I suppose I've always been much better at doing things, particularly driving fast cars, than I have about writing things down. There is no way that I could ever have been a successful co-driver; my friends and my colleagues know this very well by now. But I have had a very exciting and rewarding career in motor sport, and at last I have been nagged into collecting my reminiscences together.

Most people get around to writing their autobiographies when they reach the end of a career, but not me — Oh no! True, I've been driving all sorts of competition cars for nearly twenty years, and I've been involved in International rallies since 1961, but I'm certainly not yet ready to stop. Even if rallying is supposed to be a brave young man's sport, at the ripe old age of 36 I don't feel as if I am past it yet. My team-mate Timo Makinen is as old as me, and I'm sure feels the same.

In fact, with Ford having phased in a new Escort my rallying has now taken on an interesting new slant. But have I really driven the same basic type of rally car for the last eight years? Time has certainly slipped by, but in a pleasant and absorbing way. If Pat Moss hadn't called her own book 'The Story So Far' I might have been tempted to use that title for myself. But as for retiring — certainly not. I will stop rallying when I stop enjoying myself, and when I begin to realise that I'm just not good enough any more; I hope that that will not happen for quite a long time.

At least I don't have to start by making excuses. I may have driven some rather odd cars many years ago (the ones I prepared myself!) but since I got involved with Ford I couldn't complain on that score. My first big rallying win was in the 1964 Scottish — in my own Ford Cortina GT — and with the exception of two hilarious years as part of Ralph Nash's factory Rover team I have been loyal to Ford ever since. It must have been a long stay at Ford, because I have served under four different competition managers — Alan Platt, Henry Taylor, Stuart Turner, and now Peter Ashcroft. They have always managed to provide me with fast, strong and competitive cars, and it would have been very difficult to make excuses for *not* winning unless it was my own fault. Time and again I have been amazed by the strength and durability of these cars — particularly the last of our original Escorts, which had 235 bhp engines — when I recall the humble beginnings from which they have been developed.

Since I started serious rallying, I have seen a fantastic growth in interest, with more and more competitive cars, more and more rally-promoting countries, and vastly more spectators. I find it very difficult to understand the attitude of some newspaper, radio and TV people, even motoring writers, who still regard rallying as a rather grubby, fringe sport, without much spectator interest. I can only think that these people have never been out to watch.

There's no doubt that nowadays rallies are big news, and usually big publicity for a lucky sponsor. One effect of this has been the building of faster and more specialised cars, and an explosion in costs. I now smile at the memory of the little work I did to my own Cortinas in 1964 and 1965, which were still good enough to win for me! Fortunately, there are now plenty of firms who recognise the publicity value of successful rallying, and they are often keen to be associated through sponsoring a good car. I owe a lot to my sponsors — particularly to Cossack, who have given me such splendid support recently — and there are products from inside the motor industry without which we simply could not compete.

None of this would have been possible, and there certainly wouldn't have been a book to be written, if it hadn't been for my co-drivers. He will be horribly embarrassed to read this, but I have to say that without Jim Porter, who has bravely and silently occupied the other seat in my cars since 1960, it just wouldn't have happened. More's the pity that Jim wasn't with me when I won that RAC International Rally in 1972 that I will always count as my finest effort.

His capable deputy then, and several times since, was Tony Mason, who also understands me well. Where was Jim? Actually he was organising the event, so I couldn't really offer him the co-driver's seat, could I?

When introducing a book like this, there are so many people to be thanked, and I'm bound to forget some. But I must add that I couldn't have managed without Goo's encouragement, or without her wifely patience and forbearance in the weeks and weeks I have had to be away from home. I also needed a different sort of co-driver when it came to making sense of all my memories. I've known Graham Robson since the days when we were both doing club rallies (we even found time to win the 1965 Welsh Rally together), and I'm glad he has been able to sort it all out. If there are any mistakes in the Appendices (I never write anything down, remember?) you had better blame him!

Looking back, it has all been very exciting. Ford have sent me to some odd places, and I've done some very strange things. I never thought that Hong Kong was big enough to hold a rally until I went there, for instance, and I really must have been mad to drive a Fordsport-sponsored powerboat in the *Daily Telegraph* 'Round Britain Race'. By comparison, driving across the Canadian prairies, flat-out across the the Khyber Pass, dustily through the Australian deserts, or straddling the tracks in a railway tunnel at more than 15,000 feet in South America sounds fairly normal.

But there have been incredible happenings along the way. Rescuing Goo from the unlit gloom of a public loo in a Nairobi nightclub . . . sending a cable to Stuart Turner complaining that I couldn't find a girl at 17,000 feet in Peru, and would 17 girls at 1,000 feet be OK instead? . . . helping my mechanic Norman Masters when he had been bitten in a most embarrassing place by a fish while swimming in Africa . . . sitting in the bottom of an emptied swimming pool in the good ship *Chusan* (on its way to Perth from Bombay in 1968) after the captain had objected to rally drivers' antics . . . having my 1970 World Cup Rally Escort shunted in Uruguay, and hurting my bottom on the instrument panel . . . making the Cossack hair preparation TV commercials . . . spraying the crowd and the reporters with victory champagne at York in 1972 . . . it's been a lot of fun.

Desford, Leicestershire   *Roger Clark*
January 1976

11

Chapter 1

Getting started

ANYONE WHO OPENS this book and expects to learn how to win
International rallies may be disappointed because I don't think I can
tell them. But I can write about the things that have happened to me
on events as long as the London-Sydney Marathon or as short as the
local autocross, and recall some of the events that helped me to
develop my rally career.

I start with a big problem. I can't think of a single good reason why
I should be able to drive cars the way I do. I don't have any famous
motor sporting ancestors, and before Stan (my 'little' brother) and I
started to do local driving tests and autocrosses there was no hint of
fast motoring among the Clarks, and my father was quite nonplussed
by the whole thing. Any skills I may have developed in rally cars down
the years are purely mine — there were no 'sideways Clarks' before
me, which may encourage a lot of young hopefuls to persevere with
their own driving.

There's another thing to emphasise. In recent years, people like
Paddy Hopkirk, Vic Elford, Tony Fall and myself have had our
successes, and we're all very proud of them, but in the beginning,
when none of us had two pennies to rub together, we were no different
from all the other clubmen. None of us was born with a 'silver spoon'
in his mouth, and we certainly didn't make a start in motor sport by
the grace of wealthy sponsors. In fact, for all of us, it was damned hard
going at first. Some of my early rally cars were almost disgracefully
simple and sketchily prepared, and at times I was extremely lucky
even to finish. But I was fortunate in that I chose the right cars at the

right time, and they held together on those events where team managers were watching.

I hope a lot of clubmen will benefit from my thoughts and reminiscences, and I hope they won't find my experiences too specialised. I have driven nothing but Fords since 1966, which means that I'm now well into my eleventh year with them, but I make no excuses for being loyal to the same factory team for such a long time; I have always got on well with everyone at Boreham, and besides, they've been building the best cars throughout that time! It is also true that I haven't had to prepare my own rally cars since 1965, nor pay for them to be maintained, but I hope this won't be held against me, either.

Well now, to start at the beginning. I was born on August 5th 1939, which, for those who have a thing about dates, was just a couple of days before the last race meeting at Brooklands, and less than a month before the outbreak of World War Two. Incidentally, it was a Saturday, so I was all set to disrupt the family weekends even then! However, I don't suppose my parents gave it a thought that by christening me Roger Albert they also donated me the initials R.A.C.!

There might not have been any sporting tradition among the Clarks, but at least we were in the motor trade. My father was in business with his father, operating a local company as bus proprietors. There were between 25 and 30 buses in all, based on the same St Johns, Narborough, garage premises that we still operate as a Renault franchise, but the outbreak of war soon put a stop to the business as the buses were all requisitioned for use as troop transport.

The Clark family had to do something for the war effort, so they turned the empty garage into a machine shop for the duration. The most important products, as I remember them, were gun barrels. After the war, the family were keen to get back into bus operation, but when they saw the state in which their precious vehicles were returned from forces use they were shattered. What was left was a series of wrecks, and it nearly broke the old man's heart. No matter what the compensation would be — and it wasn't going to pay for the same number of new buses — it just wasn't on to start up the bus company again.

So there they were, back with an empty building and a living to earn. Apparently father then decided to settle down, and stubbornly — without any new cars or even the franchises from which to sell them — he started to build up a garage business. Buying and selling cars (and more often in those days just repairing the pre-war models which had to be kept going) was to be our future.

For me at first there were six years at the local Enderby primary school, then five more at Hinckley Grammar, before I finally rebelled against school life and left to make my way in the world. It was going to the Hinckley school which forged links with the town which I still retain; I lived in Hinckley after my marriage until 1974 and Brian Gillibrand now runs our Renault dealership in the town.

I suppose I must have been quite bright to get through the old 'Eleven-Plus' exams and go to the grammar school, and before I left I had chalked up five GCE 'O' Levels, but nobody could have said my heart was in it. I had become steadily more interested in practical things since I was old enough to toddle round the war-time machine shop and get my hands (not to mention face, clothes and hair) dirty. I drove my first car when I was only eight years old — not on the roads, of course, but round the two-acre field we owned, which was tacked on to the back of the garage premises. You only have to look at my successful GCEs — among them Maths, Physics, Wood and Metal-work — to realise which way my interests were developing; there was just no way I could get absorbed in things like literature or languages.

I didn't decide to leave school until the morning I should have returned to the sixth form after the summer holidays. I just didn't get up, didn't go in, and for me that was the end of schooling. Instead I went into the garage, presented myself to my father, and said I wanted to start working for him. Like everyone should, I started at the bottom — serving petrol, greasing cars and being an odd-job boy, which certainly didn't do me any harm.

School to me hadn't been so much about learning as about winning things. When I should have been studying I was more interested in swimming, water polo and rugby, and if I wasn't playing sports and games I was always making things with my hands, shaping metal and wood, and especially making model aeroplanes. Interestingly enough, cars never entered my head in my early teens, but by the time I was ready to leave school I had great ideas about being a businessman, of going into industry. I was a very good draughtsman, and thought it would be an easy step from there to being a designer. Whenever it came to metalwork or woodwork, mechanical and engineering drawing, or most practical things, I was usually top of the class.

Nobody taught me to drive. I taught myself over a period of time at the garage. There was always the field behind the premises, and a ready supply of 'bangers' and old machinery for me to hurl around without going out on to the road. I also got a lot of experience in moving customers' cars around, and generally getting the feel of driving. But that wouldn't get me through the test, so as soon as I was seventeen father made me take a few conventional lessons.

I passed the test, first time, within a couple of weeks of my seventeenth birthday, and I've had a contempt of the test ever since. Driving instructors make a very good job of teaching anyone to pass a test, but certainly not how to be a good driver. I couldn't drive any better after the lessons than I could before them, but at least I had all the flashy hand signals and the Highway Code mumbo-jumbo which was necessary to get the vital 'pink slip'. Similarly, I don't think even a more concentrated type of test necessarily proves anything, and I certainly don't need another flashy badge on the front of my cars, which explains why I have never bothered to go in for any of the more high-powered courses.

But I'm jumping ahead a little. Before then the garage had managed to get its first franchise — to sell the Renaults that are now its main activity — and a few years after that we captured Ford as well. I was as interested as any red-blooded young man in having my own transport, but I hadn't any money of my own, and the family refused to buy me a car. In the end I finished up using a very secondhand E93A Ford Thames van, which we had taken in part-exchange from the local grocer against a new van.

But what about motor sport? Well, at first I wasn't very interested at all, and it was only after several customers, members of the Leicestershire Car Club, had encouraged me to join them that I started to go along to their meetings. I wasn't very keen at first, and I suppose I only did it as a form of basic public relations, but then I started to go on one or two of their events, found it was good fun, and was hooked. . . .

Probably the very first event I did was a driving test, or even a short evening rally, but it now seems so long ago that I simply don't recall where. I do know that I didn't win, but I also know that interest became enthusiasm almost at once, and after that there was no stopping me. In those days — and we are talking now about the late 1950s — people didn't specialise at all. The cars were general-purpose

15

machines, which were used as work-a-day transport between events. I had to use whatever cars father wouldn't miss, or whatever he would least mind being bent a bit, and I would enter them in rallies, trials, driving tests, or for autocross meetings. I didn't go as far as sprints or races, but that possibility was already in view.

The old E93A van wasn't any good at all — no way, with that front suspension — and the strange little fibreglass-bodied Ford Special I used wasn't much better. I got a bit fed up with bangers after a time anyway. The Ford Special once blew four cylinder-head gaskets at me on a journey from Narborough to Silverstone to watch a race meeting; I changed them all at the roadside, not too difficult with a side-valve engine, but it was the middle of the afternoon before I got to Silverstone and I was still faced with the journey home!

It had to be something more modern, and it turned out to be a Ford 100E van. Yes, another van, but this one was basically as good as the 100E Anglia saloon, then a well-thought-of rally car, and we did all sorts of things with it. In theory it was a garage demonstrator, or at least a working van, but I still managed to fit an Elva overhead-valve conversion, a second gearbox behind the normal one (a six-speed gearbox? I think so, and it seemed the right thing to do at the time), and a lot more. It was certainly an all-happening Ford van, and after we had put side windows in it, probably without telling the Inland Revenue people, we even raced it at Brands Hatch, Mallory Park and Silverstone.

By 1960 I was a regular club tearaway, with a definite leaning towards autocross. Even then I liked the sensation of getting a car sideways, whatever the surface, and making it do what I wanted it to do. You didn't need much power to get sideways on mud and grass then, because we didn't have such things as radial-ply tyres, and certainly nothing as exotic as mud and snow treads. It was a really well-off and serious young competitor, too, who had special knobbly tyres for autocross.

But I wasn't getting anywhere in rallying. I used to enjoy them, certainly, but I seemed to have a succession of bum navigators who were either sick because of my driving methods, or got me lost down muddy tracks. I couldn't control the results by my own efforts, and this wasn't my idea of the thing at all. Incidentally, at one stage I was still using a van without windows, and therefore was supposed to be speed-limited to 40 mph on the public roads, but I didn't stop to

16

worry about that, and I was never pulled up for an interview by the men in blue. It wasn't that we were penniless, but vans, apart from being so much cheaper to buy (about £300 for a Ford 100E, I think), were also a lot lighter than the same-engined saloon and very easy to repair.

It was around 1960 that I first met Jim — Jim Porter, who became my navigator/co-driver that year and who still occupies the other front seat today, in 1976. Were we made for each other? Well, no, that would be soppy, but we came together by chance at a Leicester-shire Car Club function, and haven't quarrelled seriously since. It was pure chance. I was sick of driving my boots off and getting nowhere, while Jim had been navigating for a man who had lost interest.

We paired up in the autumn of 1960, and in the first year drove the most astonishing vehicles. There was the Thames van, of course but we also borrowed mother's Anglia once and bent all four wings, there was a 'frog-eye' Sprite that I borrowed from Stan, then Renault Dauphines, and of course the inevitable Minis. Jim keeps a record of all the events we have done together, and if you look at the table at the back of the book you'll see why he pleaded with me to close the book in July 1974. Anyway, his records show that we had our first win together in the Leicestershire Car Club's Sturgess Trophy event, in February 1961, and that the car was a Renault Dauphine Gordini. We then tried a more ambitious event, the Eastwood Rally, held in Derbyshire, and brought ourselves down to earth by finishing a resounding 33rd, but after that things got better.

Apart from the rallies, I kept on thundering round and round muddy fields in autocross, which I thoroughly enjoyed, and Stan and I even went to the trouble of building a special car for the purpose. It wasn't that special — that is, unless you could call a very disreputable-looking Triumph TR2 which we cobbled up out of the wreck of two pranged cars, a Special. Stan and I both used to drive, and I must say I always had to work very hard to beat my brother. Stan, three years younger than me, was then, and still is, a very capable driver — whatever collection of reactions I inherited from somewhere have also shown up in his abilities.

I once asked Jim if there was a time when this 'sideways to victory' driving started to show up, but he couldn't pick out any exact time. It was always obvious during 'off-road' events, but certainly not at first on road rallies. Let me be quite clear about this, if I had tried such

17

methods in the Dauphines and Dauphine Gordinis we had in 1961 it would have been pure suicide! The Dauphine, though very successful in Britain for some years, was a very fragile little car, and if you shunted it, it crumpled very quickly. Its handling was very precarious — no, let's be honest, it was dangerous if provoked. When you got a Dauphine sideways and the high-pivot swing-axles got well knotted up, there was no stopping for correction — you were either off the road, or on the roof, just like that.

Could be that's where I learned quite a lot about precision, positioning and car control, because without them we would not have been competitive. I always tried to drive a Dauphine geometrically, and keep it in line wherever possible. Anyway, I had to pay for my own preparation and repairs (bend 'em at weekends, mend 'em during the week) and I didn't fancy a lot of body-crumpling accidents.

So here I was, with a very competent co-driver, parents who, while they didn't exactly encourage me in my motor sport, didn't disapprove either, a job which meant that I was at least equipped to keep my rally cars up to some sort of level of preparation, and something that could now be called a burning ambition. No-one could call the Dauphine the best car for the job, but as Clark's of Narborough sold them I was really bound to use one. But what were my ambitions?

There was never actually a time when I sat up in bed, or in the workshop, and said to myself, 'I'm going to be the country's fastest rally driver'. It just doesn't happen like that — or it didn't happen to me. Vic Elford used to say that once he'd started driving instead of co-driving, his ambition was to be a Grand Prix driver, and as we all know he eventually made it. That sort of thing never spurred me on. I was always content to be best at whatever branch of the sport and at the level at which I was competing. Things just gradually developed in an inevitable pattern. When Jim and I thought we were good enough at our existing level, we struck out to the next level. It took time, months certainly, before we could struggle through to the top of that grade, but once we had made it we were ready to push on again. Jim and I won our first event in February 1961 at 'Closed to Club' level, but it wasn't until March 1962 that we won our first 'Restricted', the Eastwood Rally. After that we never won a National event until 1971, though a lot of other things had happened in the meantime.

In fact I gained my first factory drive on the strength of nothing better than some 'Restricted' wins, and one class win in an International event. I'm not saying that every aspiring works driver can be as lucky, especially nowadays when the competition is probably a lot stiffer, but there's no doubt that ability still counts for a lot. It would not have been any use Jim and I notching up a string of unimportant victories in piddling little rallies. The trophies on the mantelpiece might have looked good, but the factories wouldn't have been interested.

But once again I am stepping ahead. By the spring of 1961 we were getting a bit cocky and ambitious. On the strength of that first win, we decided to have a go not just at National events, but at our very first International rally. The rest of the British scene could wait — Jim and I were going to Ireland for Easter!

Chapter 2

Getting serious

IF I WAS trying to write a motoring fairy story, I would say that I went to Ireland as a novice and returned as a star. I'd like to say that — but I can't. We started our very first International rally on Good Friday, March 31st, but for all the impact we made it might just as well have been April 1st. It all seemed very important at the time, and we tried hard, but our reward was a resounding 51st overall, and 12th in our class.

But the Circuit of Ireland then was not the same as the Circuit we know today. There were no high-speed special stages and no rough stuff. Like the Scottish Rally used to be, and even the RAC had once been, it consisted of lots of tricky navigation, driving tests scattered all round the country, and a lot of spare time in which to enjoy ourselves. I had heard about Irish parties before . . . now I *knew* the Irish to be the undisputed experts at this sort of thing!

Driving tests were still one of our specialities, but this was the time when everybody except me seemed to have a Mini for their rallying. There must have been 50 of them in our class, and though none of them were Coopers (not yet announced) we were still quite satisfied to beat so many of them. And guess who won? Would you believe Paddy Hopkirk in a works Sunbeam Rapier?

Jim and I came back to Leicester feeling rather subdued. We wanted to do a lot more rallying, but in what sort of a car? If the family had been running any business other than a garage we wouldn't have had a problem, but for all the obvious reasons I had to use a make of car we sold. That meant a Renault or a Ford, and there was nothing very inspiring from either of them. Renault were very proud of their Dauphine Gordinis (I don't think any of their directors had ever driven one, otherwise they would surely have altered that dangerous rear suspension!) and in terms of performance they were the best of a dull bunch. The alternative was a Ford, a 105E Anglia looking more promising than either a Classic or a Zephyr.

But there seemed to be no way that I could beat the Minis in either a Renault or a Ford, and I was beginning to investigate ways out of the dilemma when the family suddenly solved it for me — they bought another garage with a BMC agency! The new place, about a mile away from our original premises, was little more than a filling station with a franchise to sell Austins, but it meant that I could now get my hands on a Mini without feeling in any way disloyal, and have a real go.

Not that I had solved the money problem. As newly-appointed Austin dealers we soon learned about the Mini-Coopers which would be sold in the autumn, but muggins was still having to pay for his own motor sport, and couldn't afford a brand new car anyway. In the end I settled for an old Mini which had been traded-in against something better; it was probably an original 1959 car, because it certainly had all the water leaks and other little problems for which the early Minis were famous. The nicest thing about my first rallying Mini was its registration number — XJU 2 — which would be worth as much now as the whole car cost then, I should think! I wonder if the car and the number plate are still around?

As we contemplate the splendidly prepared cars we drive today — factory drivers and privateers alike — we may look back scornfully at the junk we had to use years ago. Perhaps we've all been spoiled, I don't really know, but rally cars were so much more simple then. My Mini was. I didn't do anything to the engine, and I didn't think the suspension needed any work, either, so apart from screwing on a few extra lights and cobbling up a steel sump guard of my own design, that was how we went rallying.

That Mini was a revelation. It was the first car I'd ever owned which handled the way I wanted a car to handle, and I think I really began to develop the 'sideways Clark' technique with it. I was so delighted with it that I put in an entry for the RAC Rally that autumn. Naturally the RAC had a much bigger entry than the Circuit, and was a lot more important, too, but my own performance didn't change

21

much — this time we finished 52nd!

But that poor little car — I don't know how it survived. No-one had made. any secret of the fact that that year's RAC would be different from all the previous ones. There would be a road section of more than 2,000 miles, only a single night halt, and a lot of new-fangled and rather mysterious things called special stages. So naturally I took along a bog-standard 850 Mini, and had three people in the car. John Oldham joined Jim and I for the trip, and we set off to do the most gruelling event I had yet tackled.

It's worth harking back to that famous RAC Rally of 1961 in some detail, because it was the event that finally fired my enthusiasm; it was also the first British rally to be of real international importance. For many years after the war, the RAC Rally had been a pretty lousy event, run by people who were more interested in gracious living than in hard motoring; it had lots of boring road mileage and precious little competitive driving. The regulations and penalties were often screwy, too. The final straw came in 1958 when snow and ice caused wholesale blockages, and wide-awake co-drivers discovered that they could actually score fewer penalties by missing out controls altogether and staying on schedule, rather than flogging all the way round.

The result was an organising revolution, with Jack Kemsley taking over as the chief organiser. From 1959 the RAC Rally has never looked back, and most people agree that it is now the most popular rally in the whole world. A lot of the younger element in British rallying just don't realise how much they owe their enjoyment to Jack Kemsley. Before he changed the face of the RAC Rally, there was no such thing as special-stage motoring in Great Britain, and there were no events where we could escape from the limitations of a 30 mph road average without breaking regulations. Jack introduced closed-road sections for the 1960 RAC, which I didn't do, but the 1961 event was the very first to use forestry stages, and it set a startling trend.

None of us were quite prepared for what we had to do. We knew that these special stages would be on private ground, that the roads would not be surfaced, and that the average speeds would be set a lot higher than 30 mph. But we didn't realise how rough everything would be, and we certainly had no idea where these frighteningly new stages would be sited. There were only about 20 of them, but all were quite long, and I think we had more than 200 miles of stages even in that first year. But names like Radnor, Keilder, Culbin, Newcastleton and Dovey were all new to me — in fact they were new to everybody.

It was rough and tough, and almost everybody had trouble. Graham Robson, who was then a member of the Rootes factory team, tells me that every one of the works Rapiers was delayed when loose stones got into the engine compartment and threw off fan belts or opened radiator drain taps — even a team as experienced as Rootes had not expected such things to happen. On reflection, I think the biggest mistake we made was to travel three-up, for the event wasn't anywhere near as tiring as I had feared; the extra weight of a third crew man in the back was a big handicap to performance though, and the poor chap must have had a most uncomfortable ride.

In spite of it all, we enjoyed ourselves thoroughly. It was one of those stupid years when there was also a penalty for car body damage (on a rough road rally with special stages — whatever next?), so I was relieved that I didn't go off the road. But the front suspension kept falling apart, and we gave up trying to patch up the exhaust system when it fell off in Scotland; we kept going without one for another day, and finally had a complete new exhaust fitted back at Narborough, which was very conveniently near a control at Mallory Park. Clearly times have changed — nowadays I wouldn't be allowed to do a single stage without an effective exhaust system.

With all that, and a car floor which was peppered with flying stones and soon started to leak, it was a miracle that I had any interest or any money left to keep going, but the attraction of the forestry stages had really got me. It was like taking part in one very long autocross; there should be no chance of accidents caused by meeting cars on public roads, and I didn't have to rely as much on Jim for navigation expertise.

I wasn't quick enough to have any hope of winning my class on Internationals with that Mini, especially as the bloke who usually won the small-saloon class was a big Swede called Eric Carlsson! But I was sure now that I could drive just as quickly as many people who were finishing in front of me, and I knew I couldn't prove that unless I had something a lot nippier to pedal.

With that in view, our new Mini-Cooper demonstrator at Narborough didn't really stand a chance. Once I had driven it I knew that it couldn't waste its time giving test runs to local customers. I'm sure father didn't realise at first just what sort of treatment this

23

Cooper would have to put up with, and he certainly couldn't know how much its appearance would change in the next couple of years. After all a demonstrator car is supposed to look like those you see in a catalogue, and should perform like those you are hoping to sell. Well, OK, for the first few events it did look like most standard Mini-Coopers, with extra lamps and a sump guard just like the old 850 Mini, with the glass in the windows and a normal front grille, but I soon found the money to put a modified cylinder-head and other bits into the engine.

That was all very well, but next I modified the original grille, and masked the front with a light-alloy panel to keep water out of the engine's ignition system. The undersides, too, started to look a bit battered and frilly. Once I had put the registration number up on the bonnet all resemblance to a demonstrator was lost, and the car was a rally car pure and simple. The registration number? It was 2 ANR, new at the time and on its first rally car, but I formed a sentimental attachment to it and it has been on my own rally cars and personal cars ever since. At the time of writing it's on the garage Porsche, but before then it graced my Lotus Elite demonstrator.

We had started out full of hope with the Mini-Cooper, for it was supposed to have been developed by the Cooper racing people, and in 1962 it did well for us. But later on, old age and hard driving got the better of it, and before it was finally sold, early in 1964, having been rallied all round Britain and in the Tulip Rally, too, it must have let me down at least a dozen times with a broken transmission. If it wasn't the clutch it was a drive shaft, or a diff, or a gearwheel, or something else. Mine, at least, simply wasn't strong enough to stand up to a lot of rallying.

Mind you, the Cooper had a hard life; apart from an intensive rallying season I took it to any driving test, autocross or even sporting trial that I could find. Any weekend that passed without my doing at least one event seemed like a waste, and I wanted to broaden my experience in all types of competition. Jim and I had set our sights on the local East Midland area rally championship, which didn't leave time for many larger events. But I still found time for three 'home' Internationals — the Circuit, the Scottish and the RAC — plus the last of the navigational London Rallies, then Britain's most important domestic event.

The Mini-Cooper's rally career had started on a high note. I prepared it in the February, and took it out on the Eastwood Rally in March, which it promptly won. It was all very exciting — my first 'Restricted' win, in which Jim earned his keep because the Eastwood always had a reputation for being very navigational, and because there was a lot of snow on the roads — and guess who couldn't afford any studded tyres? We finished second in another area qualifier just a few weeks later, and before the end of the season were placed in four more rallies, including a brace of outright wins in Rolls-Royce Motor Club and Dukeries Motor Club events (no, the Dukeries didn't go anywhere near the forests in those days!).

It's nice to look back on those days now, especially when everything I do now seems so professional, expensive and serious. Driving through the Andes on a World Cup Rally, or across the plains of Canada, couldn't have been a more remote possibility then; the East Midlands and its championship were all-important.

Even in the bigger events there was a lot of encouragement. We just missed a place in the top ten of the London, but on my second trip to Ireland there was great rejoicing. I didn't have to come home and talk about positions in the '50s' any more — this time we took fourth overall and won our class! The Mini-Cooper was absolutely ideal for the Circuit of Ireland. It was quick enough for the night-navigation sections (and Jim now had a year's experience to help him point me round those very strange Irish ordnance maps), but more important was its ideal handling and response for the driving tests that helped to settle everything.

Paddy Hopkirk, Cecil Vard and Bobby Parkes got there before me. Doing as well as this was satisfying enough, but I also discovered that at this sort of level all sorts of people begin to pay you money for success if you've made sure to 'sign up' with them beforehand. That sort of thing hadn't actually happened to me before, but I could see that I was going to like it if it happened more often!

So I was looking forward to my first attempt at the Scottish, even though Jim couldn't come with me (exams or something equally as boring, I believe). In his place I took Roger Marriott, who hadn't been with me before. The Scottish looked very much like the Circuit, but with more sun, even more night halts where we could enjoy ourselves, and a lot of those new-fangled Forestry Commission special stages which I had liked so much on the previous year's RAC.

The special stages, the Mini-Cooper and me all seemed to go well

25

together, and even though the car was still barely modified above standard performance, the only car I couldn't quite catch was Andrew Cowan in a works-prepared Sunbeam Rapier. Right up to the last day I was holding second place, and looking forward to more lovely bonus money — then Roger got me lost! It was one of those simple navigational errors where you take the wrong road, but in Scotland where there are so few chances to cut across to retrieve an error (especially in this case as Loch Ness was in the way!) it can be disastrous. We lost something like 20 minutes at the next time control, and that was that. From second place we dropped to 'nowhere'.

The RAC Rally wasn't much of a week, either. There were a lot more special stages — 38 of them, twice as many as in our first year — and the format was much the same, but the Mini-Cooper disgraced itself by wrecking its transmission for the first time.

But at least 1962 wasn't a complete disaster — we managed to win the East Midland Rally Championship after all, which was good for local publicity. It was also a year, incidentally, when I got my first sponsorship deal, and I didn't even have to ask for it. The Capital Finance company came along and offered me £200 — a princely sum to me when I was probably scratching for £20 to buy a modified cylinder-head — so that they could use my name in their adverts in the Leicestershire area. One of the adverts I still have says 'Roger Clark is a man obsessed by cars, and whose recommendation really means something to keen motorists. He recommends Capital Plan . . .' I don't know about being obsessed about cars, even then, but I was quite happy to recommend one finance company ahead of another if they paid me to be loyal. And we *did* put all our garage's hire-purchase business their way . . .

I suppose that winning the area championship was a great spur to my ambitions. It was still only a fairly modest achievement, of course, but after all I was still having to pay for my own preparation and rebuilds, and up to then I hadn't really gone far to look for bigger successes. Outside the Midlands, Jim and I were still not well-known, though I was very pleased with that success in Ireland.

By now I really had the big-time rallying 'bug'. It wasn't something that exploded suddenly inside me, but a feeling that developed over a period of time. Jim and I progressed from club events to area, then on to Nationals and Internationals, without feeling out of our depth at all. If we could finish fourth in the Circuit, I was quite determined to prove that I could do even better in 1963. We decided to enter as many of the best British events as was practicable, and fortunately Jim could spare quite a lot of time from his college work to be with me. We had to look after local Restricted events, tackle the *Motoring News* series (then *much* more important and significant than it is now), and do Nationals into the bargain.

The year started very well for the Mini-Cooper. We had a win in the Lincolnshire Rally, a very exciting night as I recall it. Nearly all the roads were covered by snow or sheet ice, and I still didn't have any studded tyres! There were no serious gradients in Lincolnshire, but most of the route had long straights with a sharp corner at the end — and if you didn't get round there was usually a river or a dyke waiting over the edge. After that we notched up third overall on the Cat's Eyes (a National, and *very* snowy — it was that sort of winter), fourth on the Welsh Marches, then second on the Eastwood.

However, the Cooper was getting tired, having been a very hard-worked car. In the four Nationals and Internationals I did in March and April it let me down every time. It even blew up in Ireland for the Circuit, where I had wanted to do well, and it left me stranded somewhere in France on the Tulip Rally, which John Oldham and I tackled as my very first Continental rally.

It was a great relief and pleasure, therefore, when the little car held together for five days of rough and tough forestry-rallying on the Scottish. Once again it was Andrew Cowan in a Rapier who won, but this time I was with Hal Patton, who made no navigational mistakes, and we finished very strongly in second place, not far behind. It was only my fourth forestry event, and I was now well into the swing of things. Special-stage events were still quite new here, so I had no idea of the way those acres of pine trees were going to become so familiar in the coming years.

But that was the Mini-Cooper's last fling. The rest of the year was a disaster, with retirement in the RAC Rally (transmission again), and in the following January yet another breakdown in the Welsh. I was thoroughly disillusioned; the Cooper was failing through a combination of mechanical old age and the sort of long events it was forced to do.

Choosing a replacement was easy, for we had the Ford agency at our original Narborough garage, and Fords had suddenly become interested in competitions. From the days of entering a team of individualists in Zephyrs, Anglias, or whatever else had been prepared for them at the very cheerfully-amateur workshops at Lincoln Cars, in Brentford, Ford of Britain had been told to go in for 'Total Performance', following the lead of the American factory. They now had a new workshop, purpose-built for the job at Boreham Airfield, their testing ground in Essex, and a full-time competitions manager.

The cars, too, were looking up. The Cortina GT had been announced in 1963, and was already very popular for racing and rallying. The factory teams were using them, and developing lots of screw-on parts, so there was really no problem. I sold the Mini-Cooper, but kept the registration number, and in February 1964 put it on a brand new white two-door Cortina GT. Looking back, this was probably the most momentous move I could have made. It was the very first of my modern rallying Fords — more than twelve years later I am still driving them.

But it still wasn't a case of rich young garage owner building himself a works replicar. Oh no! For a start I wasn't rich, and I wasn't interested in spending the sort of money on extra bits and pieces that Boreham were quoting. Just about the only thing I needed from Boreham and couldn't get anywhere else was an homologation form, and when that arrived I sat down to see what could be done.

I'm not modest about my rallying Cortina 2 ANR. It was quite famous, first in its white paint, and later with a new body in scarlet. It did well for me, and it had a hard life, so it will surprise a lot of people to know the way I prepared it. To start with I did nothing, nothing at all, to the bodyshell and structure. I cobbled up a steel sump guard myself, and put a guard around the petrol tank, which was low down behind the back axle.

The only cash I spent on the car was for an Alexander cylinder-head and big jets for the Weber carburettor. I even had the nerve to go along to Michael Christie and plead poverty, so that I got the modified head for £10 exchange price, and as far as the engine was concerned that was that. I needed a better gearbox, or at least better ratios, and it just so happened that we had a Lotus-Cortina in stock, secondhand, so its gearbox (we called them 'Bullet' ratios later, on the Escorts) finished up in my car. It's all a long time ago now, but I have an idea we sold that Lotus-Cortina with the Cortina GT gearbox in it; I wonder if the owner ever found it?

I did the same thing with the back axle. I needed something lower than the 3.9 diff. that was standard, and as we had an old 5-cwt van in stock which might have done more than 50,000 miles but did at least have the desired 4.44 diff. we did the swop. That diff. lasted my own Cortina for nearly two seasons, and was still going strong when I sold it. Incidentally, there very definitely was a Ford 5-cwt van in Leicestershire with a 3.9 axle, and if the engine had had enough power it would probably have done at least 90 mph!

The suspension was standard at first, completely standard — I didn't even fit uprated shock absorbers. I took a set of wider wheels from the same Lotus-Cortina, but the brakes only had the usual Ferodo competition pads and linings. Inside you wouldn't have known that it was a rally car apart from the rather better Lotus-Cortina seats, and a miserable little flexible map-reading lamp for Jim. There was nothing else, no special steering wheel, nor any special instruments, and on navigational events Jim even had to estimate distances from the speedometer on my side of the car, and considering that this was not recalibrated for the 4.44 diff. it must have been a long way adrift.

By today's standards this must sound like a laughably under-prepared rally car, and even then I didn't think it was anything special. You also have to remember that the first Mark 1 Cortinas were fairly flimsy things — the bodies were very light, and after a lot of rallying, even in club events, they started to bend in the middle. The recognition points were a crease between the door pillars across the roof, and kinks above the top of the rear wheel arches! Quite a lot of people carried on using their cars long after the tell-tale marks had appeared, and some people swore that the handling actually improved thereafter. We didn't even know that there was a special 'export' bodyshell, and that if you talked long enough and persuasively enough the factory would build a right-hand-drive example for home delivery!

However, the Cortina and I really 'clicked' together, and right from the start I knew that its handling suited my methods very well. I'd been developing this rather extreme sideways-into-corners technique for some time, and here was a big, soft, floppy saloon which encouraged me. I didn't have to think very carefully about the technique at all — just rush up to a corner, turn the wheel, and leave the Cortina's natural balance and my reactions to balance the result. It was a tiny bit long for that sort of thing, which meant that the rear corners were a bit vulnerable to rocky banks and brave trees, but we seemed to miss most of them. Apart from the fact that a white Cortina with 2 ANR on the nose started to get a bit notorious anyway, people used to say they could tell when I was coming when they recognised the front door and competition number before they saw the nose. It might have looked rather horrifying, especially on a car whose suspension was absolutely standard, but it felt quite safe from my angle.

I used the new car for everything, for rallying, autocross, and all day and every day. It was the hardest-working car I'd had, and incidentally it was the first *new* car I'd ever had. It started well with a third place on the 1964 *Express and Star,* then blew its dynamo on the Circuit at Easter time, and went on to cover itself with glory by helping me to win the Scottish outright!

My first win in an International event, and what a relief. I might have looked casual when it was all over, but this was a barrier that I'd been waiting to crack for some time. The Scottish, too, was a real rally by now. There might be lots of night halts, and a number of very beery parties to enjoy, but the rallying was serious, and very fast; Forestry Commission land was used, of course — this time with no less than 44 special stages in the 1,600-mile route. I've just had a look at the reports of that event, and seen the names of the villains who finished right behind me — Adrian Boyd, John La Trobe, Eric Jackson, Robin Richards and Alan Allard. That must have been quite a week!

I shunted the white car on the Gulf London — very aggrevating because of a phenomenal £1,000 waiting for somebody as first prize (big money for 1964), and it then fell to pieces on me in the first of the 1965 Welsh Internationals. I say 'fell to pieces' because the body started to fall apart. A rear spring actually punched its way into the bodywork with a piece of spring hanger still attached, which made such a mess of the rear end that a new bodyshell was needed.

It was then that Ford began to take a real interest, and Alan Platt, who was competitions manager at Boreham by then, offered me a new works bodyshell. 'Works' meant a scarlet body with all the latest strengthening bits and an up-to-date facia with lots of instruments, aeroflow ventilation, the lot. It was still 2 ANR, and most of the old parts went into it, but it all looked brand new and sparkling.

We took it out on the Circuit of Ireland for the first time, and to get away from factory-entered cars we did some minor things to make it non-standard and ran as a Grand Touring car. The Circuit had changed a lot even since 1962 when I had my first successes. The driving tests had been swept away, while special stages and sections over closed public roads had come in. In fact, the whole of the British 'home International' circus now ran to the same format, with more and more off-the-road stages to sort out the men from the boys.

There was lots of works support for the Circuit, with cars from BMC, Ford, Rootes and Standard-Triumph. Ford were helping me quite a bit, with some service assistance and a lot of encouragement, but that didn't mean it was going to be any easier to win. It was a long, hard Easter, and none of the Fords could quite beat Paddy Hopkirk's works Mini-Cooper S; Vic Elford's works Cortina GT beat me into third place, and Brian Melia's car finished right behind.

It was the beginning of a beautiful friendship. Ford made it clear that they appreciated our efforts, even if they couldn't do more in the way of direct support, and they made sure I was kept informed, and given any wayside service they could spare. Some of their drivers didn't appreciate being challenged by an outsider, but Henry Taylor in particular couldn't have been nicer. I didn't know it then, but I think Henry did, that he would soon be exchanging a driving seat for the team manager's chair, and he was kind enough to invite me to team discussions, to eat with the team at hotels, and generally to get me more and more involved. I must say it was all a nice change from 1963, when nobody seemed to want to know me.

June 1965 was a busy month for the red Cortina and me, and one that probably shaped my career for years ahead. Jim and I entered both the Scottish and the Gulf London, which were to be run only three weeks apart, so if we shunted or broke down seriously in Scotland we wouldn't be able to attack the Gulf. We were as interested as ever in Gulf's £1,000 prize *and* free petrol, so I was hoping to survive the Scottish without trouble!

The story of the Scottish is that Ford entered four very fast works cars for Vic Elford, David Seigle-Morris, Brian Melia and Henry Taylor, and were happy to look benignly on me. As it happened, both Vic and David rolled their cars on the first afternoon, Brian Melia tried to establish a world record for distance off-the-road, and Henry Taylor's car smashed its differential cage in the middle of the Kirroughtree stage. All of which left me battling away against

31

Paddy's Cooper S and Timo Makinen's Austin-Healey 3000 for the next four days. The advantage was that I got instant full factory service — Alan Platt's mechanics had no-one else to look after — and they spent the rest of the week patiently screwing on the secret factory bits and pieces. The car was in much better nick at the end of the rally than it had been at the start, and I was very happy to win quite easily. But there is one picture showing me going off the road *after* the end of the very last special stage, and almost turning that nice red car into a banana. At least I've had the guts to print it in this book . . .

In spite of all the factory help on the Scottish, we nearly didn't make the start of the Gulf at all. What with one thing or another, it took such a long time to rebuild that I was tempted to cry off. I believe I was seeded in the first five, but I was so late finishing the car and driving down the motorway to the start from London Airport that I rang up and asked for a late number. That is why the pictures show me running at number 64, which was a lot further down than I would have liked. Not that it mattered after a day or so. The Gulf was a phenomenal marathon for a British event. David Seigle-Morris was the chief organiser, and had come up with the bright idea of timing the road section at 30 mph on public roads, and 50 mph on private land. This road timing had nothing to do with special stage penalties, and if you work it out it means that the road section was one hell of a scramble as well! A lot of navigators never picked this up at all, and when they took service after stages they suddenly realised that they couldn't make the next time control without penalty. Jim didn't fall for it, and we never ran late, but by the time we got to the finish, 40 stages and 1,400 nearly-non-stop miles had completely knackered me again. Of the 100 cars that started, only 15 of us finished. I managed to win again — which made two International victories for the red car inside a month.

One funny story I can tell against Tony Fall came from this Gulf London. Roy Fidler's works Triumph 2000 had broken down with a shattered rear axle in the middle of Dovey, so he was trekking forward on the stage to find a service car, and passing the time making rude signs at the opposition as they passed. Tony Fall flew past in his Cooper S, returned the rude signs and laughed so much that he went straight off the road at the next 'open-air' corner! That was him out, but a few minutes later his team-mate Chris Knowles-Fitton arrived, got bemused by the sight of Tony's Mini down the bank, and promptly spun off to join him. It made quite a party, because Vic Elford's works Cortina was in there somewhere as well. I didn't have time to see it, and as it was near the end of a 30-mile stage Jim was sound asleep in the other chair at the time. Asleep? Oh, yes — he did quite a lot of it, and he hasn't improved over the years.

Two wins inside a month was nice, and though I didn't realise it at the time that was also a swansong for the car. The Gulf London in 1965 was the last event I ever did as a private owner, and it was also the very last one I ever did in my own car. For well over a year I had been living a dual existence. Sometimes I would be in factory-entered cars in big Internationals, and at others I was back on my own; the way into a works team was chancy, and not without its disappointments. People now may link my name with Fords, but it took more than two years and three other factory teams before I finally made it, and I'm sure no-one could have forecast the car in which I was to start my works career.

Chapter 3

Factory drives at last

BY 1963 I was making no secret of my ambitions. I reckoned I was good enough to get into one or other of the factory teams, and the sooner the better. But to do it I had to show more results, and that Mini-Cooper was letting me down far too often. In National and International rallies, where a good result really mattered, the situation was depressing. Before the end of April I had started in four events and achieved precisely nothing — I had retired in every one of them. I never crashed the car, but the Mini-Cooper's transmission had let me down every time (the early Coopers often broke this way, and it took some time for Stuart Turner's department at Abingdon to find a solution). It was the sort of run that every rally driver hates. No matter how hard he tries (and I was driving the wheels off the Cooper most of the time), he never reaches the finish and there's no mark in the record book to prove anything. It was no way to impress any competition managers who were looking for talent, unless they happened to be watching before I broke down.

It proved to me something that I have remembered ever since. No matter how fast my car is, before it can win anything it is first necessary to get to the finish. Every new rally car I have built for myself since the Cooper has been first of all reliable and strong; high performance has followed on after that.

As I was running a Mini-Cooper I was naturally attracted to the possibilities of a BMC drive, but as Stuart Turner was busily building up his team of Finns, plus buying Paddy Hopkirk from Rootes, I had no chance there. Anyway, at that time I just didn't 'get on' with

Stuart. After my car had broken down on the Tulip in the spring I had asked him for help in getting it repaired and brought back to England, but I was given a very firm brush-off. He just didn't want to know about helping me; as far as he was concerned I was just one more private owner who was a nuisance and possibly a sponger on his facilities.

When my father did his best to get me some help, by contacting Abingdon as a BMC dealer, he also got a very firm 'cold shoulder', so even if I had had an offer from BMC I might have thought twice about accepting. There were lots of other British factories active then — it was a time when works-sponsored rallying was popular, and when most factories had money to spend on competitions. Apart from BMC, there were cars from Ford, Rootes, Rover, Triumph and Vauxhall in most of the important continental events, but none of their team managers seemed to want to know me, and considering the lack of results I'd had so far in 1963 no-one could really blame them.

However, even before the Scottish in which the Mini-Cooper finally held together, I received a phone call quite out of the blue, which must prove that there is a Father Christmas after all. It came, not from one of the big factory teams, but from the little Tamworth company of Reliant, and the caller was Arthur Rusling. The name didn't ring a bell immediately, but then I remembered that Arthur was running Reliant's competition effort. "Would you", he asked, "be interested in driving a works-prepared Sabre Six in the Alpine Rally, the legendary *Coupe des Alpes?*"

I didn't hesitate for a moment. I don't believe I actually asked him to hold on to the phone until I reached the Reliant factory at Two Gates, but I was over there not much after that! I was overjoyed that someone, at least, thought that I was good enough, and even if Reliant had yet to win anything in international competition, it would give me the experience that I lacked. So what if the cars were entered in the same class as Stuart Turner's all-conquering Austin-Healey 3000s?

I hadn't a clue how Arthur Rusling had singled me out for an offer. He certainly couldn't have decided from a study of results in *Motoring News,* and I knew I hadn't met him or seen him anywhere before. Later on I discovered that it was Bob Aston (soon to take over Reliant competitions) who had recommended me for this drive. Bob lived in Coventry, and had been doing many of the same events as I

35

had, in his own Saab, and I presume he had brushed with me somewhere along the way.

It would be very nice to write that my works career started with a bang, bringing great success and lots of headlines, but it wasn't quite like that. It was asking a lot for an untried rally car to out-perform the opposition in Europe's toughest and fastest rally, especially as Reliant had not tackled the Alpine before, neither had I, and for this event I wouldn't be able to get away to do any practising. Before the invitation arrived, I hadn't even sat in a Sabre Six; it had only been announced the previous autumn, and this would be its very first rally. Reliant had given the engines a complete Raymond Mays tune, which was supposed to produce a lot of power, but the cars were barely finished before they had to leave for France, and as I also knew that they didn't have much of a reputation for roadholding, it promised to be quite an epic!

When the team gathered in La Ciotat, before the start, it was all very strange. Bob Aston was to be my co-driver, and the other team members were Jimmy Ray (he won the RAC Rally way back in 1955) and Bobby Parkes. Gerry Cooper had done some sort of recce for the team, and had even produced crude pace notes for some of the speed hill-climbs, but then — as now — I wasn't keen on trusting other people's notes. The cars were very raw, and needed a lot of work even before we started from Marseilles. The engines were giving a great deal of trouble — on the Alpine the cars could be at sea level or as high as 9,000 feet, which was hell for the carburation — and they were never right all through the event. It wasn't until we got home that it was discovered that the ignition timing was all wrong, and that my engine was considerably retarded, which explained all the spitting and banging we had to endure for five days.

I never reckoned much to the handling or the balance, and when I looked underneath I could see why. There was a dreadfully crude-looking chassis with a most complicated rear suspension — all sorts of brackets, rods and springs tacked together, and a weird semi-swinging-arm front end. It looked for all the world like a big Ford engine at one end and a petrol tank at the other tied together with steel members.

Quite frankly I didn't get on well with the car at all. Just about everything was basically wrong with it as a rally car, and we couldn't be expected to win anything. It was a miracle that we finished, but

what was even more of a miracle was that one of the cars *did* win after
all. Quite unexpectedly, all four of the works Austin-Healeys (driven
by Paddy Hopkirk, the Morley brothers, Logan Morrison and Timo
Makinen) fell out, and though Jimmy Ray's Reliant retired, the other
two finished, Bobby Parkes' car winning the unlimited GT class —
and you can get an idea of how slow mine was when I say that Bobby's
car broke a pushrod and was only running on five cylinders at the
finish.

I can't pretend that I was proud of this performance, because I
wasn't. In a way I was proud of getting the Sabre Six to the finish,
but I didn't enjoy the drive at all. I must have made this very clear to
Bob Aston, too, because after he became competitions manager a few
weeks later I wasn't asked to drive for the team any more! Reliant
asked different drivers (including Raymond Baxter) to take cars on the
four-days-and-four-nights Liege-Sofia-Liege a few weeks after that,
and I was out in the cold again.

But this time it wasn't for long. No sooner had the news got around
that I was 'on the dole' than Graham Robson contacted me about the
Liege. Graham was then running competitions at Triumph, while still
remaining very active in British events himself, and he asked me if I
would take a Triumph TR4 on the Liege as a try-out. There were no
firm promises, and nothing was written down, but I thought this
might lead to a more permanent seat if I was lucky. As it was, I knew
that I owed this drive to a broken leg and a written-off car.

Mike Sutcliffe had been sacked by Triumph after his Alpine Rally
shunt — not his first with the team by any means — and his
co-driver, Roy Fidler, who was just about to be promoted to the
driving seat, had broken a leg in the same accident. Roy's leg
wouldn't be mended in time for the Liege, so I was offered the spare
car.

The Liege was probably the world's toughest rally at the time, and
possibly it hasn't been beaten in this respect since. From Tuesday to
Saturday, in early September, through the dust and rocks of
Jugoslavia, there was virtually no rest for the car — there was no
night halt, just a single hour's rest at Sofia half-way through. I was
sure I needed a co-driver in the driving sense rather than a navigator,
and as once again Jim had to stay at home (I think he understood!) I
asked Brian Culcheth along in his place.

But our luck was no better this time. Though the TR4 was a

fully-developed rally car, with better performance than the Reliant even though the engine was only 2.2-litres, it wasn't the sort of car that could expect to do well on such a rough event. We started off in fine style, but before we bounced and graunched our way round to the Adriatic coast at Titograd the exhaust system had been torn off and the flames had cooked some gearbox seals. How the system managed to come off (for it was tucked away *inside* the chassis cruciform) is a mystery, but that was that. Triumph had service cars, of course, but they couldn't afford an umbrella system; in any case Jugoslavia is so big, and the roads so remote, that the chances of being near a service car if you broke down were small, and we weren't lucky. So we loaded the car on to a train for England, and trekked home with the sad news.

Triumph didn't seem too unhappy about this, and they entered me in the RAC Rally with Jim. That should have been more interesting, but in the end it didn't happen because the European railway system took so long to get the broken Liege car back to Coventry that it couldn't be re-prepared in time, and since there were no more spare cars I was out of a drive again. Jim and I had to use my own Mini-Cooper, which broke its transmission yet again.

Even then Triumph were talking seriously about a series of drives for 1964, but then there was a policy change that made them withdraw cars from Europe for a time and send the TR4s to Canada to do the Shell 4000 Rally. I wasn't invited along, and quite early in the new year it became clear that there wasn't likely to be a car for me in the new season. It was all a great pity, because their cars for 1964 included the Spitfires, which eventually became very fast indeed, and the big 2000s, which were still being used with great success by British Leyland as recently as 1971. The 2000 was just the sort of car that I might have enjoyed taming, though at the time I hadn't started slinging big saloons around.

I was very peeved. I just *knew* that I was quicker than some of the drivers who were retained, and I had an idea that I might be quicker than all of them. It was very disheartening to be dropped twice within a year, and for a time I was very low. It's now something of a consolation to know that Graham Robson admits to having been wrong . . .

I could see no sign of a place in one of the top teams when suddenly I had another approach, though at first it was rather discreet and 'through the back door'. Quite unexpectedly Richard Martin-Hurst

38

asked me, "How would you like to do the Acropolis Rally in May? We'll share the driving." There were all sorts of snags — I didn't know Richard well, and I wasn't at all sure about the car, which was to be nothing less than a Rover 3-litre. But as Richard was the son of Rover's Managing Director, and the car had been factory-prepared, it was a lot better than standard, and it helped that the factory team were there in strength with four 3-litres of their own.

The original agreement was that we should share everything, driving and navigating turn and turn about, so I want to make the point that I was expected to do some map reading. A lot of people are very rude about my navigation these days (that's because I make Jim do everything except actually drive the special stages) but on the Acropolis it turned out that I did just about everything. I had to, because Richard wouldn't let me drive. As we had agreed, when we set off from Athens in the evening Richard drove the first stage, then handed over to me to do the next one. I drove it fairly quickly, and I suppose it must have been very sideways from time to time. Anyway, at the end of that stage, Richard mumbled something that might have been "Thank you very much", took hold of the steering wheel, and wouldn't let me drive again until after the finish! All very strange — had I frightened him that much? So it was mainly through Richard Martin-Hurst's driving and my navigation that the big Rover finished ninth on that Acropolis.

It was only a try-out, but it must have been enough to satisfy someone, because Ralph Nash of Rovers immediately asked me if I would drive for the factory team for the rest of the year and for 1965. The one thing that sticks in my mercenary little mind is that this was the first time anyone had mentioned driving for money — apart from getting expenses, I was actually being offered a fee to do each event. Not that it was one of these huge 'telephone number' fees that the Italian teams throw about now — it might seem unbelievable, but I believe I was paid either £50 or £100 per event, and I was very grateful for that.

Rover had a very odd, but efficient set-up. Their team manager, Ralph Nash, was really the experimental department shop superintendent who was squeezing a few extra hours into his week. He started in 1962 not knowing anything about motor sport, but by the time I joined the team he was as crafty and wily as any of the opposition. Toney Cox was in charge of the workshops, and he really settled the specification of the cars. The team had started with heavy old-fashioned Rover 3-litres, so they had scarcely attracted the fastest drivers in the business, but now the Rover 2000 had arrived on the rally scene, and when I joined the other drivers were Ken James, Peter Riley and Anne Hall. The four cars we were to use had consecutive registration numbers — and you can work out why I took a particular liking to 4 KUE for my own car.

I fell for the Rover right from the start. The 2000 was an all-new design, and though it was very heavy and underpowered, it was fantastically strong and very forgiving. With the Cortina I had developed this very sideways technique on rough or smooth roads, and I was never happy unless I could throw a car about and get it all balanced when cornering. The 2000 was superb. It had lots of wheel travel (one of the pictures I have chosen proves just how much) and excellent steering. It had only 90 bhp in standard form, and the competitions department never modified their engines very much, so it was always a struggle to keep up the pace, which meant that we all had to drive the cars even harder than usual.

Until I really got used to the Rover, and found out what tremendous handling it had, I didn't know just what liberties I could take with it. I'd never driven a car flat-out for so long; you could go so far sideways and stay in control it was almost ridiculous, but it was essential. I remember going over the Turini once, on the 1965 Monte, where there was snow on the ground the whole way. David Pollard started a minute behind me in a works 'all-happening' Group Three Imp, and passed me on the way up, but I caught him up just after the summit, and actually beat him on overall time. So we must have taken more than a minute off him downhill! That's how good the Rover 2000 was.

Being so tremendously strong and with such good handling and brakes, the cars gave us great confidence. Of course something had to give from time to time, and I have to admit that we could break the gearboxes, while my cornering methods, more than other peoples' perhaps, could also do nasty things to the chassis-mounted differentials, especially as I would insist on leaning the back wheels on things at the outside of corners.

People sometimes used to ask me how I could possibly drive a Rover 2000 like that, but these were usually people who hadn't driven the cars for themselves, and thought that all Rovers were like the 'aunties' of the 1950s. As far as the 2000s were concerned, the only changes Toney Cox and his mechanics made to the suspension were to stiffen up springs and dampers (I honestly think they did this just by upgrading by a certain amount — there was no scientific testing involved) and to make sure that everything else was absolutely 'just so'.

The way I drove the rally cars didn't please everybody. It amused those who found it incongruous, but one or two of Rover's management didn't think it was quite the thing. There was one famous occasion when I was driving a rally car round the Solihull test track. I was out with Toney Cox one day trying different things and as time was short we decided to nip out from the workshops to the test track, just round the corner from the main factory. I hadn't used it before, and I was skating round in my usual slipshod way. Though it was all tarmac, it was a patchy wet-and-dry day, so we were throwing it around. I think some of the directors were also on the track that day, trying a new car for themselves, and they must have seen me getting all crossed-up. When we had finished I was introduced to them, and Spen King started to chat. Spen was then in charge of new design projects (now, of course, he is Technical Director of British Leyland as a whole), and was one of the creators of the Rover 2000.

"I've been watching you drive round our test track", he said, "and I don't think you're doing it properly. I don't think that is the best way to drive a Rover 2000. Anyway, it doesn't look tidy, and it can't be the quickest way to go round the corners. I'll show you how to do it". Spen was no mean driver himself, on a race track, and he wanted to show me the way round a track he knew very well, keeping the car in a straight line, and going round like a racing driver.

So we jumped in, with me in the passenger seat (I never drove him at all) and we set off. Almost the next thing that happened was that we went into one corner with no hope of getting round on a proper 'racing-driver' line; the car charged straight off, and cleared up a row of marker poles, on my side of course! He had the car beautifully set up in a racing line — the only trouble was that the corner kept on turning and he didn't have a chance. There wasn't a lot said after that, and nobody tried to discourage me any more. I think the rest of the management party were highly amused!

I had an absolute whale of a time driving for Rover in 1964 and 1965. Because the cars weren't really competitive (in Europe they

41

always had to face the big Citroens) we couldn't be expected to win very often, but that didn't mean that we didn't try; I certainly drove my car flat-out the whole time, and if very occasionally it got away from me I thought I could be excused.

In fact I never completed an event in the Rover the first year — the back axle fell to pieces on the Alpine, I blew the engine on a Jugoslavian *autoput* on the Liege when the gearbox jumped out of gear, and I fell out of the RAC Rally in November with another blown engine. 1965 just had to be better — and it was.

On the private front, I had a bad start to the year when my old white Cortina GT broke down on the Welsh with a structural failure, but as this had had to be fitted in round our practice for the Monte there hadn't been a lot of time for preparation. Jim and I did a lot of practice for that year's Monte, something I had never had to do before. At first I could grin and bear it, but before long I found it a great bore. It might sound all very glamorous, to be sent to the South of France for weeks to charge up and down hills in someone else's car and at someone else's expense, but why not try it yourself? We must have spent a week doing nothing else but driving up and over the Turini, correcting the notes, then driving up and over again (the test was used both ways as usual), correcting the other notes, and so on. Not my idea of fun, and something I came to dislike thoroughly.

We had drawn number 136, and were starting the Monte from London. Everything was straightforward on the trundle round France (I've never liked that either — it's just another way of getting everybody tired out and irritable), but soon after we reached St Claude the snow really began to bucket down. From there to the end of the rally conditions couldn't have been more ideal for us. All that snow and very little grip meant that the Rover didn't have its usual handicaps, and I really began to enjoy it. I'm not one for statistics, but it is interesting to note that 237 cars started and only 35 reached Monte within the hour's lateness limit. Mine was the only one of four works Rovers to make it.

But not even the heavy snow, as a great performance leveller, could make it all equal. We'd already had five long special stages, and more than two hours of them at that. The road section was almost impossibly tight. We lost 11 minutes from Chambery to Monte Carlo and more than 17 minutes on stages behind Timo Makinen in a works Cooper S. It was good enough for seventh place at that stage.

All that remained was the final Mountain Circuit, with another snow-covered 380 miles and half-a-dozen special stages. I had all Rover's attention as their only runner. What happened that night really does read like a fairy tale. I felt good, the car couldn't have been better, and by seemingly going sideways from the minute we left the *parc ferme* to the minute we finished we had a completely faultless run. The fairy tale was that in the fabulous excitement of that night two of the factory Citroens disappeared, there was a bit of reshuffling, and not only did we end up in sixth place, but we won the class and lifted the complete touring car category. I've done better on the Monte since then, and won more important events, but nothing could take away the excitement of that morning.

Rover's management went potty. In all their planning they hadn't expected anything like this to happen, and I don't suppose you could blame their publicity machine for being unprepared. I think they got even as much pleasure out of the televised 'TV-Monte' racing that the BBC organised in Sweden the following month, particularly when I beat Bengt Soderstrom's factory Cortina GT in conditions that he should have relished.

It's difficult to remember now just how important that Monte success was. I suppose I'd been trying to break away from the 'Roger Clark-driving hooligan' image for some time, and I had to agree that my driving record with three works teams hadn't been up to much. The Monte success changed everything. It proved something to the factory and to the press, and (possibly as important) it proved something to me. The 1965 Monte was a complete watershed in my driving career. After that I never had any doubts about my own abilities — it was just up to me to put them to best effect in the future.

Even so, it was the high-spot of my driving with Rover. I drove better after that, and the cars improved somewhat, but we never achieved the same sort of results. In the mid-1960s, the Monte was still *the* rally as far as the press and radio/TV people were concerned. Most of the professionals preferred the Alpine or the Acropolis, but you couldn't convince a pressman about that. The Monte was the oldest, the coldest, the most glamorous, and it was traditional — there just couldn't possibly have been a better place to shine. It was very important to Rover, and just as significant for me.

There was another happy result of this performance — Rover suddenly got all keen about their rallying. Ralph Nash, on the other hand, was not happy about having to hold down two full-time jobs — it couldn't have been easy for him to be planning a rallying programme one minute, and holding a meeting with shop-floor union men the next. I was settled into the team, too, so it was all very satisfactory when Ralph suggested that Jim Porter should go to work for him. In fact it was very brave of Ralph because he'd tried the same sort of thing a couple of years earlier with a very well-known navigator — a rather disastrous experiment as I recall!

Not that it was all that easy to arrange. Though Jim had completed his college education, he was by then with the British Beef Company, as a management trainee. Jim thought long and hard before deciding to move over to Solihull, and since there was a tradition of meat management in the family there was also quite a bit of family resistance to be overcome. In the end, in the spring of that year, Jim made the break and took over all the day-to-day administration of the rallying team from Ralph Nash. I should make it clear, here, that although Rover also had their BRM-chassised Le Mans car at the time, it was developed in a separate department, and neither Jim nor I ever got our hands on it.

The first event Jim and I tackled together after he had joined the firm was in Greece — the Acropolis — and it couldn't have been a worse way to impress his new boss. We had gone all professional, had actually spent some time practising the difficult stages, and were proud of our set of pace notes. It was one of those typical Greek roads — all ball bearings and tortoises — slippery, smooth and very greasy (for it *does* rain sometimes in Greece, even in May).

The pace notes were fine, and we were tramping on well in the 2000, but nobody had warned us that the local council would be digging up the road just before the rally arrived. The road works had cut out a couple of bends, the pace notes didn't fit any more, we got back on to the original road where the new hardcore had spread all across the bend, and promptly flew off. It was just like driving on marbles, on top of the usual Greek grease, and as we spun off we hit a signpost with a back wheel and the rear wing, then disappeared down the hillside. We managed to get the wreck back on to the road, but the swipe from the signpost had clobbered the back axle, and we were out. What annoyed me was that other team-mates who were using the same notes (Andrew Cowan, Logan Morrison and Anne Hall) didn't go off, which meant either they were driving better than me, or that I

44

was going far too fast.

I seemed to have more than my fair share of shunts in the Rover 2000s, but the reasons were not obvious, except that the cars were so beautifully balanced that it was always very tempting to drive them absolutely on the limit, and occasionally over it. Structurally the Rover was a splendid car, but when we were faced with the might of the Citroen and Volvo teams it was essential to row the car along with the gear lever and get it into the most incredible situations. The RAC Rally in 1965 was a good example. From the start of the Yorkshire section to the end of the Welsh section days later there was snow and ice everywhere. The 2000 had good traction, and we were not too worried about the conditions, but somehow it wasn't our week. We must have been off half-a-dozen times, usually just an 'off-bang-engage reverse-drive out' occurence, but well before the end the car looked fit only for the scrap heap. The rear bumper had gone, the front was askew, and just about every panel was bent, including the roof because at one point the car had fallen gently over on to its side in Keilder and had rested gently against a tree.

Earlier in the year, on the Alpine, we had done better. The previous year we had crunched the back axle, but in 1965 my usual 4 KUE held together. We ran 'Group One', or in Rover terms absolutely bog-standard — a considerable handicap when one remembers that Groups One and Two were combined, which meant we had to fight against the Lotus-Cortinas and works Lancias as well. It really was a ridiculously tight Alpine that year, as far as road penalties were concerned, and I was very happy to get away with only a single lost minute, but it would have been nice to notch up a *Coupe des Alpes* for a clear run. We didn't win anything, not surprisingly in that field, but we finished tenth in the Touring category, and incidentally ahead of all the GT cars, which had much more severe road timings to beat.

By the middle of the year, Rover had started to use prototypes of their 2000TC cars wherever the regulations allowed it, and these were quite a lot quicker. They would be homologated for the 1966 season, when it looked as if they could have the beating of the Triumphs and Citroens in the 2-litre class. Even more interesting was the talk floating around Solihull of the V8-engined 'Rover 2000' project, which was all supposed to be very secret, but about which the competition department soon got to know. Everybody was getting a bit excited about this until we learned that it wouldn't be offered for sale with a manual gearbox. I've heard about rallying in comfort before, but I didn't fancy having to do it with automatic transmission.

It all looked very promising, but in the meantime I had made things a lot more complicated for myself. While I was driving factory cars for Ralph Nash, I was still driving my own Cortinas at home. Those two big wins in the Scottish and the Gulf London had sparked off interest elsewhere, and I soon had another offer for my services. Between July and the autumn, big and far-reaching decisions had to be made.

Chapter 4

Into the Ford team

IT WAS EVERY rally driver's dream to be asked to drive for BMC or Ford, but most of us thought we'd never make it. Even after I had won the Scottish in my own white Cortina GT I still wasn't sure how much Fords thought about me. Probably that Rover drive in the 1965 Monte did the trick, because soon afterwards Alan Platt (Ford's competitions manager at Boreham) started to make encouraging noises. The first signs came when he provided me with the works bodyshell to replace the old white one which had begun to bend, having been shunted more than once.

Alan talked vaguely about works drives during the year, which was exciting but also awkward; I couldn't have gone straight into the Ford team at that point, even if there had been a place for me, because of my agreement with Ralph Nash at Rover. Although there was no question of a rigid contract, it would have been quite wrong for me to leave Rover for a better offer in the middle of the year, and in any case I was very happy to drive the Rovers. However, when I wasn't needed to drive a 2000 I was free to go off and rally on my own account.

This suited me very well, so when Fords duly offered me a ride in the Tulip Rally that April I was delighted. It was really a trial run for the future, though I didn't know it at the time, and because I couldn't take Jim as my co-driver Brian Melia sat alongside instead. We did a good recce session, which I didn't enjoy (because the Tulip was really just a collection of speed hill-climbs with a lot of mileage in between) but as it turned out this was all a waste of time. Of all things there was heavy snow in the Geneva-St Claude area, which made life very difficult because the factory hadn't supplied studs! It's all very well being brave downhill without studs, or even on the level, but climbing 7,000 foot passes on snow is no joke. We kept going — just — with Brian spending some of the time in the boot to give me more traction, but later the engine's electrics went on the blink and we were forced to retire. It wasn't a good start, but the second Scottish Rally win in my own Cortina made up for it.

After those wins in the Scottish and the Gulf London a few weeks later Fords made it very clear that they wanted me in their works team as soon as possible. Even during 1965, when I was already in another works team, I had always looked on Ford works drivers as little gods, and whenever they were nice to me, or helped me along with spares, service and advice, I felt rather privileged. Now I had the chance to join them, but first I had to sort out my relationship with Rover.

Ralph Nash was anxious that I should stay with him, especially as his team could look forward to better and faster cars in 1966. He had Jim Porter working for him, and he even offered me more money. However, apart from the sheer size and professionalism of the new Ford outfit, of which Henry Taylor was to become the new manager, there was the attraction of using the latest Lotus-Cortinas. These had been fragile and unreliable at first, but by 1965 they were rugged and very strong.

There was a great mental tug-of-war of loyalties before I made a decision. In the end I had to tell Ralph that I would be moving on, and he was really very nice about it. Poor Jim wasn't very happy, though; just when it looked as if my prospects were very bright, he couldn't be around to enjoy them. He had only started work in Rover's competition department in the spring, but as their team was still going ahead he was prepared to stay.

Apart from the potential of the cars, and the prestige of the team, I couldn't ignore the attraction of the money. Incidentally, don't believe all those 'telephone number' figures which are bandied around for driver fees, because they were never as high as all that. Stuart Turner has often said that a top-grade rally driver makes as much money as a Cabinet Minister, and is worth much more than that in terms of the prestige he brings his country. He may be right. For 1966, I wasn't being paid at that sort of rate, but an initial fee of £2,000 for the season, plus every sort of generous expense, was something new to me.

Jim and I with the Renault Dauphine which we used for the Circuit of Ireland in 1961. (Leicester Mercury)

I really did rally some odd cars a long time ago. This was a Renault R8 owned by the garage in a local Derbyshire Championship event in 1963.

The hard-worked Mini-Cooper, 2 ANR, on the Welsh Rally in 1964, with Tom Romanis counting us down at the start of a stage. We retired with a broken gearbox, *again!* (C.D.Soden)

My first works drive, with Bob Aston in a Reliant Sabre Six on the 1963 Alpine Rally. We finished second in our class, but the car was desperately slow and under-developed. Nevertheless, I always thank Reliant for giving me my first chance in a team. (Photo Junior)

Jim Porter, my long suffering and faithful co-driver for so many years. We have shared many successes, but his work behind the scenes of the RAC Rally prevents him from accompanying me to any successes I may score on that event.

This must be the limit of roll on a Rover 2000. We were tackling the snow-free Levens hill-climb, near Nice, on the Monte Carlo Rally, and we went on to finish sixth.

Suspension-testing a Group One Rover 2000 on the 1964 Alpine Rally with Johnstone Syer. (Rover)

This was the third bodyshell to carry the number 2 ANR, my Mini-Cooper being the first and my white Cortina GT the second. This one, painted red, is on its way to a first-time win in the 1965 Scottish Rally.

A close call! This near-miss happened after the finish line of the final stage on the 1965 Scottish Rally, when the Mini in the foreground stopped and blocked my line. Fortunately the Cortina survived unscathed.

My first rally – and my first win – in a Lotus-Cortina. This was the second Welsh Rally in 1965, when Graham Robson was my co-driver. (C.D. Soden)

That dust on the East African Safari gets into everything – and I do mean *everything!* This was the Mark 1 Lotus-Cortina which Gilbert Staepelaere and I drove into the ground on the 1967 event.

This could be Wales, but in fact it is Canada, when I tackled the 1966 Shell 4000 Rally with Robin Edwardes, and finished third.

Wedding day with Goo, and I find a useful resting place for my topper. Henry Taylor supplied a fleet of Lotus-Cortina rally cars as wedding transport, this one being my 'British events' car throughout 1966 after it had helped me win the 1965 Welsh.

Brian Melia and I at the start of the 1966 Acropolis Rally in our Mark 1 Lotus-Cortina. We finished second overall behind the sister car of Bengt Soderstrom and Gunnar Palm.

Very relived to finish the 1966 Alpine Rally. Brian Melia and I finished second to Jean Rolland's Alfa Romeo GTA, by 67 seconds, while our team-mates Greder and Staepelaere finished fifth.

Goo joins me at the end of a Safari. I was tired out – and it shows!

In any case, rallying for Ford made a lot of sense. I had been using my own Cortinas for a while (lately with help from the factory team, of course), the Narborough business still held the Ford franchise, and best of all, the Lotus-Cortinas were probably an even better potential bet than the Mini-Coopers from Abingdon.

When I moved into Fords it wasn't going to be easy. Though I think I was probably Rover's 'Number One' driver (though they didn't have hierarchies, as such), at Ford I would be the apprentice. Manager Henry Taylor had only recently retired from driving, their fastest road driver was certainly Vic Elford, and no-one could argue with Bengt Soderstrom's abilities in the forests, or on snow and ice. Incidentally, Vic had started his works driving career with Triumph, and had been very strongly attracted to an offer from Rover just before I went there.

For 1966, Ford planned a very busy programme for me, which would also involve a lot of practising and a lot of time away from home. The factory wanted me to take the department's navigator, Brian Melia, as my regular co-driver. I also learned that Boreham operated a system of one mechanic-one driver, where a nominated workshop mechanic specialised in building and preparing cars for one particular team driver. It was in this way, purely by chance, that I met and grew to know Norman Masters. Norman had been David Seigle-Morris' man, and since I replaced David in the team we got together that way. If you saw someone mending my Escort at the side of the road in 1975, it would still have been Norman; after nearly ten years we get on even better than ever.

In fact I started driving for Ford as soon as I had completed that last event, the RAC Rally, for Rover. There were two Welsh Internationals in 1965, the second being in December. Henry rang me up and said, ''Why not start in an event you know well and take one of our Lotus-Cortinas? If you like it, that can be your own car for British events next year.'' It would also be my very first event in a Lotus-Cortina. Naturally I had driven one before, but never in anger and certainly not over Forestry Commission tracks. It all looked very interesting.

Naturally I couldn't take Jim with me, so I asked Graham Robson (by then writing for *Autocar*) to weight down the left-hand side of the car. Left to himself, Graham would now probably chip in and point out that since this one event we never rallied together again, which

65

must surely prove something! Anyway, I know he is bursting to make a short contribution to my book so here are his comments about this rally:

"No-one could have been more shattered than I was when Roger asked me to do the Welsh with him, and I was petrified at the thought of letting him down by doing something really stupid. Apart from the rally itself, I have an idea that the RAC Rally Championship was also at stake. As Roger has mentioned, there were two Welsh Rallies that year, one in January and this one in December, and Roy Fidler and I had led the January event until the last night when his works Triumph 2000 suffered engine trouble, so I was hoping for better luck this time.

Roger was new to his car, I was new to him, and everything was very strange. It didn't help that I had often watched this young lunatic driving Rovers and Cortinas at quite impossible-looking angles through British forests, and I wasn't at all convinced that I was up to it. Anyway, I was supposed to have stopped rallying when I joined *Autocar,* hadn't I? Roger was really very kind about the whole deal, particularly as I knew he would rather have had Jim Porter alongside him.

I suppose it could all have been a bit of an act, a touch of nervousness perhaps, but at first he made much of the strangeness of the car, that he didn't know much about Lotus-Cortinas, and that it worried him. The first bit of competitive motoring was over the tarmac of the Eppynt ranges in very frosty conditions, but as we 'cleaned' them both without any danger I should have been reassured.

When, at last, we got stuck into the forestry special stages there was no more need to worry. The Lotus-Cortina was obviously just as nicely balanced as his own cars, and had about 50 bhp more into the bargain. He flew . . . he really flew. I was belted in alongside with virtually nothing to do but keep checking the clocks and spot the stage direction arrows, while this fellow did indescribable things at the wheel, on the pedals, and to the gear lever. For the first few minutes I was completely horrified. It was all happening so very rapidly. I'd never experienced anything quite like it before, and as far as I was concerned his performance was just the prelude to a very large shunt.

I don't think he knew just how frightened I really was at first, and he didn't have much time to find out, anyway, because I suddenly began to have second thoughts. It was probably when we were rushing steeply *downhill between trees* in Coed-y-Brenin, and he engaged top gear and stamped on the throttle pedal, that I knew. Perhaps this madman really *did* know what he was doing, and perhaps there wasn't a death wish after all? After that it became extremely enjoyable; even though it was always a very tight battle with Simo Lampinen in the works Triumph 2000 he was incredibly relaxed, and even found time to explain a few points on driving technique in mid-stage.

It might not be the same story, and certainly not as relaxing, to repeat the experience in a 240 bhp Escort, but even in 1965 a very 'sideways' Lotus-Cortina was exciting enough, and it didn't take me long to realise that sideways is fastest if the Clark technique was used.

In the end, of course, he won the rally without much help from me, though it *was* me who found an error in the published results which showed Lampinen to be winning! But he didn't let me drive much, which I now know is a bad sign . . . I think it might have been because I couldn't find him any lunch on the first day when the organisers had boobed. The prestige was very flattering, and the party was fun. I haven't enjoyed a rally so much, ever again.''

Well, thank you for those kind words. Yes, that first Lotus-Cortina was different. All the controls, the general layout and the overall size were exactly as I was used to, but the power output was a whole lot better than I had ever had before. As Graham has said, it didn't change the balance, and I didn't have to change my style. The nice thing was that here, at last, was a car that would accelerate strongly uphill as well as down, and I didn't really have to be as brave going downhill as before!

His comment about not getting to drive very much is interesting, particularly as I was already well on the way to this reputation for being idle and liking to sleep a lot. But it rubs in something I have emphasised so often at forums and other talk shows — that you have to get used to a co-driver, and that the best way to do this is to find one regular partner and go with him all the time. Even if Jim had two heads and was coloured bright green that wouldn't matter to me, because he is a perfect co-driver for my requirements, and that is all that matters. Incidentally, he hasn't and he isn't — which is a great consolation to all of us!

Almost straight after the Welsh, I had to go off to France and practice for the next Monte Carlo Rally. The record books show that I didn't figure in the results, but is it really so long ago that we have all forgotten why? Yes! That was the notorious 'disqualification' Monte, where all the winning British cars were thrown out on a very flimsy technicality involving headlamp bulbs. There is some sort of justice in that everybody interested in motor sport remembers it as Timo Makinen's victory, but if you look in the history books the winner is given as Pauli Toivonen and his Citroen DS21. First, let's remember that 'on the road' the first three finishers were all Abingdon Mini-Coopers (Makinen, Aaltonen and Paddy Hopkirk), and yours truly was very happy indeed to be fourth. But we were all thrown out. Why?

The core of the story is that the 1966 Monte was run for Group One cars — standard cars with virtually no modifications allowed. The cars were so standard that the off-duty driver had to make do without a reclining seat unless the car was sold from the factory with one fitted, and the driver had to make do with a standard seat, too.

Even before we started there was a general feeling that this ruling was meant to give the best possible chance to the Citroens, and with so much snow about at the start they were firm favourites. But surely everybody knows now that both BMC and ourselves wiped the floor with the Citroens, with Toivonen's car fifth and Neyret's eighth? I should have been very pleased with fourth, especially as the front-wheel-drive Minis were supposed to be that much more controllable on the snow, but in fact I was even a bit disappointed. Before the final night and the Mountain Circuit I was ahead of Paddy Hopkirk, who pipped me for third before the night was over.

Yet we were all thrown out, and there was a really king-sized rumpus about the decision. We couldn't help having the feeling that the organisers were looking for any reason to get rid of the British cars, and in the end they said we were using lighting systems which didn't comply with the Group One ruling which, even when read carefully, was easily misunderstood anyway. The Fords were using single-filament quartz-halogen headlamp bulbs, arranged so that to dip them we switched over to the auxiliary fog lamps. This was not exactly as production, certainly, but both Henry Taylor and Stuart Turner (of BMC) thought they had cleared their own interpretation with the CSI before the start.

Even now, ten years afterwards, we are none too clear about the real reasons, and I don't want to risk any libel actions by making any more of it. Most of the press, and even quite a number of our continental friends, thought that there was such widespread dismay when a French car could not win a rally whose regulations were designed in its favour, that every effort was made to find some way in which the British cars might be wrong.

We knew there was a lot of pro-French hysteria about when we heard it suggested that both BMC and ourselves were using non-standard cars, that homologation papers were fiddled, and that at times we were even swopping cars for race-tuned versions to tackle certain tests and hill-climbs! Now I *do* know of cases in certain foreign teams where this has happened, and there was one famous case on the Liege where a driver was carted all the way through Jugoslavia on a bed in the back of a service car while a mechanic drove the easy bits, but this is ridiculous.

It all pointed to hysteria by a group of very nationalistic people. They just couldn't believe how we could all go so fast, and somehow they just had to find a way to disqualify us — that's what the rumours said, anyway. What the opposition didn't know was that BMC and Ford both had access to superbly up-to-date information on road surfaces, and were able to choose the most suitable tyres at all times.

At the finish the organisers stripped the winning Minis almost to the last nut and bolt, *but they left the Lotus-Cortina alone;* they could find nothing at all wrong. In retrospect this was very strange because a few weeks later Vic Elford lost the *Rallye dei Fiore* because the organisers found that his Lotus-Cortina and the homologation paper didn't tie up; we then discovered that the sheet was wrong! Anyway in Monte Carlo they eventually fell back on this feeble excuse about the lights, though nobody seemed to notice that the French Citroens had been using white bulbs in their lamps (French law required yellow), or that the swivelling mechanism on their DS21 headlamps had been disconnected.

But let me make it quite clear. We were not cheating. We were not using non-standard cars. We didn't substitute cars at any time. Believe me, my Lotus-Cortina was about as standard as a rally car can be. The reasons BMC and Ford were faster were that we had practised better, had planned our tyres better, had provided ourselves with better service, and had excellent ahead-of-the-rally support. We had better cars than everybody else, and — dare I say it? — we had better drivers, too.

There are several others things to remember about that Monte. Pauli Toivonen didn't want to be a winner in this manner and said so, but Citroen made him put a brave face on it; he vowed never to drive a Citroen again, and so far as I know he never has. Another thing was that both BMC and Ford probably gained more publicity by being disqualified than by winning; there were reverberations in the press for weeks.

Everybody will recall our own performances (I will certainly never forget, even if it's only because of those standard seats!) and at the time there was no doubt about the direction of the public's sympathy. Only the French press tried to brazen it out, but Stuart soon trimmed their sails. He offered Timo's winning car straight out of the scrutineering bay, unaltered, for a French journalist to try up a hill-climb behind Monte Carlo. The same man then tried an unprepared demonstrator car found in a Nice showroom, and he was quite shattered and very puzzled to find that he was actually a bit quicker in the standard car!

So that was the start of my rallying with Ford, and the beginning of a very hectic rallying year. Somewhere in that programme I also had to find time to get myself married, because Goo was beginning to nag about it. She had a point.

Goo and I first met after a local Leicestershire Car Club driving test meeting, when she says she took an instant dislike to me. I'd just returned from my first works drive with Reliant in 1963 and had celebrated by winning this local meeting in the Mini-Cooper. Goo was in the same pub afterwards, where some of us were trying to cause a local bitter shortage, and it all started from there.

But why 'Goo'? It was because when she was very young and learning to talk she couldn't pronounce 'Judith', which came out as 'Goo', and the nickname stuck. Goo says that when we met she wasn't at all interested in motor sport. In fact I've just had a smart set-back to my early image with Goo's recollection of our first meeting: "This little red Mini was charging round in the dust, between posts and things, and someone said, 'That's Roger Clark'. I'd never heard of him, so then someone else said, 'He's just come back from the Alpine Rally', but I'd never heard of the Alpine Rally either . . ."

When we actually got round to setting a wedding date, it had to slot in between all the rallies, and we couldn't possibly have got off to a more hectic beginning if we had tried. The first week in May I was in Canada, rallying for Ford, we married the week I got back, and in theory our honeymoon was in Greece, not too far from the Acropolis Rally recce that Bill Barnett and Brian Melia were to do. The Acropolis was to follow, after which we were all due to fly back to Scotland to start the Scottish in another car!

We had a good gimmick at the wedding, far more appropriate for me than the traditional Rolls-Royce or a veteran car. Henry Taylor provided my own works Lotus-Cortina rally car for the bridal carriage, all in bright red with white ribbons, of course, and he sent up another pair of rally cars to use as taxis. Very colourful, and it made for some nice souvenir pictures.

Before then I hadn't travelled outside Europe at all, but once with Ford I really began to globe-trot. There were to be some very out-of-the-ordinary trips in the future, but just for starters Henry Taylor decided to send me over to Canada to tackle the Shell 4000. At first glance it all sounded very interesting, but there were some nasty doubts in the back of my mind. I didn't know many people who had done the Shell 4000 before me (though Henry Taylor had finished third the previous year) but from what I had heard, or had read in the 'comics', it all seemed such a waste of time and that I wouldn't be suited to it at all. And so it proved.

Here was this fantastically wild country, underpopulated and with lots of space, and what looked like enough ideal rallying country and roads to keep us busy for hours on end. But what happened? It was just as we feared. Faced with a nation-wide 65 mph speed limit (even less at night) and obstructive police, the Shell organisers set a six-day navigator's nightmare, with all sorts of 'Mickey Mouse' problems, absolutely stupid regularity sections, and virtually nothing for us to do at all. Henry had warned me, but I simply couldn't believe it would be so awful. Not that the organisers seemed to be aware of our disgust — there were very few Europeans anyway (Rosemary Smith came along in a Rallye Imp and took the Ladies' award) and most of the North Americans were quite used to this sort of dawdle.

My co-driver was Robin Edwardes, from Quebec, who had pointed the way for Henry Taylor in 1965, and I must say he came well equipped for all these mobile guessing games, with those queer little 'pepper-pot' Curta calculators, accurate watches, charts of average speed data, and a very studious look. Me? Well, I just sat there like a

71

dummy, turning the wheel this way and that and generally trying to keep awake.

There were precisely eight special stages — the Canadians called them 'closed sections' — from the start in Vancouver to the finish at Quebec, which gives you an idea of how unimportant was my contribution. Marking was on a class-improvement system on the stages, so the two works Fords (Paul MacLennan was driving the other Lotus-Cortina) resorted to dropping marker dyes along the stages to show the other car how far they had gone in a certain time. There was so much difference between car performance and ability that I was badly baulked several times on stages, and with so much dust on strange roads I just had to sit there and wait.

We were placed third but we should have won. Robin and I had arrived early at one of the controls, and while he filled the car up I gave a press interview. Then we left on the next section . . . but a couple of miles up the road we realised that Robin had forgotten to clock in! That was worth a five-minute penalty, which made all the difference. I wasn't very impressed by the event, but as the Canadian market was important to Ford they were quite right to send team cars out to compete. Apart from that silly mistake, MacLennan and I had beaten everybody else — and it showed in the times.

The rest of that year blended into a mixture of flying to and fro, practising, competing and having very little time off to relax. I had Brian Melia with me for every major event except the RAC Rally at the end of the year, and he tried to make all the routine as painless as possible. One of Brian's advantages was that he was also a very capable driver, and he would often do a lot of the practising himself before I even appeared.

Not that it always worked to my advantage. After our wedding the theory was that Goo and I would honeymoon in Greece, then I would disappear for a few days to complete a race and compete in the Acropolis Rally immediately afterwards. But after three days we had an anguished phone call from Bill Barnett saying that Brian had hurt his back and couldn't carry on without resting, so would I please start work in his place! As Goo says, how do you explain to anyone else from Britain that you are on your honeymoon, that your husband has gone away in a car, and that his co-driver is staying with you in the same hotel and has hurt his back?

Rallying abroad in 1966 was more fruitful than at home. Jim and I fell out of the Circuit of Ireland when I landed the car hard on its sump-shield, which then punched the sump and the oil pump out of place. Then Brian and I dropped out of the Scottish early on when the diff. failed, and darn me if the same thing didn't happen again to Jim and I in the same car on the Gulf London.

In Europe, Brian and I managed second place in the Acropolis (team-mate Bengt Soderstrom won, but that was the year Paddy Hopkirk *should* have won, except that he was penalised for servicing too near a control), we were fourth in Poland and a miserable 19th in Finland. That's the only time I have ever tacked the Thousand Lakes, and I didn't enjoy it at all. Somehow their roads were not at all the same as our own forests, and I didn't relish flying through the air among all those trees. But no excuses — the Finns obviously loved it.

Brian and I managed second overall in the Alpine at the end of the holiday season, rather more than a minute behind Jean Rolland's Alfa GTA, and I captured one of those rare *Coupes des Alpes* awards for a clear run on the road that I had missed with Rover the year before. What a splendid road race — they don't run them like that any more — but those were the days when you could compete in a road rally without annoying everybody; the Alpine had a great tradition, and was firmly controlled by the French police, who stood no nonsense at all.

A couple of weeks later I was in the garage at home when the phone rang. It was Henry Taylor with the most surprising news. ''We've persuaded your namesake, Jim Clark, to do the RAC Rally! He'll have a Lotus-Cortina just like the regulars, and I'm sending Brian Melia with him as co-driver. I want you to come down to Bagshot to show him the ropes.'' I was flabbergasted — me, show a World Champion the way to drive?

At least I was thoroughly accustomed to being at Bagshot, which helped a lot. We seem to have been going to Bagshot for so many years that it is difficult to remember a time when it *was* strange. I believe it was BMC and Stuart Turner who first found the place, a tight and very demanding test circuit in forestry land owned by the Armed Forces. The MVRDE used it mainly for proving out new designs for 'off-the-road' use, but as soon as the rallying teams found out about it there was a queue at the gates. For controlled testing in the right sort of conditions Bagshot was ideal, and of course we still use it a lot for testing, though perhaps we're now a bit too familiar with its twists, brows and rough patches — I sometimes feel that I am driving there in my sleep.

I was quite nervous about meeting Jim, and of helping him with his driving, but I needn't have bothered. We had a complete day together. First I showed him the way round the course, slowly, to let him settle in and relax, then gradually went quicker and quicker. Before long I was flat-out as usual, and he was getting interested.

When it was Jim's turn to leap in and drive he was all over the road at first, but the way he improved was quite fantastic. He learned *everything* so very quickly, and by the end of the day he was just about as quick in the car as I was. At first he couldn't get used to the idea of the car's attitudes being so extreme, and he would get himself into a bit of a knot when the back was a long way out of line, with his arms all anywhere, but he soon had everything under control. There's no doubt that he had 'the gift'.

He was a bit taken aback by the sheer pace of rough-road driving at first, but then became impressed by the amount of grip there was, and how much braking you could get on that sort of surface. Racing drivers don't really like getting the tail well out of line, and they tend to do all their braking in a straight line, but Jim picked up the technique tremendously quickly.

His only real problem was this business of reeling in a car that is all sideways — and a Lotus-Cortina always was! Jim wasn't used to the idea of winding away at the wheel to keep it on the track, and the tail used to wag about until he captured this. But there was never any question of him being slow, or frightened of rough surfaces, fresh-air corners, trees or anything like that. He was only interested in learning — if he wasn't asking questions he was saying, "Do that again", like jumping a bit askew, or flick turning, or even seeing how I drove with one hand. It was a real pleasure to be with him, and I know he was enjoying himself.

Incidentally, Graham Hill also did the RAC Rally that year in a Cooper S, and a year later in a Lotus-Cortina. But with Graham it wasn't the same. I got the impression that it wasn't quite his scene, and he wasn't really interested. He seemed to be doing it mainly for publicity, or for money, or perhaps for a joke, I don't know which, but he didn't find driving in unusual circumstances as easy as did Jim Clark; he was still very impressive, but somehow he didn't appear to be a 'natural', like Clark, for whom everything came so easily.

I know Jim then went away with Brian and did quite a bit more practice before the event started, so by the time he turned up at London Airport there was no question of him being slow or a novice, although that didn't matter to the daily papers, who made a lot of it.

What actually happened on that RAC Rally is a bit embarrassing. It was this Clark and not the other one who went off the road first — worse still, it was permanent! I was very pleased to have Jim Porter back in the left-hand seat with me, and we started out in fine style by setting fastest time on each of the first four stages. Then on the Puddletown Forest stage (it's near Dorchester, but we haven't used it since then) my car slid off the outside of a gentle downhill bend, the nose hit a tree head-on, and we split the radiator. I wasn't quite used to the new type of limited-slip differential in the car, which is no excuse, but normally any 'off' at this speed wouldn't have been fatal. This time it was. The radiator was split, we lost all the water, and before we could even get to our next service car a few miles away the head gasket had blown.

Jim, on the other hand, made a lot of headlines. He went off in a minor way at least twice, but then had a huge accident in Achray, near the half-way halt. That reduced the off-side of his car to scrap, and he then had a final shunt when he flew so far off into the scrub that nobody else could see the wreckage! Brian Melia says that both accidents were caused by trifling things that we only learn by experience — like how difficult it is to steer a car when the front wheels are off the ground! — but his performance was no joke; he made fastest time on a few stages, and was somewhere in the top six on most of them.

I didn't fare any better on the Welsh a few weeks later. This time I had another absolutely freak accident, the sort I am sure I would have if it happened next week with an Escort. Jim and I were running first on the road in the Lotus-Cortina, it was a dark and dirty night, and we charged over a brow to land smack in the middle of a very large pool of water. The problem was that it only covered one side of the road, and it pulled the steering wheel clean out of my hands. We spun, hit the bank, and the wretched thing fell over. That was that, we couldn't get the car on to its wheels, everybody else laughed like drains when they came past, and we had to walk off in the rain.

I have just looked up my driving diary for 1967 and found that it was a very thin year indeed for me. We started the year without a Lotus-Cortina in production at all (though the old car was still homologated) and for various reasons connected with the money they were spending at Cosworth, Ford management had decided on a very quiet rallying year. The team had changed a lot, too. Vic Elford, who was probably a bit quicker than me on tarmac rallies, had finally broken away from the team (he never got on all that well with Henry, I think), and Ove Andersson from Sweden had joined Bengt Soderstrom. So now I was the only Briton on the strength — something I would get very accustomed to in the next nine years!

After the Monte fiasco in 1966, Henry Taylor kept his word and didn't enter us for the next event (in fact we didn't go again until 1970), so it looked as if I would be staying at home, but I was in for rather a rude shock. I had a call from Ford of Germany, who proudly asked me if I would like to drive one of their latest Taunus 20Ms? They seemed to think that because it had a bit of a sloping roof line, and an optional limited-slip axle, that it ought to be a racer, and they were out to prove it.

Jim and I practised quite hard and really set out to do our best for them, but as it transpired it was all a bit of a joke. Not that we treated it as such, but there was just no way that the Taunus could go quickly. It didn't have much urge, the limited-slip didn't limit . . . and we were in the wrong category anyway.

All too often there seems to be a lot of messing about with regulations in rallying; that's why I like a straightforward 'forestry race' so much. On this Monte you could either opt for eight marked tyres (all to be carried in the car), or have unlimited tyres and a 12 per cent handicap applied to stage times. Ford thought it worthwhile going for unlimited tyres and chose that category.

They were wrong, and we finished nowhere, not that the choice would have mattered, anyway, because the Taunus looked and went about as well as a Cologne taxi. We flogged ourselves to get the best possible result, but nearly all the stages were steep uphill and down again, which favoured the 'power' cars. If you look at the results they show R. Clark's position as 67th (and that's no misprint), even though we were 22nd fastest on scratch times.

I see that Jim has crept back into the story without an explanation. After I moved on from Rover, Jim stayed behind to administer the team, and then found the department closed down around him. Both

Rover and Triumph decided to pull out of rallying in 1966, which left Jim out on a limb at Rovers from February. In fact he stayed on to work with Ralph Nash in the engineering department for a time, but obviously he was free to go rallying with me again if he could find the time. By 1967 Jim had got thoroughly browned off with earning an honest living, and went back to rally driving instead! Henry took him on as one of Ford's first contracted co-drivers, where he's been ever since.

I'm very sorry that Jim has missed out on one or two of my more exotic trips — usually for a very good reason. 1967 might have been a thin year for my sport (the foot-and-mouth epidemic didn't help at the end when the RAC Rally was cancelled quite literally at 12 hours' notice), but I had not one, but two far-flung trips. Henry sent me to Canada again, this time for the Shell 4000 which ran to the site of the enormous Expo 67 exhibition, and I had my first taste of the Safari.

There isn't much to say about the Shell 4000, as it was much the same as the previous year. The nice thing was that this time I won it — my first 'International' win out of Britain — and I used a Mark 2 Lotus-Cortina to do it. It was still very much of a long-distance grind, with only 12 stages (totalling about 250 miles, so that was an improvement) in eight days between the start in Vancouver and the finish in Montreal. I see from the pictures that the Lotus-Cortina was a 'left-hooker', the first left-hand-drive car I had driven in competition.

Africa was something else. There had been Safaris since 1953, and they had always been won by local East African drivers. The Hughes organisation of Kenya, who sold Fords, were very keen to knock over this reputation, and they were delighted when Henry decided to send over a huge team of five cars, plus two works-assisted entries. Publicity dictated that the new-shape Cortinas were to be used, but as the new Lotus-Cortina was not yet homologated, four drivers had to use the new Cortina GTs, while I was delighted to be given an old-model Lotus-Cortina. To hell with the publicity — I had just the car I needed.

There was something about the new Mark 2 Cortina body that was only just becoming known. If you drove them hard enough and jumped them high enough the whole body started to bend, not like the original Cortinas, which the Boreham mechanics had put right by strengthening the shells, but in a more serious way. After a lot of rough work they started to crumple in the scuttle and front door hinge area, and if a car was painted with Lotus-Cortina stripes you could see a definite kink in the supposedly straight line as it passed from front wing to front door. Sometimes we had difficulty opening and closing the front doors, so no wonder we got around to calling them 'sausages' or 'bananas'.

Our solution back at Boreham was to throw the bodies away after every rough rally; there wasn't much point in trying to develop the trouble away because we all had an idea we might not be using them in 1968. That was still a most interesting little secret that comes later in the story.

But back to Africa. It was all very strange at first, and because of the distances involved and the nature of the event I decided to take Gilbert Staepelaere (who was driving Fords in Belgium) as my co-driver. Because the Cortina GTs were not nearly as quick as my Lotus-Cortina we were expected to go faster at first, though I don't know if they expected me to finish. In practice we learned very quickly that the flat-out all-sideways technique would not do where a tight section might go on for hours. Getting away from somebody else's dust was most important, which meant going flat-out for a time to get by and then sprint away from them, but apart from that preserving the car was all-important, and after looking at the target averages we were not at all sure it was possible. Ford had won the Safari in 1964 (locals Peter Hughes and Bill Young, driving a works-built Cortina GT), but survival was more difficult then in a very wet and boggy event.

We had the most hilarious problems beforehand. There was one occasion when Norman Masters had taken Goo to the local Nairobi night club (I was away practising). They hadn't been sitting up on the balcony for long before an enormous and very cocky African came up to Norman and offered to buy Goo! Now even Norman, whose eyes light up at the sight of money, wasn't going to have that, and he turned him down flat. What Norman didn't realise was that his reaction was the normal way to start any sort of business negotiation in Kenya, and the African took it to be an invitation to start bargaining! The next thing was that he said he just wanted to borrow Goo for a while, and he tried to trade her for a number of African girls he controlled. Norman soon caught on to this and played him along to see what the limits were, but Goo got thoroughly alarmed. As she said, ''I didn't mind the bargaining, even over me, but by the time

Norman was being offered ten African girls I thought he actually might agree!''

It wasn't even entirely safe to stay inside the splendid old Norfolk Hotel in the town because the local boys were always trying to sell us something. It was on the same trip that Norman and the other mechanics went for a swim in the sea off Dar-es-Salaam, and the poor man met up with a fish that rather fancied his big toe and took a big bite out of it.

After all that the rally might have been an anti-climax; in fact just about everything happened, and even if we did finish nowhere I could never have been bored. First of all we broke a half-shaft (Stuart Turner says in his latest book *The Way to Win* that 'half-shaft' will be found engraved on his heart when he dies, and I know what he means!), then the dynamo stopped working, and next the rear dampers punched their way through the bodywork. Later on a marshal gave our route card away to another competitor at a busy check point, and then an engine mounting collapsed. No — it wasn't my year, was it?

I only did two big events at home all year, and it was good news and bad news. Jim and I won the Scottish fairly comfortably, though the car was white with a green stripe so it demonstrated its bends very well indeed. On the Gulf London Ford went in for a bit of experimentation, and I was faced with fuel-injection on a rally car for the first time. I had a new car for the Gulf (the 'banana' was loaned to Tony Chappell) and the fuel-injected engine was intended to take advantage of the rules of homologation which allowed alternative 'carburation' if you had sold so many sets. Where Fords had sold *any* sets for the Mark 2 Lotus-Cortina I never found out, and by their performance on this rally I don't think their owners would have been very pleased. I didn't even see the set-up until my car arrived at scrutineering in Manchester, and I was appalled.

The injection was by Tecalemit-Jackson, a system that was supposed to be cheap and simple; what it actually meant was that there were lots of little things buzzing and whirring around under the bonnet. There were pipes, belts, wires, pumps, nozzles — you name it — and all sorts of strange noises to keep us company.

There looked to be so much more that could go wrong — belts to break, timing devices to slip, precision this and that — and it was not my idea of a good rally car at all. I have to be fair to Henry Taylor, though — the set-up did bring lots of extra performance to *racing* Cortinas, just when they needed it, but it didn't do a lot for me.

The engine never gave any extra *usable* power in the special stages, and when an oil pipe split and leaked all the sump's contents into the middle of Dovey forest I can't say I was sorry. I never did come to terms with 'things that go whirr in the night', but funny that five years later I should have another make of injection on the car that gave me a very big win indeed. That was the end of my rallying for 1967. There should have been a titanic RAC Rally, of course, but an epidemic of foot-and-mouth disease put an end to that. Nobody could blame Jack Kemsley and his team for trying to run an event in the face of all the odds, and we actually got as far as scrutineering in London, with revised routes being worked out at very short notice, when it all had to be cancelled.

There was the most monumental party in the Airport Hotel after the announcement, but I also remember that the foreign teams were very depressed the next night when Prime Minister Harold Wilson appeared on TV to announce devaluation. Most of the teams had turned all their expenses into British money the day before, and were faced with a big loss when they tried to turn them back again on the way home! Because I was the only British driver in the Ford team I was the only one available at short notice for development and testing. I was quite used to receiving a phone call asking me to scoot down to Bagshot or somewhere like it to do more work, or even to do some demonstration driving. In 1967 there were Grand Prix drivers entered for the rally again, but this time Jim Clark couldn't make it (he had to stay out of the country for tax reasons, I believe). Graham Hill was down to drive a Lotus-Cortina with David Seigle-Morris, while World Champion Denny Hulme was taking a prototype Triumph 2.5 PI with Graham Robson as his co-driver.

By chance they both arranged to turn up at Bagshot on the same day for some practice on the rough roads. Graham Hill was making a serious attempt to learn the game this time (a Lotus-Cortina was much more his scene than a Cooper S) and he was thrashing round and round and round. We kept seeing him thundering up the hill towards the control hut, turning off into the trees and back round the circuit, with his moustache bristling and a look of fierce concentration on his face. Suddenly it all went quiet; the car had stopped.

A few minutes later he arrived back at the control hut, on foot, grinning broadly, and announced, "The windscreen's broken, so I left it out there for the mechanics to collect". He was right — the windscreen *had* broken, but what he hadn't said was *why*. It wasn't because of a flying stone, but because the car was way off the road, neatly parked on its stoved in roof; the screen was missing completely!

Denny Hulme wasn't quite as serious about it as Graham Hill, mainly because the practice car provided by Triumph was nearly standard. However, we managed to get him a lot more interested when I was talked into trying out the Triumph 2000, putting him in the passenger seat, and thrashing him round a few times.

In those two years I also managed to put in a lot of motor racing. Not the serious and dramatic single-seater stuff, but racing in saloon car classes with Cortinas of one sort or another. In 1966 I simply used the Lotus-Cortina Henry Taylor had provided for British rallying, and because it would be racing one weekend and rallying the next we never found time to set it up for the tracks. It wasn't a very special car — we used to race it on steel wheels for instance — but it went round in a very special way. In the dry it simply wasn't competitive, but in the wet it seemed to grow horns and really enjoy itself. It was set up very tail-happy for rallying, and on a wet circuit it used to behave in the same way. I didn't like 'wet' racers, which were almost useless at the time, so I used to turn up on the starting grids with great fat knobbly tyres!

The stewards didn't know what to make of this, particularly as there was no rule on which they could exclude me, but there were three meetings at Silverstone when they called me in and read the riot act. They had a point though — we were using the Club circuit, which made Woodcote a sharp, slowish corner, and I would persist in going round there absolutely sideways in the wet, steering with one hand and shaking my fist or making suitable gestures at someone on the end of the pit counter!

Some of the old diehards nearly had heart failure, or apoplexy, or something, and I was told "That is *not* the way to go round corners; it's not the quickest way. You should learn". I was reminded of what Spen King had said, and offered to take any of them round to demonstrate the difference, but nobody took me up on it.

The car was never competitive — no, that's not true — it simply wasn't a stripped-out specialised racer, and it was a lot too soft and a lot too heavy. But in *really* bad weather conditions I could see off nearly all the pansy racing drivers who liked sunshine on their bonnets. Sideways all the way round Gerard's Bend at Mallory Park was one of my specialities.

A year later we were all a lot more serious. Henry Taylor was keen to get me a bit more involved in racing, so when a Mark 2 Lotus-Cortina set up for track racing suddenly became free I was asked to drive it. This was a car built up by John Young, the Ford racing preparation specialist, for Calypso (the cigarette people), and it had subsequently reverted to Boreham. Calypso set up a season of British saloon car racing, Mick Jones and David Wood looked after the car, and we had a good time.

None of the Boreham mechanics were used to racing or to racing saloons, and the first time I took the car out they had put in only a little petrol in order to keep the weight down, but after a couple of corners there was so much centrifugal force that the pump refused to pick up anything but air and the car just stopped — on its first ever lap! I also shocked them by demanding knobblies the first time it rained, and the Calypso directors didn't think much of it, either.

Somehow we couldn't get very serious about the car, and the operation was soon known as 'Collapsible Racing' because that's what happened more than once. It was, however, a lot more competitive than the Mark 1 car, and on occasions it went very quickly indeed.

Henry Taylor wanted me to do more racing, but he also kept me very busy in a rally car and there simply wasn't time to do both. Colin Chapman went through a period of looking for new talent from the rally drivers (Andrew Cowan actually had a go once or twice in a Formula 3 car), and Henry Taylor once asked me if I would like to take up single-seater racing. He could guarantee me a drive straight away in a Formula 3 car, and if I wanted it, in a Formula 2 car within a few months. After that it was up to me; I could have had all the support that Ford and Lotus could provide. But I turned it down, figuring that racing wasn't for me if I had to get serious about it; even in the short saloon car races I had been doing I was likely to get bored towards the end unless the weather conditions were really bad.

So that was 1967, and a not very successful year at all, not that we minded so much at the time because for at least half of the year we were hugging a secret that we thought was about to revolutionise our chances in coming years. I was in on the ground floor of this project, and it was all very exciting; Ford had decided that they couldn't beat specialised rally cars from other factories with modified production cars of their own, and they meant to do something about it. They were right — 1968 was one of the most extraordinary years I have ever witnessed, and I had a completely new car to play with.

Chapter 5

The Escort and me

IT ALL STARTED in the spring of 1967. Some of us had known for a long time that a new small Ford was due in 1968, but we didn't think it would mean any more to us than the existing Anglia. At first there was no intention of selling any really white-hot versions, but the Escort Twin-Cam duly appeared in the same line-up as the other Escorts — for which you can really blame Stuart Turner. I don't mind blaming him, because he is now benefitting from the consequences.

In 1967 Stuart was in charge at Abingdon, and his BMC Cooper Ss were getting ridiculously quick, whether racing or rallying. The Lotus-Cortinas could still beat them in some conditions but not all, and our latest versions were heavier than before; we were in trouble. Henry Taylor and his boss, Walter Hayes, got their heads together, agreed that they didn't like being second-best at anything, and resolved to do something about it.

After I had returned home from Canada in May I found a nice congratulatory letter from Walter Hayes waiting for me, which ended like this, "I hope that we may have something even more interesting for you next year, but I imagine Henry Taylor has talked to you about things in general". That 'even more interesting' project was to be a very hot small car, a special version of the Escort, which Boreham were to design and develop.

I wasn't in at the birth of the thing, because at the time the drivers were not needed. Bill Meade and the Boreham mechanics spent a complete weekend (all the days and most of the nights too, by all accounts) squeezing the Lotus-Cortina mechanicals into the bodyshell of a prototype Escort GT. They weren't allowed to keep the car at that point, and were told to strip everything out and return the shell to Ford Engineering! That gives you an idea of the low priority we sometimes enjoyed at Boreham, even in 1967. It also gives an idea of the way the Escort Twin-Cam was 'designed' — by push, grunt and hope rather than by pencils on paper. Incidentally, when the first prototype was finished off, later in the summer, one of the mechanics, Johnny Rule, wrote it off on its first shake-down run when some vital structural welding came adrift.

I got involved with development towards the end of the year, before the car was announced, and before announcement day in January we were already testing a Twin-Cam at Bagshot. I liked the 'J25' (as we coded it) right from the start and I soon realised that this was *the* rally car for me in the future.

Most of the mechanism was already very familiar and well-developed, but the basic car was smaller, stiffer and more precise. There wasn't all that much difference in length — just under a foot, and only 3.5 inches in the wheelbase — but somehow the Cortinas felt a lot longer, especially when they were all sideways on a narrow special stage.

My first impression was that there was much more precision built into a Twin-Cam, and it demanded more precise driving from me. Part of this was due to the rack-and-pinion steering, and part because of the way Mick Jones and Ken Wiltshire had set up the suspension; it felt a lot more 'nervous' on twisting tracks — not quite as much difference as racehorse against carthorse, but there was a completely fresh feeling. The electrifying tingle of a car built for competitions, and nearly right from the beginning, was something you just can't describe, but the Escort had it. The right tool for the job, at last, and no compromises.

People look at Escorts now and think that the Twin-Cam conversion must have been very easy to engineer. No way. For a start, the engine simply wouldn't go in to the body at first, which is why every Twin-Cam or RS1600 ever made has a cock-eyed drive-line with the nose of the engine pushed well over to the left. The Cortina gearbox was a very tight fit in a body designed for a smaller component, and we had to lobby like hell to get more space for bigger wheels and tyres; the Escort was only meant to have 12-inch wheels, and the basic jobs had quite narrow rims.

We lost out on headlamps, and had to live with those dreadful rectangular units for some time. It was stupid, and all a matter of 'product planning'. The cheapest Escorts had round units, but the more expensive ones had rectangular units. Therefore, said the product planners, as our Twin-Cam was to be the most expensive Escort, it had to have rectangular lamps, too. We stuck with them, or a messy conversion kit, for a long time, but at least every RS1600 car sold reverted to the best arrangement.

When it was time to see how an Escort stood up to a pounding, I spent a lot of time at Bagshot trying to break the bodies, tear the suspension out, and develop a lightweight sump-shield. Mick Jones and Ken Wiltshire had got over all their troubles with the rear suspension by then — they had wanted a Panhard-rod arrangement, which fitted in well but repeatedly broke in testing. Eventually they had to revert to radius arms instead, which stayed in one piece.

There was one particular hump at Bagshot where we could jump very high — to test dampers and things — and there is a splendid sequence of Ford publicity pictures which show me flying higher, and higher, and higher . . . we thought we should stop after one run when the car jumped so high that it landed on its nose and nearly did an end-over-end for photographer Ken Shipton's benefit! I see that John Taylor jumped a Mark 1 Escort very high indeed for its last publicity shot of all, but we were not shown what happened when it landed.

The original car we used for all this destruction testing — the first prototype, XTW 368F — was eventually sold to Barry Lee, who won an enormous number of events in it. That car has had quite a life — I even used it to win a rallycross at Croft just after announcement in 1968.

We have been using Escorts for such a long time — eight years to the end of 1975 — that you might think we were all getting thoroughly bored with them. But over the years we have carried out so much detail development and experimental work on them that they have rarely remained the same cars for long. The specification settled down in 1973 and 1974, but following the arrival of the new car several big improvements have already been tried in rally conditions.

The Twin-Cam was so much quicker, smaller, and more precise that the Lotus-Cortinas that we were really in paradise that first year. It didn't take long to get homologation, though it certainly wasn't on the strength of 1,000 cars, which was the requirement. The Boreham workshops actually assembled the first 25 cars, which explains why we weren't very active during the winter and early spring of 1968 — there simply was no room in the workshops for rally cars to be prepared.

Ove Andersson had the honour of taking the Twin-Cam on its first ever rally, in Italy, where he came third, but I gave it its first win at Easter in the Circuit of Ireland. My principal opposition there was Paddy Hopkirk, in the latest of 1275 cc Cooper Ss, but there was such a massive power difference that I didn't have to work very hard to beat him.

April, May and June were fantastically successful months for us. Jim and I followed up the Circuit win by going off to Holland and France to lift the Tulip Rally (Ove's Twin-Cam finished right behind me), followed it up with another win in the Acropolis Rally then came home to tackle the Scottish in my Circuit 'rough road' car and win that as well. Four wins from four starts was a splendid way of getting to know the Escort, and I've been in love with them ever since. It was quite an anti-climax to be sent out to practise for the Alpine Rally in a full-house Escort with a Formula 2 FVA engine and have it blow up on me.

The sudden arrival of the Escort revolutionised British club rallying. For years, it was necessary to have a Cooper S to win, or, if you were brave with a larger car, a Lotus-Cortina. But Coopers were notoriously hard on their transmissions, whereas the first Twin-Cams were very reliable. It *was* possible to spend a lot of money on an Escort (Boreham were already in the homologation business, and selling goodies to support this) but even an un-tuned car, made stronger with a good set of skid shielding, was competitive. Certainly we thought the team cars were fast enough at first, but strong competition from Europe soon made us think again.

I think it would be very revealing to have to drive an Escort Twin-Cam prepared to the first 1968 rally-car specification in a 1976 rally. I think we would be amazed at the things it couldn't do that we are now accustomed to expecting, for there really isn't much comparison between an early Twin-Cam and the latest in RS1600s or RS1800s.

Since 1968 we've had engine transplants, gearbox transplants and back axle transplants. The rear suspension has changed, the front struts are different, we've changed our minds many times on seats, controls, safety belts, instruments, roll cages — there isn't a lot left.

To satisfy the "Wottle she do, mister?" brigade, I should say that since 1968 we have pushed up rally-car power outputs from 145 bhp for a Twin-Cam to around 245 bhp for a Brian Hart 2-litre RS engine. Top speed means very little, because on a rally car it is the 50 mph to 90 mph acceleration band that is vitally important on high-speed stages. We have five-speed gearboxes now, so there is a ratio for every need, but top speeds are really meaningless. My first Twin-Cam was geared *down* to less than 100 mph whereas the production car reached 112 mph. Even now a full-house five-speed 2-litre is rarely geared for more than 115 mph as we don't expect to see that lick anywhere other than in Yorkshire on an RAC Rally.

Boreham never, but never, has time to do performance tests on its own rally cars, so it is only by the seat of our pants, and the times compared with the opposition, that we know if the thing has been improved. There have been times when we thought that the Escort was finished, the most desperate being when the 'racers' we built for the 1970 Monte failed to make any impression on the Alpines and Porsches, but even at the end of 1974, when the old Escort was going out of production, it was still fast enough to win in Finland and in the RAC Rally.

From time to time, our rally cars have been tested by the motoring press, and the results make very interesting reading. The snag is that these tests are usually carried out on the car *after* it has finished, and often won, something important, and we have no way of knowing if the performance is still up to scratch. I have ignored the figures taken by some of the less reputable 'comics', because their methods are sometimes crude and unreliable. On the other hand, Escorts have been loaned to *Autocar* and *Motor* from time to time, where the results recorded are always accurate and repeatable.

I have written out a table of performance comparisons of four rally car tests, along with figures for the showroom models, which tell you all sorts of things:

What rather puzzles me is that according to these test figures, the rally Escorts haven't really got a lot quicker over the years, not, that is, in terms of flat-out acceleration. According to them, the quickest of all in a straight line way my 1800 Twin-Cam of 1969, which couldn't possibly have been giving more than about 170 bhp even when fully fit. Even my very first Twin-Cam, tested after it had won

Rally car performance figures compared

Car	Standard Twin Cam	1968 Rally Twin Cam	1969 Rally Twin Cam	Standard RS1600	1971 Rally RS1600	1974 Rally RS1600
Tested	Autocar 6-6-68	Autocar 11-7-68	Motor 31-5-69	Autocar 30-4-70	Autocar 20-1-72	Motor 28-12-74
Engine and Power Output	1558cc TC 106 bhp	1600cc TC 150 bhp	1800cc TC 175 bhp	1601cc RS 120 bhp	1800cc RS 210 bhp	2000cc RS 235 bhp
Rev Limit	6500 rpm	7500 rpm	7000 rpm	6500 rpm	8500 rpm	8500 rpm
Gearbox	Standard	'Bullet'	'Bullet'	Standard	ZF 5-spd	ZF 5-spd
Axle Ratio	3.77	4.9	5.1	3.77	5.14	5.3
Maximum in each gear:						
Top	113	99	—	113	113	—
4th	—	—	—	—	96	—
3rd	81	77	—	85	87	—
2nd	56	58	—	60	63	—
1st	38	43	—	40	49	—
Acceleration through gears:						
0-30 mph	3.8	3.5	—	3.4	2.9	2.5
0-50 mph	7.2	6.2	4.7	6.8	5.5	5.3
0-60 mph	9.9	7.9	6.3	8.9	7.0	6.4
0-70 mph	13.0	10.1	8.3	12.4	9.0	8.3
0-80 mph	16.8	13.0	10.6	16.1	11.9	10.8
0-90 mph	24.2	16.8	13.5	22.6	14.9	13.6
0-100 mph	33.6	21.2	17.1	32.3	20.3	17.7
Standing ¼-mile	17.2	15.9	14.7	16.7	14.7	—
Top gear 50-90 mph	22.3	13.1	—	22.0	10.7	—
4th gear 50-90 mph	—	—	—	—	9.4	—
3rd gear 30-70 mph	12.5	9.4	—	12.1	6.9	—

its first rally in Ireland at Easter, was nearly as quick through the gears as the 1800 RS which Timo used in 1971 on the RAC Rally. However, in any particular gear the later RS was quite a lot quicker, which is part of the answer, I'm sure.

But that doesn't give all the answers, and because I'm no boffin, someone else will have to explain it to me. I have always said (sometimes *very* loudly at Ford forums) that I don't think the Escort is a very quick car, especially on tarmac. I've also said many times that I haven't really been able to identify any great change in performance over the years.

So where has that extra 90 bhp become useful? Or conversely, where has it gone? After all, 90 bhp is more than a Mexico had altogether in standard form. One answer is to look back at my performance in the RS2000 which I used for the Mintex Dales in 1974, when I won by just a couple of seconds after working very hard indeed. That car, which I never drove again, produced around 160 bhp, or about the same as an original Twin-Cam, and it felt much slower than my normal machine. The differences were most obvious at high speed on a really quick Yorkshire stage, where the last 10 mph never appeared at all.

There are two other factors which complicate the issue. One is that we have seen very important advances in traction in recent years, and the other is that all rally cars have become a lot heavier as various lightening allowances, such as plastic windows, have been withdrawn and big strong roll cages have become compulsory. I wouldn't be at all surprised if a 1975 RS was at least 300 to 400 pounds heavier in rally condition than a 1968 car. The really interesting thing would be to put all the modern improvements on to a 1968 specification Twin-Cam and try it out again.

For a time, as we built up experience with the early Twin-Cams, the car was good enough. We won events all over the place (and of course other people wiped up the opposition on the race tracks), and we only had trouble with the occasional Porsche and Alpine on special events. The Mini-Coopers were wiped out; in 1967 they had been top, and in 1968 the team started to break up — it was as sudden as that. But by 1969 we were having to enlarge engines to keep up, and by 1970 we were struggling. People like Waldegaard were winning tarmac, rough and snowy rallies in Porsches, and the Alpines looked as if they might have a winner, too.

We knew that a new engine was nearly ready, but meanwhile the fact that we had a very good practice, loads of studded tyres, and virtually trouble-free runs on the 1970 Monte didn't help us much. My own particular triumph was in beating Timo and Hannu, but I only notched up fifth overall, behind three Porsches and one Alpine-Renault. It was a question of traction and sheer power. The power improvements were promised, but traction was — and still is — a problem.

However, before this, we had another big upheaval in the team. Quite suddenly, and with virtually no warning, we heard that there was going to be a change at the helm. Henry Taylor was moving on and — of all people — Stuart Turner was coming in as our new competitions manager. I say ''of all people'' because this was rather like asking Harold Wilson to be leader of the Tory Party! Stuart had been in charge at Abingdon during the Mini-Cooper success period, though we had had business links with him after that when he was publicity manager at Castrol, our oil suppliers.

I wondered what my future with Ford would be now? We all knew that Stuart Turner was firmly convinced that the Finns were the best drivers in the world, while there was also the fact that he and I had never really hit it off in recent years. Henry Taylor and I were very firm friends — his life-style and mine were similar — but Stuart was, and still is for that matter, one of those dedicated men who are very difficult to really get to know.

The relationship started rather badly, mostly because of the way things developed at Boreham and in the team. After Stuart had arrived at Abingdon he had brought Rauno Aaltonen and Timo Makinen into the team within a year; when he arrived at Boreham he confirmed Hannu Mikkola's appointment, and had taken Timo Makinen into his team well within the year. Not long after that he recruited Rauno Aaltonen for the World Cup Rally, and my place was beginning to look shaky. It didn't help when Stuart did a BBC ''Wheelbase'' TV interview and said that inside two years there wouldn't be any British drivers in his team because Scandinavians were quicker and tried harder.

I don't think I actually had a row with Stuart then, but it came mighty close once or twice, and if I hadn't felt so loyal to the rest of the team, the mechanics and the cars themselves I would have been tempted to say ''Stuff it'' and go off to look for other drives.

Now we get on very much better, and perhaps we respect each other's views more completely. Stuart has often had the kindness to pull his own leg at forums by reminding people about his TV remarks and then pointing to my RAC Rally win; I get my own back on the same platforms.

Soon after this there was a build-up of staff at Boreham. Several ex-Boreham or ex-BMC mechanics and specialists arrived, and as both Timo and Rauno had come from BMC, too, there was all the makings of a good personality split right through the department, especially as at this time some of the mechanics were very loyal to

91

their own drivers, but not to the others. I wouldn't say that Norman Masters would actually ever have thumped anyone over the head with a spanner, but it wasn't wise to walk around him at Boreham singing the praises of some Scandinavian drivers!

Things have never recovered completely. Even in 1975, when Timo and I have been the only regularly retained drivers, there have been mechanics who don't particularly like testing with Timo because of his great attention to detail and his occasional rushing off up a blind development alley; 15-inch wheels were a case in point, but the story of these comes a little later.

The biggest upset, which affected us all for a time, was Stuart's insistance on a change in workshop building methods. Until then Henry Taylor had worked a one-man-one-car philosophy where, for instance, Norman Masters would build me a new rally car, starting from the bare bodyshell, and finishing when the completed car was driven out of the gates; he would accept engines from the engine specialists, a gearbox from the stores but built by a gearbox man, and so on, but the car would be a Norman Masters car, for me. A car by Robin Vokins for Timo might theoretically be the same, but there would be all manner of tiny differences that Timo and I could spot.

Stuart changed all this. For a time he insisted on a production-line method of building, where the same men did the same things to a whole series of cars, so that a set of identically-prepared cars came out at the far end. The trouble was that because the mechanics could no longer 'identify' with a driver they lost a little, just the sharp edge, of their professional pride, and they were still faced with the problem of personalising each rally car before we could start an event. I'm happy to say that this approach didn't last too long — certainly for the last four years Norman Masters has been building my Escorts, and that's the way I like it.

Norman and I have evolved this fantastic understanding about my rally cars. I know that if he was to build up a new car for me, without me knowing, paint it up to look like the last one, and present me with it at the start of an event, I probably wouldn't even notice it was new! This may sound like a waste, but it isn't. Everything I want, such as my favourite seat, the control layout, the setting of the lights, the spares list and where they are stowed, dusters and rags, safety belts, spare wheel stowage — everything would be right. Usually I don't even have to check the tyre pressures.

As a confidence-builder this is outstanding. It has got to such a stage nowadays that I don't have to allow any time before scrutineering at the start of a rally to 'get it right'; if Norman has built the car it *will* be right. If I am ever pushed for time getting to a start, I may miss the scrutineering beforehand, and on more than one occasion I have stepped into a car in the *parc ferme* for the first time since I saw it on the previous event.

Just occasionally there can be a few snags. On two occasions I have turned up at the start and found no car waiting for me! There was the time in 1974 when Norman took my Esso car to scrutineering before the Dukeries on one set of tyres, changed them to knobblies to come back to the garage, went off on slippery tarmac, and came back to me with an ignition key but no car . . .

Sometimes we find ourselves in scrapes together, like the occasion when we had all gone down to the South of France for the Alpine Rally. It was a lovely evening, the cars were ready to be used, and we all drifted off down the cost to Cassis for a few beers. We were down by the harbour, one drink led to another, we started singing, and before we knew what had happened it was one o'clock in the morning.

Now there's never any way to explain this sort of thing afterwards, but at the time it seemed to be a good idea to take a boat — not our boat — and row back to the hotel in the pitch black! We 'found' this boat, and started back by sea, which wasn't easy, because we couldn't see much, and neither of us knew much about boats. To make sure we were OK, or possibly just to wait for the splash, Mick Jones and the other mechanics trailed us back on the edge of the water.

There we were, rowing away and singing at the tops of our voices, and before long we were back to what we thought was our beach. The only trouble was that when we turned into land we saw a night guard — one of the chaps who was paid to look after all the boats — and he was hopping up and down with rage!

There was only one thing for it — we had to turn round and row most of the way back, and beach the damned thing near our starting point. It was a long walk home, too, and after all that exercise we were flaked out. Need I say that I got no sympathy from any quarter? Or that it was the night before the start?

The drawback to this sort of close relationship (or so Stuart has assured me from time to time) is that I tend to trust Norman in everything he does, I am usually completely satisfied with a new car, and don't voluntarily do enough testing and niggling to see if improvements can be made. This is what Stuart had to say recently when questioned on the subject:

"If you put Roger in a London taxi on bald remoulds and sent him off to Bagshot, he'd probably be about as quick as usual. He just gets in and goes round, gets on with the job, and enjoys it. There's none of the Jackie Stewart's 'I want a quarter-inch off this, a few thou' on that'. Timo, on the other hand — well, we have mechanics who think Timo's a damned nuisance. But in a way we need people to be damned nuisances. Unless they keep ringing up Peter Ashcroft and suggesting crazy things like sideways engines on the roof, 19-inch wheels on one side, seven-speed gearboxes . . . you need to keep pushing. Once you stand still, you start to go back."

Stuart is also very firm about contracts — he doesn't believe in rigid legally-phrased contracts. I'm happy about that, because I don't really want to get involved in any of the situations which are rife in motor racing. Did the Peterson.— Lotus — UOP-Shadow business early in 1975 do any good for motor sport in the end? I don't think so.

Stuart's approach to driver-team arrangements are simple. Every year, all that happens — assuming he remembers — is that I get a letter like this:

"Dear Roger,

As agreed when we chatted over a few pints the other night, we would like you to drive for us next year. We will pay you £x. If you would like to borrow a car for the coming year for your own transport we will provide one. We would also like you to go to a number of motor club functions, we'd like you to do at least 20 Ford forums and other Ford occasions, and we might want to use you in Ford advertising or dealer promotions from time to time. We will pay all your out-of-pocket expenses when you are working for us."

There will be little more than that, and all I have to do is to sign a copy of it and let Ford have it, so they know I agree.

It is a sort of annual contract, I suppose, but quite un-enforceable. It would be possible to have a contract that tied up everything, but what would be the point? Ford could have a piece of paper witnessed by everybody in the Houses of Parliament which said I had to drive for them when required, and I'm sure a High Court judge could make me do it, but if I was really browned off with the deal there's just no way they could expect me to drive all that hard. That's where legal contracts in motor sport make no sense at all. In the end it is driver flair, effort and dedication which bring results, and if a relationship has gone sour the performance will certainly have suffered.

Here's one very good example of how contracts can be self-defeating; Ford were very happy that I went out and found my own support for a rallying programme by enlisting Esso as a sponsor. This worked very well until we had a big event like the RAC Rally, when I had to be part of a Ford team which was backed by Shell, the Milk Marketing Board or Colibri. Esso rightly thought they had exclusive use of my talents and my car in British events, which was something that I'm sure Ford must have found inhibiting, although it simply wasn't worth getting into a lather about it.

The development of the cars has usually been of more immediate importance to us, and I am rather proud of the great improvements we have made to the Escorts since 1968. We have always been hidebound by the limitations of homologation (a horrid word that I don't propose to explain), which basically meant that whatever we needed on a rally car had to be available for sale to private owners.

The improvements we made can be split into three categories — those to make the car stronger, those to make it more nimble, and those to make it quicker.

What surprised us all was how strong the original Escort bodyshell proved to be. Twin-Cams and their successors, the Mexicos, RS1600s and RS2000s, have always used the heavy-duty Type 49 bodyshell, but apart from changes to get in the extra homologated parts such as fuel tanks, damper turrets, ZF gearboxes and the like, they haven't needed a lot of attention.

By comparison with the Mark 2 Lotus-Cortina bodies, the Escort body is very robust. Back in the mid-1960s it was common knowledge that a works Mini-Cooper S would only do one, or possibly two, rough-road events before you had to start again, but the Escort hasn't suffered like that. My first famous blue Esso car is a good example of this. 'LVX' had a new bodyshell for the 1972 RAC Rally because somebody had rolled the previous one at Boreham in a filming session. (Who? No names . . .) This rebuilt car won the RAC Rally and went on to win two more Internationals (the Welsh and the Scottish), plus eight more RAC Championship Nationals, all with the same body and basic equipment. It was good for more, but I was due for a new Esso car so we sold it to Adrian Boyd, who promptly shunted it!

Boreham got its Mark 1 bodyshells ready prepared by Maurice Gomm's metalworking people. In the early days we used to find that an Escort that was really getting old would give itself away with a bit of windscreen pillar cracking. That was before we used full roll cages. Now that we stiffen the whole shell by our roll bars, which follow the screen pillars very closely, the Boreham mechanics have to look elsewhere. Latterly, Mick Jones tells me, the first traces appeared in the form of cracks around the base of the rear windows.

With the new 'Brenda' (the Escort with the latest body), we have slightly different problems, but since the underpan is the same I haven't experienced too much trouble there.

The Escort's power possibilities have been going up steadily, and although my own rally engines have settled down at about 235 bhp in the last couple of years, Peter Ashcroft thinks there may be more to come yet. We started with just about 150 bhp in the 1,594 cc Twin-Cams, though the racing Twin-Cams could often call up 170 bhp for short events.

Because I was the only British team driver, and because I did more local events (home Internationals like the Circuit and the Scottish) I tended to be the guinea-pig for new engine tunes in rally cars. We stuck with the original engine for not much more than a year, before Peter Ashcroft's engine shop stuck an 1800 Twin-Cam unit into 'BEV' for the 1969 Circuit. That was the maximum *practicable* Twin-Cam engine stretch for rallying, where you have to flog on for hour after hour. A few of the racing teams went in for boring right out and re-sleeving to 2-litres, but these engines didn't last long, and anyway they broke most of the homologation regulations, too!

By the end of that year, 1969, we knew that the rear-engined cars had the beating of us on most counts, and I was delighted to hear rumours about the new Cosworth 16-valve engine. Keith Duckworth had designed a soft-tune BDA version of the Formula Two engine (the FVA) but with belt-driven camshafts. Don't ask me why, but Ford then put it in a prototype Capri and said they would be selling Capris like that in the future.

Nothing happened for a time (even Keith Duckworth was in the dark about the BDA's future when he first met Stuart Turner at a dinner party in the Midlands), but once Boreham had explained its needs, the BDA engine was scheduled for the new Escort.

I drove the first BDA-Escort from Boreham, took it on the Circuit in 1970, and won by nearly half-an-hour from Chris Sclater's Twin-Cam. We probably had only 170 or 180 bhp from the first BDAs, but a lot more torque than before, and with a great increase in reliability.

Since then we've been progressively stretching and tuning the BDAs. I had the first 1800 BDA unit on the RAC Rally in 1970, which pushed out 200 bhp, quite enough to chew up gearboxes and half-shafts at the time, and it's interesting to note that mine was the only RS1600 in the works team that week, because both Timo and Hannu had the 'old-model' Twin-Cams.

The BDAs got stronger and stronger, but no bigger, until the first of the light-alloy-block engines was built. That block, designed by Brian Hart for his own use in racing cars, came as a complete surprise to Peter Ashcroft when he almost fell over it on a visit to Brian's workshops. Apart from offering a great weight saving, it could also be bored out to the full 2-litre class limit and it gave us the final boost we needed.

I used an alloy-block 2-litre engine for the first time on the Jim Clark Rally in June 1972, it was homologated towards the end of the year, and the team used them on the RAC Rally in November.

It's worth remembering that for this particular RAC Rally, which I won, my engine was fitted with an experimental Lucas fuel-injection system. It was a much more sophisticated system that the other layout on the old Lotus-Cortina, but it still *looked* more complicated than the simple old Webers we knew so well. In terms of power there wasn't a lot in it. We had started with about 215 bhp at 8,500 rpm with the first of the alloy-block 2-litre engines, which Peter Ashcroft's boys pushed up to more than 230 bhp for the RAC Rally. My injection engine reputedly gave just a few more — about 240 bhp — but certainly not enough to give me any great 'edge'.

Since that RAC, we have not used the fuel-injection system again. During that winter the test beds worked away, and for quite a time now our standard policy has been to fit Webers, though even bigger and with larger-diameter chokes than before. At the end of the book there is an index showing the car's build schedule and its engine details. We abandoned fuel-injection for the time being because I wanted to keep the equipment simple. That's something that I return to time and time again — less complication means something less to go wrong, and it doesn't matter how expertly designed or built something is, on a rough rally there is still plenty of opportunity for it to go wrong!

As we kept pushing the power up, we inevitably ran into transmission troubles. After all, the original gearbox design dated back to the 1200 Cortina (and in philosophy to the 105E Anglia of 1959!) and I've already pointed out that back-axle parts could be swopped between Lotus-Cortinas, Escorts and 5-cwt Thames vans! By the time we were ready to use highly-tuned 16-valve Cosworth BDA engines, everybody at Boreham knew that different, stronger, gearboxes and back-axles would be needed. Then, incidentally, all mechanical links with the Lotus-Cortinas would be gone.

The axle problem was easy to solve — or so we thought at first. Ford of Germany had a big robust axle underneath their RS2600 Capri, and it was going to be used in the British 3-litre Capri. It coped with the racing version of a Capri V-6, so we thought it ought to deal with 2-litres of high-revving BDA. It did, and until we reached the stage of fuel-injected 240 bhp screamers it was even over-strong for the job. The snag, not to be ignored where roadholding was concerned, was that it was a great big heavy lump. It was yet another example of the way that Escort weights have crept up every time we have been looking for more performance or improving durability. RS1600s and RS1800s are not actually built from new with the Atlas axle (as we call it) but it is freely available as one of the homologated options.

When we first fitted Atlas axles they were amply strong enough for racing, and for Escort rally power on smooth roads. The two big troubles rough-road rallying exposed, which no amount of racing could betray, were half-shaft breakages, and the fact that lots of high jumping could bend them!

This was the cause of Stuart's remarks that the words 'Half-shafts' will be found engraved on his heart when he dies. For a time we were in continuous trouble with half-shafts being chewed up, and on one RAC Rally, in particular, the entire team suffered breakages in the middle of stages, and even though our limited-slip diffs. gave traction to the other wheel and allowed us to crawl along to our service cars, the wrong sort of breakage sometimes let the wheel fall off, and that was that.

We needed to do a lot of painstaking detail development, and it was here that the value of Bagshot's rough-road development potential proved itself. The Bagshot track is very specialised, and probably a lot more severe than most special stages, but it is absolutely predictable. Even though we may want to compare the results of work done one week with something done months earlier, we can rely on Bagshot results. The track is used by the same sort of military vehicles, day in and day out, to earn its bread and butter, is re-graded regularly, and we can now rely on it for our conclusions.

The high-speed course, indeed all the courses, are 'one-way only', which means that we never have to worry about people coming the other way. The track itself is private and strictly reserved to permit holders, which gets rid of the thought of peasants and rubber-neckers straying on to the track. It also means that over the years we have got used to the idea of thundering over blind brows and round the edge of a big tree, with complete confidence that there should be nothing there in our way. From time to time we find military vehicles using the same facilities, but they often stop to watch us enjoying our testing, and leave the track to the competition cars.

With all the severe uphill and downhill gradients, jumps and bumps, Bagshot was an ideal place to sort our half-shaft problem, especially as we could guarantee to snap them much quicker than on normal special stages. Bagshot is so severe on a rally car that we could go out with one set of shafts in a hard-working old test car and perhaps break one in 12 laps (that's less than 20 minutes), change the shafts, go out again and this time break them on the 13th lap. There was always some sort of pattern. Then we'd try a slightly different design, with sharp radii removed. This time we might get 20 laps, 21 laps, 19 laps, but once again a recognisable pattern. To be completely sure of correlation it had to be me driving, and it had to be the same car, but we never found ourselves being fooled. When eventually we found a set of shafts that could last 50 laps — that was long enough, believe me, because even I was getting bored of the track by then — we knew we had the job beaten.

We still change axle shafts regularly, perhaps after three events in the RAC Championship, but one set ought to be good enough to complete a full-length RAC Rally. Fortunately Norman Masters knows what sort of deterioration to look for, and if we catch the shafts at that point a change is quick and easy.

I'm told I hold the lap record at Bagshot, for what it's worth, but as I'm usually competing against military 4 x 4 trucks I don't think I'm going to start boasting about that. However, if I was asked to drive an Escort with a new engine tune, and it suddenly became worth three seconds or more, I'd know that we had found a useful improvement for a rally car. Bagshot is so useful for that sort of thing. Absolute performance is always hard to define, but if we can compare one thing with another, and pick up something definite and different, then Bagshot has done its job.

We needed a new gearbox behind the BDA engine because the Ford box had simply run out of torque capacity. In the end, when we were reaching towards 200 bhp, with a lot of extra torque, we could strip third gear out of the old 'Bullet' box in no time at all. By 1971, when the big new boxes were available, Timo and Hannu used them on the RAC Rally, while I was sent off with the best and strongest 'Rocket' box we could build. It was chewed up before Jim and I even got out of the Lake District, well before the half-way mark.

We had been fiddling around, looking for an alternative gearbox for some time. Apart from the usual problems of cost, commercial and political clashes and reliability, we had to be sure that the box could be fitted inside the Escort's slim floor pan. Apart from 'Rocket' ratios inside the existing shell, we had also looked at the Hewland five-speed creation, which was used in racing Escorts and didn't have any synchromesh.

For events like the Safari, or for long-distance Marathons where we needed a really tall top gear to give high maximum speed and relaxed cruising, we also needed a low bottom ratio to act as a 'stump puller' for dragging out of mud patches. For this sort of requirement, a four-speed gearbox couldn't do the job, so we had to look around for a five-speed gearbox that someone would be willing to sell us. It had to be an independent make, of course (one couldn't expect British Leyland, VW, Fiat or even a Japanese company to sell their stuff to a rival), and soon ZF got to know of our needs, through the German Ford operation.

The ZF gearbox looked promising, not only because it was German and had a good reputation for strength and long life, but because ZF had a lot of experience of building racing transmissions (including some for Lotus Formula One cars and for Ford's GT40s) and for being an adaptable organisation. The unit they proposed was already in production for the Fiat 130, and I believe it was optional on a BMW or two. That made it economically viable for us, but the big bonus was that there were alternative ratios, too. One, with a wide spread of ratios and a very low bottom gear, we now call the 'Safari' set, while the other, with really close spacing, is used for most of the normal type of events.

It had its problems for us, particularly at the beginning. ZF had never designed it to be thrashed around behind an engine that might pull more than 9,000 rpm, and although it was fine up to about 7,000 rpm, above that the synchromesh cones became overloaded and the selectors in particular gave some trouble.

We found that when we were making hurried changes at high revs, it was sometimes possible for the gear lever and linkage to over-ride the selectors. This meant that after we had engaged that particular gear, the gear lever would be flapping about in the breeze and we couldn't shift it. Many is the special stage I have finished with the car in this state, and before long Norman and the other mechanics were absolute experts in getting the top off the box, poking about with a screwdriver, and sending us off again.

The first thing we had to do was to design our own selector mechanisms, and as far as I know the ZF boxes now arrive from Germany without them, so that we can fit Ford-developed items. ZF have now recognised these problems, and have modified their own linkages in line with our thinking; I hope the Fiat and BMW customers are pleased!

The ZF shell is quite a lot larger than our own Ford box, which was itself bulkier than the Escort box for which the gearbox tunnel was designed, so getting it into the body was quite difficult. Quite a lot of work is necessary to a new body to make room for the ZF installation, and on our team cars it doesn't help that I have one idea of where the gear lever should be and Timo has another! The mounting point on to the body, just in front of the front seat positions, is different, but in our case Gomms make the change when they are rally-preparing the bodies, putting on the new fittings, seam-welding the structure, and adding the shocker turrets.

We don't reckon to do gearbox changes any more because the ZF is so strong, but because of the size it makes clutch changing difficult. In the old days, we could have a box out, change the clutch, and have it all stitched up again in about 25 minutes. On the 1974 RAC Rally, both Timo and I needed a clutch change on the last morning (the linings were quite literally worn out after 2,000 miles of forestry

101

stuff). The mechanics had the use of a garage ramp in Thornton-le-Dale, but it took about 50 minutes of blood and sweat to change Timo's clutch. Mine followed later, and they got it down to 35 minutes. Most of the difference, incidentally, would be because Timo insists on the long selector housing, which makes it that much more awkward to remove.

The ZF has its drawbacks. It is a heavy, notchy old thing which refuses to be hurried, and you have to change gear deliberately, but if you learn to respect it it's bomb-proof. It makes horrible noises and rattles like hell, because it's one of those boxes where everything is in mesh all the time, and because the rally BDA doesn't idle at all smoothly the backlash in the gears has a terrible time. There are so many noises in my sort of Escort it's really quite an education, and if the average driver got into one he'd wonder what he was taking on. But we're never alone in an Escort, because the diff. talks away to us as well. Still, it's an old, but true story — you only have to worry when any of these little noises stop happening; then you really *are* in trouble!

The other big changes in Escorts have been wheels, tyres and brakes. We've had very close co-operation with Dunlop for a long time over rallying tyres, and they still build the best rough-road stuff in the world. We don't do as much development on studded equipment any more but with Timo in the team there isn't any lack of expertise where we need it. It was Timo who did much of the work on the original M & S Dunlops in 1971, and since then the improvements have been mainly in tread refinement and puncture-proofing. A long time ago we switched from Goodyear to Dunlop, not solely because we thought Dunlop made the best tyres, but with a mixture of good old British patriotism and a bit of money in the equation too. Our rallying Goodyears were as good as anything around when we were contracted to them, and I don't think they would find it difficult to match Dunlop again if they had a major works team nagging away at them for improvements. The question of wheel size on Escorts has been causing controversy for a couple of years, and I return to this later.

On brakes, we soon had to go over to an all-disc set-up for extra power and to ensure a stable front-rear balance in all conditions of use, and the latest development, of course, is to use ventilated discs. We also started to use a separate hydraulic handbrake to the rear wheels, which gave us a really good 'corner tweaker', and we ditched the original cable system.

That was all well and good until a policeman local to Boreham pointed out the fine print in the Construction and Use regulations, and suggested we were actually breaking the law. It was all a matter of having a 'separate mechanical system' on the handbrake (which ours was not), so now we fit the original cable type of set-up as well.

One big advance we have made is in knowing how to tune the car's braking balance between front and rear wheels. In the early days of Escorts we used to change the balance by swopping rear wheel cylinders, and rebleeding, but somehow we never got it right, and sometimes we used to run out of time. If we came out of a forest, and the next stage was on tarmac, the car might have to be set up for forests with too much braking on the rears, and not enough on the fronts for the racing tyre set-up I needed on tar.

When twin-circuit systems became available, we quickly went over to them; these, of course, had two master cylinders and an adjustable balance bar. Now, after a lot of experience, I can have the bar screwed along and set up very easily within a couple of minutes. Normally we need a bit of fine adjustment after the next couple of stages, but I know roughly where it needs to be for most track conditions. We also know that we have to come back so many turns on the adjuster when changing from M & S tyres on the loose to racers for tarmac — I can guess at how many turns by now.

On wheels, we haven't deviated from Minilites. I know that these are very expensive for a private owner to consider, but for us they have so many good points that we can forget the cost. However, I do remember that when Stuart was circling in a plane watching Timo and Henry change a wheel on the Safari, then throw the punctured Minilite into the bush, he nearly had a fit!

We went in for knock-on Minilites early on with the Escorts, but we had trouble with retaining nuts working loose and the wheels tending to be thrown off. Very embarrassing! The need for knock-ons was so that we could save time at service points, but apart from the Safari (where you *never* have any spare time at all) the time available for service has actually increased in recent years, so to keep it simple — there's that word again — we went back to conventional fixings.

The story on suspensions is that once we had successfully converted the rally cars to leaf springs and a full radius-arm location set-up, we have left them alone. I certainly haven't done any serious handling or damper development testing for a long time, and fundamentally there hasn't been any change since about 1971.

The damper story is simple. I regret to say that no British company has been able to match the performance of Bilstein struts and dampers, certainly as far as Escort rally cars is concerned. It's a question of damper performance, fade resistance and life — the areas where Bilstein absolutely excel. I know that some factory engineering departments have tested rally Bilsteins on their laboratory test rigs, and found that their standard fade tests don't touch them.

The fact that we haven't changed our suspension systems in a long time also explains how I almost lost one British National event in 1973. Peter Ashcroft was getting a bit worried that we didn't seem to be doing anything to improve the traction, so he suggested that we tried the latest Group Two racing set-up (coil springs and a different linkage) on a rally.

I started the event (the Lindisfarne, I think it was) but the rear end was completely undeveloped for rallying and seemed to be floating around a bit. Poor Norman — I rushed into one service point with a lot of time in hand and demanded a complete change, back to my old system. He didn't even flinch, and of course he managed to do it in no time at all. What else could I expect?

There was no real advantage with the coil-spring set-up after all. Its object was to ensure precise wheel control at all times, but there's no point in doing that on rough roads; you can't get any more grip if the wheels can't follow the road all the time. With a normal system on rough roads the wheel angles don't matter whereas on tarmac they obviously would. The world isn't flat, and that's often proved on a forestry event.

It seems an appropriate point here to mention the rallycross seasons I put in with Escorts and Capris. With an Escort there was no novelty — it was just rather a gimmicky sort of rallying or autocross racing. For me, all the interest came from the Capris we were asked to drive, particularly the ones that bellowed their way around the circuits in 1970 and 1971.

The Capri was announced in January 1969, but within a couple of weeks I had appeared at a Croft rallycross meeting in one. Not just any old Capri, either — mine was a 3-litre car (the production version wouldn't be ready until the autumn) and it had four-wheel drive!

If ever there was a legendary beast it was the four-wheel-drive Capri, and if ever there was a car that didn't live up to its legend, this was it. The theory behind four-wheel drive for a rallycross car was obvious — there ought to be that much more traction for starts and to sling you out of a muddy corner. That was the theory — the problem was that I don't think anyone had told the cars about it, and they didn't always behave themselves.

I think the original idea for four-wheel-drive Capris came from Henry Taylor. The Escorts and the Cortinas were all poor off the start line, with bad traction, and at about that time Ferguson Research were building a few four-wheel-drive Ford Zephyrs and things for the police forces. I think they even built a four-wheel-drive Capri for demonstrations. The Zephyrs obviously had the same basic engines and transmissions, so Henry approached Tony Rolt of Fergusons to make us a couple of rallycross specials.

Boreham built up three cars from bits supplied by Ferguson. Two of them had Weber-carburettor 212 bhp 3-litre V-6 engines, while mine had a 3-litre V-6 with Weslake cylinder-heads, all the bits, a Lucas fuel-injection system, and something like 250 bhp! The gearbox, incidentally, was an early five-speeder from ZF, and the front axle ratio was slightly different from the back axle ratio, which didn't matter much because all of the wheels were spinning all of the time. Actually we did try a rather different front ratio once, but that soon led to disaster. We had a limited-slip diff, but for some reason there was no limited-slip in the front. The Ferguson centre diff. also had its own spin-limiters as usual.

The record shows that the cars were competitive enough for Stan and I to drive fast, and in fact we won a championship in them. But after just one season they were put away and have rarely appeared since. Rod Chapman bought the remaining two from Ford in 1971, and as far as I know he still has them. But why did we put them away when they were winning? Basically, we ditched them because they were an enormous amount of trouble, not just in reliability, which was dreadful enough, but because they were absolute pigs to handle. Four-wheel drive was splendid from the start line, but in muddy corners it was a different story. I hesitate to say it, but I never mastered those Capris, not even after a full winter with them. They had minds of their own, and they changed their minds far too often.

It was the same trouble as with the experimental Grand Prix cars

105

being produced about the same time. If we had driven front wheels we suffered from too much understeer, and to kill the understeer we had to back right off the power delivery to the wheels; in other words it was a self-defeating exercise.

You could also get into a situation, sometimes, where the front wheels were sliding about on mud, and you just didn't know which way to turn the steering wheel for the best. The steering was very heavy anyway, and there was no feed-back to the driver.

With an Escort in rallycross, it was possible to place the car to within about six inches, but with the Capris we had to hang back a bit in case the damned thing didn't want to help. Sometimes everything happened beautifully, and we could get out of a corner in a full-power four-wheel drift with big silly grins on our faces. There was that tremendous noise, too, but get it wrong and — Oh boy!

Once the car was in an oversteer situation, everything was superb, but getting it there — that was the problem. Once into a corner in an understeer slide there was no way out, so we had to slow right down, get into gear again, point the right way and set off. Conventional correction didn't work — if we lifted momentarily the front wheels tended to brake themselves, and trying to boot the back wheels into a slide only spun the front wheels straight on even harder.

We tried everything, and I mean everything, to sort things out. Mick Jones was the poor sod who had to do most of the development work. We fiddled around with the front/rear torque split, but finished up with a 40/60 per cent split, biassed to the rear. We were so desperate at one time that we even started dismantling prop-shafts, and on one occasion I actually tried it as a front-wheel-drive car only. We played with wheel sizes, tyres sizes and rim widths, but we never controlled the understeer.

The traction in a straight line was fantastic. You could get to a start on ice or mud, bury your right foot in it, get wheelspin for about six inches and . . . wham, away to the first corner. Whether or not we could win races depended on the organisers. One lot gave any four-wheel-drive car a five-second race penalty on its time — which didn't matter because if we could out-drag everyone into the first corner I could usually make the car wide enough to stay ahead. The other organisers made us start five seconds behind the others. Catching them up was usually no problem, but actually getting past with a car handling like the Capri was a different story.

It was most fun on hard dry circuits, but then a two-wheel-drive car was as quick. When traction was vital we gained, but on the same days we lost out in cornering power.

We had a lot of problems. The engines weren't very reliable (mine used to eat a set of bearings every meeting — a life of about 20 miles, perhaps) and Mick Jones used to say that the cylinder blocks were made out of Weetabix and a bit of lamp black! We were forever breaking front drive-shafts — there was a bit of poor geometry built-in during the many instances when the suspension was on full lock and full droop. The joints would 'neck' and we could snap them like carrots. It was virtually a full time job for two mechanics to repair the damage to the cars during the week, that Stan and I had done at the weekends.

The other odd thing was that Tony Rolt had said originally that there would be very little extra rolling resistance, but those Capris were heavy, hard beasts to push around. I think the transmission power losses must have been ridiculous, and it needed several strong men to heave the things up on to trailers for the trip home.

We had a lot of fun out of them, though, and it was always a challenge to us to get the best out of them and their little ways. The object was publicity, and we certainly didn't lack that, but my car still made me feel a bit of a buffoon at times.

Finally, a comment on left-hand or right-hand drive. In sorting through pictures to use as illustrations, it's obvious that I have spent a lot of time on both sides of the car. Up to my Escort days there was never a problem — the cars were all right-hand drive, and under Henry Taylor I was never asked to drive a left-hooker.

When Stuart settled in at Boreham, and demanded his 'production line' build and preparation methods, it made sense to standardise on cars. It wasn't only a question of steering, but of instruments, brakes, wiring and pedal gear. As odd-man-out in the team (before long all the others were to be Swedes or Finns) I soon lost my choice, and had to learn to drive left-hand-drive Escorts.

Actually, I was agreeably surprised. The transition was not as difficult as I feared, and before long I could more or less jump into anything and go as fast as usual. Occasionally I would start practising in a left-hooker and hear Jim take a few sharp intakes of breath — I would be getting a bit close to drops, walls or rock faces, but that phase didn't last long. Changing gear with the wrong hand was the biggest problem, but once we had ZF gearboxes with a very deliberate truck-like change I had time to think what I was doing.

I rallied a left-hand-drive car for the first time on the 1970 Circuit of Ireland, then stayed with the layout until my blue Esso car was finished a couple of years later. It made a lot of sense, in those two years, because with most of our events outside Britain, in countries where one drove on the right, a left-hooker was right for the job. My Esso car, on the other hand, was meant for British events only, so could be built up like a British car. The first Esso car, 'Old Gold', was an ex-Ford France 1971 machine, and kept its left-hand driving position until the end of its work with me.

All this talk of left-hand and right-hand drive does rub in the point that we have rallied all over the world, not just in Europe, either, nor even Africa. There have been trips to Hong Kong and Australia — but this is all another story. For a man who has a reputation for idleness, I seem to have been involved in all sorts of long-distance events — one of which, at least, should have been my win, yet must rank as one of my greatest disappointments.

Chapter 6

Safaris and Marathons

BY 1968 rallying was in a rut, all over the world. Events like the Monte or the Safari were not exactly dying on their feet, but they were being run to the same old pattern, and there wasn't a lot new happening. People would sit down at the end of a rally and say ''Wouldn't it be nice if we could do this, and go there?'' but nothing came of it. Every now and then there would be talk of another Peking-to-Paris race, and somebody even suggested running a long-distance sports car race over the motorways of Europe.

One rumour, however, refused to go away. During the autumn of 1967 stories of a dramatically different event had been spreading in the business, but none of us dared to believe them, so when Jack Sears and Tony Ambrose called a press conference in Monte Carlo after the 1968 rally they caused a sensation.

The *Daily Express* had been persuaded to put up the sponsorship for an incredible marathon, all the way from London to Sydney in Australia! Now that really *was* different — enough for lunatics like me, who thought they'd seen everything, to be very interested. And who wouldn't be attracted to a drive half-way around the world and Christmas in Australia if someone else was paying?

Then we had a look at the schedule. The organisers said there were more than 10,000 road miles from London to Sydney, and apart from a long sea trip from India to Australia they were going to make us drive non-stop! There wasn't to be any cissy business about night halts in Turkey, or a rest in the middle of the Australian desert. It might just as well have been a motor race, but to keep governments and insurance companies happy there would be a few controls here and there.

I rather think we had the wrong idea at first. Just because we hadn't been beyond Bulgaria in rally cars we thought the Middle East roads might be very primitive. Not many people had actually driven the whole way from India back to Europe, and those who had usually got a lot of publicity out of it. A lot of scare stories were dredged up by the national press, and the *Daily Express* did everything they could to whip up the 'adventure' side of it.

The timing was such that we would leave London at the end of November and take seven days to get to Bombay. It would be late autumn in Turkey and Afghanistan, and there was talk of snow and very cold weather. The race across Australia, from Perth to Sydney, would take just three days, so the whole driving part (if we were on time) would take just ten days for 10,000 miles.

It was a huge undertaking, and not enough people realised just how much it was going to cost a team in terms of manpower, machinery and plain money. Today I believe enthusiasts realise how difficult it is for a competition department to find extra money for extra events, but seven or eight years ago it was assumed that everybody would enter cars, and that nothing else would suffer.

This of course was nonsense. Henry Taylor had sorted out Ford's 1968 rallying programme months before the Marathon had even been heard of, and finding something like £50,000 for it was difficult. We already had an intensive year planned for the new Escorts, but I think it's significant that Ford didn't go to Africa for the Safari that year.

Almost as soon as I had heard the details I was on the phone to Henry to tell him I was interested, but so were Eric Jackson, Bengt Soderstrom, Ove Andersson, old Uncle Tom Cobley and all. For months we weren't at all sure how many team drivers would be going on the Marathon, and without a generous extra supplementary budget from Walter Hayes there wouldn't have been the massive team effort that finally took the starting flag from Crystal Palace.

I was very sorry that we had to duck out of the RAC Rally. Quite a few rallying writers were angry that the Marathon should start so close to the RAC Rally (only four days after the finish *and* in the same city) and its entry that year was very thin.

The two big decisions that had to be taken quite early on were over crews and cars. Don't forget that in 1968 nobody had done a

Marathon before, and we couldn't be sure about long-distance fatigue and the endurance of the cars. Looking back, it really is amazing that we didn't even consider the Escorts at all. Our thinking then was that the Escort was too small, and that we needed a lot more space to pack spares, provisions, safety equipment, survival gear and the rest. For a time we thought we were going to need three-man crews (BMC actually took three people in their cars), and we didn't reckon an Escort would take three in any comfort.

As we know now, the Escort bodyshell in its Type 49 form is one of the toughest little shells in the business, and would have been ideal for the Marathon. However, after flirting with thoughts of Zodiacs, Boreham plumped for a set of Lotus-Cortinas — the cars we had already abandoned as front-line competition cars. There was a lot of discussion about the quality of petrol we would have to use, particularly in the Middle East (ironic that there, of all places, we might not find the right stuff), and for a time it looked odds-on we would use 1600GT engines instead of the Twin-Cams. Then it looked as if the loaded cars would need all the power they could get, so we decided to use Twin-Cam engines and hoped for the best. That decision probably lost me the rally, but no-one could be blamed.

I was so busy rallying all over Europe with the new Escorts that I didn't do any practising at all, so I led the Marathon until the last day having seen not one yard of the route before. I didn't even know the way through London from Crystal Palace to Parliament Square and on to Dover — all that stuff would be up to my navigator, or those who had been able to recce the 10,000 miles.

But what about the crew? We argued it all through, on the evidence of recces, and decided we could manage with two to a car. As it happened, we were absolutely right — I was so fresh when we reached Bombay that I was able to go out on the town and enjoy myself. There was never any doubt in my mind that mine should be a two-driver team. It was a mighty long way, and I knew there would be times when I was tired and when the other driver would have to press on much harder than I could expect from Jim. Jim understood this completely, I know.

But who? Suddenly I had a brainwave. Why not Ove Andersson? He was a team-mate, he was quick, and by all the evidence of his driving for Ford he was also very safe. We were already good friends, and we thought we could live together for ten days without problems.

Henry Taylor was doubtful at first, and others were incredulous. "Two drivers without a navigator? When Clark can't navigate? When he likes to sleep when he isn't driving? And what about Ove? They won't even get to Dover!" Ove and I were quite convinced, and stuck to our guns. As it turned out this was just about the happiest event I did, and we never had a single problem. No wrong route-taking, no arguments, neither frightening the other — it was just perfect.

What is interesting is that Ford made all the right decisions about crews and tactics in 1968, and BMC got it all wrong, and that in 1970, when we were faced with an even tougher challenge, the same thing happened again. The secret was to rely on fit two-man crews, and not add the third man; BMC got it wrong on the Marathon, and again on the World Cup Rally.

Some of us had done Safaris, Lieges, and other endurance rallies, but we couldn't get to grips with the scale of this Marathon, and the fatigue factor was a worry to everybody. There was also the fear that people would break down and have to survive for a time in a wilderness — it was all very frightening, but as it transpired we were all worrying too much.

Anyway, it was thought to be good policy that we should get ourselves fit, and learn a bit about survival. Me, getting fit! My idea of being fit before a rally was having my eyes open when needed and being able to lift every pint glass put in front of me. Mind you, I didn't have as much of a problem as Bengt Soderstrom, who must have weighed 16 stone, even when stripped down to his rallying gear.

There were a couple of Army people who had entered the Marathon in a Cortina who turned up at Boreham looking for help, and as a return for the help we gave them they offered us a short sharp course in survival training. I have pictures of me doing all sorts of odd things like PT in the gym. We had a couple of days in their barracks at Bramcote (near Nuneaton — trust me to fall on my feet, it was only a few miles from home) then we all went away for a weekend to North Wales on a training course which involved diets, survival packs and first aid, and we were introduced to emergency Army rations. They were quite good, too — when you've been in a car for ten days almost anything tastes good! Incidentally, it was the 'old man' of the team, Eric 'Round the World' Jackson, who turned out to be the fittest of us all, and the Army were very pleased with him.

I enjoyed every minute of the Marathon, and that's no exaggeration. Ove and I couldn't possibly have been happier together in a rally car. It helped that we were leading nearly the whole way, but we sang songs to each other, fed each other with sweeties, and generally enjoyed ourselves. It didn't seem to matter who was driving when, because we both seemed to drive at about the same pace and in exactly the same way. It was a complete picnic.

There wasn't any seeding, so the works teams were spread right through the entry of 100 cars. I had drawn number 48, with Jean Denton's *Nova* magazine-sponsored MGB in front of me, and Nick Brittan's works Cortina right behind. Paddy Hopkirk was right behind Nick in his BMC 1800 and John Sprinzel was next up with his Midget, so until we got separated it was going to be quite a party.

The Marathon is history, and very happily-remembered history too, but I must make one thing clear. It wasn't the flat-out endurance test some people had prophesied, and though there wasn't an official night stop between London and Bombay we certainly didn't go short of sleep. I reckon that by the time we rolled in to Bombay, I had had more good sleep than I normally get, and most of it in beds, too. We slept on the cross-channel boat, in beds in Turin, Belgrade (about 11 hours), Istanbul and Sivas, and all of this was before we had been given a single hard-working competitive section. Then there were many blissful hours in Teheran and Kabul, and a rest in New Delhi, before we arrived in Bombay with plenty of time for a check over before handing over the car to the controllers and their shipping company.

It was a long way, of course, but there was no question of fatigue affecting any of our performances. In the whole of that seven-day trip to Bombay there were just 220 miles of flat-out driving — nearly three hours of it Turkey and an hour of it in Afghanistan.

To cut the story short (modesty forbids, and all that . . .) I drove both the 'impossible' sections (Sivas-Erzincan, and Kabul-Sarobi) and we were easily quickest on each. It meant that unless we did something stupid on the other road sections we would lead at Bombay, and that was what happened.

If either section had been in a shorter event I think we could have cleaned them without difficulty. As it was, we loafed through them, trying quite hard but not *that* hard, and lost six minutes and five minutes, respectively. Ove was urging me on to go faster the whole

113

time, but it felt about right and it was good enough. On the long section, Andrew Cowan, who eventually won, dropped 21 minutes, and the best performance behind me was Simo Lampinen's German Ford Taunus, which dropped 14. It was all a lot closer over the Lataban Pass, for Simo and Andrew Cowan dropped just six minutes in all.

I must have been a great disappointment to the press assembled at the end of the section (that wasn't the first, nor indeed the last time, I'm sure). Most of the amateurs were making all sorts of lurid comments, but to me it was just another road.

After that, all that remained was the long slog down to Bombay, a bath, a celebration and the start of a couple of weeks of boredom. Guards gave a very splendid party, a trophy and a most acceptable £2,000 cheque for the leaders at Bombay, and we were very happy to collect. I seem to remember that I already had a considerable tax problem that year, so I did a deal with Ove. He kept the money and I kept the Guards Trophy!

The next two weeks were purgatory. All 72 cars which made it to Bombay, their crews and many of the mechanics, were all cooped up on the P. & O. cruise ship *Chusan*. Apart from over-eating and over-sleeping there was nothing else to do except walk and try to keep fit. We swam and we sunbathed, but to be honest it was one long bore. The next time this sort of rally was run off, I swore I would come home again to get some work done in the interim if it was at all possible.

We had David Benson of the *Daily Express* and one or two other journalists on board, who were racking their brains for some new news story for their papers. One day they even had me driving the ship by hand (usually it was on 'automatic pilot') but I couldn't resist taking it off the straight and narrow to make at least some change in the pattern of the wake. I don't think I actually made it turn round in circles, but it was enough to make the captain work out how much extra money it was going to cost P & O in increased mileage! Benson and the others had me quoted as saying I didn't like the response and thought nothing of the understeer — neither of which I uttered, but it was all harmless.

To alleviate the boredom there was a lot of horseplay. It got so bad at one stage around the ship's pool, with people being flung in fully dressed, that the captain ordered the pool to be emptied. I treasure to this day the solemn way in which some of us, beer glasses in hand, sat on the bottom of the emptied pool and held a protest meeting!

We were all very glad to get off *Chusan* at the far end of that trip, and I think Paddy Hopkirk summed it all up well when he was asked by a newsman about his voyage: ''It's the best advert I can think of for flying''. I had a nice surprise on arriving at Freemantle; Goo was waiting on the quayside. We hadn't planned anything, but Henry Taylor and Walter Hayes were so pleased with our performance so far that Goo had been flown out to Australia as a treat.

The Australian crews, who had started the Marathon thinking they were going to win it but found themselves nowhere at the Perth re-start, had done their best to frighten us with horror stories about the desert roads. What they didn't realise is that most factories had practised, and knew the route even better than them.

The rally would be all over in 70 hours, without a break. We were due to leave first (the re-start was in classification order) and we were raring for action. Gough Whitlam, later to become Australia's Prime Minister, flagged us off, and for another glorious 30 hours we led easily. The much-feared crossing of the Nullabor desert was a 15-hour bore. It was all looking very comfortable, but I should have known better.

I was driving and Ove was asleep. We were in no hurry — we estimated we would have more than two hours to spare at Quorn, the next control — when suddenly there was a bang from the engine, a clattering noise, and we only had three cylinders. A quick look in the darkness (it had to be dark, of course!) showed nothing, but I suspected something serious. All I could do was crawl on and hope for the best.

Eric Jackson's Lotus-Cortina, half-an-hour behind us on the road at Perth, caught up, stopped to see if he could help, then rushed ahead to warn Bill Barnett, Mick Jones and Ken Wiltshire. But what could they do? We might be in a works team, but it wasn't a million-dollar effort. We literally had two mechanics in Australia, and they were not carrying any engine spares.

We were still up on time when the car spluttered into our workshops at Port Augusta, but even though the cylinder-head was lifted very rapidly we knew we were finished. A valve had broken and damaged a piston. After 8,500 miles in the lead it was all over — or was it?

115

Just as the head had been laid on a bench, Eric Jackson came back in to collect his own car, still healthy and well-placed. "What's up?" said Eric. "Roger's done a valve" was the reply. Eric, bless him, only thought for a second or so, then said "Give him the head from my car. He can still win!" It was one of the few occasions when I've been near to crying. Eric was throwing away the chance of a high placing for me. There was only one response I could make: "Thanks, mate."

After that, it was up to the mechanics. For about half an hour there were cylinder-heads, spanners and chaps everywhere. Ove and I kept out of the way until it was nearly time to go, but we knew our lead was ticking away. A last-minute problem with the distributor timing, then we were away. Fort Augusta was 26 miles from the control, and we left just minutes before we had been due to clock in. I don't think I've ever driven faster on unknown roads — later I was told that those 26 miles took only 16 minutes, and I don't want to repeat the experience, thank you very much.

We were back in, but now third, just five minutes behind Simo Lampinen's German Taunus. We flogged on and soon passed him, but so did Lucien Bianchi in the big Citroen. There was time — just — to catch the French car, because the last night was the real 'sting in the tail'.

But it wasn't to be. Half-way to Murrindal there was a crash from the back axle, and the car lurched to a stop. Later we found that the pinion bolts had loosened and sheared — they were not Loctited or anything. You can bet that Loctite has been a prominent item in my cars' equipment since then!

We were out of the biggest rally once again, only hours from Sydney. But what followed was sheer pantomime. No factory mechanics could help us, but perhaps a private owner could? It was only just breaking dawn, but very soon an unsuspecting fisherman drove up in his Cortina. We flagged him down and made what I thought was a very reasonable request: "Please can we buy your back axle?"

At first the fisherman thought we were mad, told us to get stuffed, or some such Australian phrase, and drove off. But quite soon he came back and said something like: "You're Roger Clark, aren't you? Take my axle and anything else you need. I'll help you change it!" It was a real sacrifice, and it left him without a car for his fishing trip, but it got us mobile again. Not that it made much difference to the results. You don't change axles in minutes, and by the time we were going up the road another couple of hours had passed. Our final reward was tenth, and a mere £100 in prize money. It might, just might, have been glory and £10,000.

The only way to sum this up is to quote Walter Hayes' telegram to me: ''Please don't commit suicide because we need you. You could not have driven any better. Many thanks for a magnificent effort.''

After that first Marathon, everybody seemed to want to jump on the bandwagon. It was all very easy to talk about running another, but the money needed to back such things was hard to find. Anyway, it was obvious that even the biggest and keenest factory teams couldn't support a long-distance thrash every year.

Sir Max Aitken had already promised another *Daily Express* Marathon for 1972 (which, as it transpired, never happened), so as far as the professionals were concerned they could only envisage one event in between in 1970.

It wasn't many months after we had returned from Australia that the *Daily Mirror's* World Cup Rally was announced. There was even something of a geographical excuse for running this one — a rally which would start from Wembley Stadium, where the last football World Cup had been held, and finish in Mexico City, where the next one was due to start in June 1970! I don't think anyone ever found out how much the *Daily Mirror* had committed to promote their marathon although I heard that originally they had budgetted for more than £100,000 and had finished up paying out more than £200,000. John Sprinzel was the organising genius behind this one, and Tony Ambrose joined the team well before the start.

The 'World Cup' — it was never called anything else by most of us, which must have been very annoying for the *Daily Mirror* — was the biggest, the wildest and certainly the longest rally that any of us had seen. It wasn't just a direct drive from London to somewhere else this time — that would have been difficult, anyway, as between London and Mexico there's a lot of ocean. John Sprinzel had laid out a real rally — 16,000 miles of it, with a long European section from London to Sofia and across to Lisbon, then a fantastic circuit of South and Central America, starting at Rio de Janiero and finishing up in Mexico weeks later.

There were to be a few over-night halts, true, but there would also be Primes (another word for special stages) of a length and ferocity we

117

hadn't experienced before, ever, anywhere. You couldn't just treat this as any other marathon, not when there were Primes like the Route of the Incas, 560 miles long with an eleven-hour target — nearly all at altitudes above 12,000 feet!

There was never any doubt that Ford would enter a team of cars, and Stuart Turner, our new manager, was quite determined to win this one. But for months, from the event being launched in the spring of 1969, we hadn't a clue what sort of cars to take. There were all the old arguments to settle — large or small cars, tortoises or hares, two-man or three-man crews, tuned engines or standard units. We were going to need a lot of practising and a lot of testing.

It's worth remembering just how much mind-changing there was about the cars. The only car we really didn't consider taking was a Lotus-Cortina, even though it had nearly won the Marathon for me. We thought about Escort Twin-Cams, Escorts with very odd engines, German Ford Taunuses (Ford of Germany had won the Safari that year in a Taunus 20MTS) and there was even talk of taking Mark 4 Zodiacs.

The problem was all about endurance, speed, strength and car-and-driver durability. We can all look back on this now and laugh, but at the time the indecision got us all on edge. Stuart sent me off to do the Alpine that year in an Escort fitted with the German 2.3-litre V-6 engine, which might have been a solution to the World Cup entries, but wasn't — mine did everything from boil all its water away when climbing hills to handling like a pig because of all the weight up front.

Relays of team drivers and co-drivers went out to practise and survey the route. Europe was familiar to all of us, and we were sure an Escort in one form or another would do the job there, but South America was a closed book to the whole team, and there was so much of it. Timo and Hannu both came back looking worried and shaken — something you wouldn't expect of them, at least. ''Much too long for a two-man crew. Need three men. Need big cars. Need oxygen. Awful roads, terrible mountains, big drops''. These were just a few of their comments.

Stuart was desperately worried about this. The last thing he wanted was to enter cars that the team knew little about, and the way his Finns were talking we would need Taunuses or Zodiacs. Just in case, he sent Jim and I off to do the Three Cities Rally in Eastern Europe in, of all things, a Zodiac! Poor old Clark was coming in for all the

118

odd-ball jobs, which was one reason why Stuart and I were nearly at each other's throats in 1969.

Just in case it was all a disaster, Stuart had the car prepared by British Vita under Brian Gillibrand, though the car was Ford-owned. But the big Zodiac turned out to be not as much of a joke as it might have been. No-one expected us to achieve anything with it, but it lumbered round rather well. Somebody once said that driving a Zodiac was like driving an aircraft carrier and I saw what they meant, but I could throw it at the corners, and by the time Vita had done their job it was a safe and interesting car.

It had a lot of character but not a lot of performance. Vita had screwed Bilsteins on it, plus a few lights and a sump shield, and any of the engine tweaks they could think of. It was so uncompetitive that we could never get very serious with it, but we were beating BMWs up hills and it was a great deal of fun.

Actually this great barge won its class for us, and a lot of good publicity for Ford. It also proved to me that it wasn't the right car for the World Cup. We knew through the grapevine that British Leyland would be using Triumph 2.5 PIs (they made a decision very early indeed), and here we were at the end of the year without a settled idea in our heads.

It was my turn to go out to South America in the winter (between the RAC Rally and the Monte because Boreham was also running a full programme while we were testing) along with Henry Liddon. We picked up the route in Rio, and drove right round, through Argentina, Chile and Bolivia to Peru. I packed it in at Lima and came home, but Henry carried on all the way to Mexico.

Before I got to Peru I was puzzled, but when I left for home I was quite convinced. Tony Fall had won the Rally of the Incas in Peru and had come back sweating about the huge drops over the edge and the oxygen problem at those heights, and the Finns had also gone home saying that they needed three-man crews in a Taunus. It didn't look like that to me. It was horrible, and it was long, and I didn't fancy the heights one bit, but if we were all properly fit I couldn't see the need for three-man crews at all. Stuart was very kind in his latest book, *The Way to Win,* when he wrote that "Roger Clark's appraisal of the Andes quite emphatically won the London-to-Mexico for Ford". I certainly got home and said I wanted a fast, light Escort with just one other man in the car.

Our practising sessions were quite hilarious. Henry and I borrowed Fords of one sort or another from the local importers, and the theory was that we handed them back when the job was finished. What usually happened was that we phoned them up to say where we had left the wrecked machine! The nicest car we had was a Ford Corcel, made in Brazil, but I don't want to confuse you all too much when I say that a Corcel is really a Renault 12 with Ford styling; it's also interesting that the Corcel was on the market in Brazil before the Renault 12 was sold in France. That was a sweet little car, and we had lots of fun with it.

On the other hand, I also remember a bloody great American thing — a Fairlane, I believe — which we tried to drive across Argentina. The Primes were supposed to be across the deserts, but when we were there there was a lot of deep mud, rocks, stones and general rubbish in the roads. We seemed to cross the country from lock to lock in this barge. Its petrol tank was right behind the back axle, we absolutely peppered it with stones and soon it began to leak like a colander. We didn't know what to do about this, but we stopped in a local village where somebody gave us some jam. Jam? Apparently punctured tanks were a regular affair there, and the locals had found out that the very hard jam which they bought in squares to eat was also a good sealer. Henry and I were sure they were joking at first, but we bunged some into the tank and it did the job. Petrol couldn't touch it, apart from making it a bit plastic, which proved a lot to me about the jam.

Everything else that could go wrong on the Fairlane did go wrong. We got it stuck in bogs several times, it finished up without an exhaust pipe, the power steering failed, the radiator leaked (jam wouldn't do the job there, the water was too hot), couldn't get any gears, the clutch was on its way out, and we had only one round wheel left. It was a real junk heap by the time we hobbled into a local Ford factory.

It wasn't just me who did this to cars. After he left me, Henry Liddon flew off to Mexico and Central America to do more surveying with Timo. They ran out of cars at one point and Henry was even forced to buy one! He sold it again at the end of his trip, but it wasn't worth much. Stuart had a lot of trouble reconciling Henry's expenses after that, because buying and selling cars wasn't part of the deal at all.

We have a good story that we tell at forums about testing our stamina with the aid of the girl at 17,000 feet or the 17 girls at 1,000 feet . . . I wish it was true, but it isn't. Our serious instructions were to drive up to that sort of extreme altitude, up the Agua Negra, then get out of the car, run around, change a wheel and use the jack, and see how we got on. We also took portable oxygen kits to assess if they helped.

I wasn't affected as much by oxygen starvation as some of the others (one of the travelling marshals, Erle Morley, asked John Sprinzel: "What happens to the rally if I get up there, start working, then turn blue?") which must have surprised some people. My recommendation was that we should carry oxygen kits but not use them unless we were in terrible distress. Not many of the team actually had to do so.

Height and oxygen starvation do funny things, though. When Tony Fall and Jimmy Greaves tackled the Incas Prime in their Escort they had a series of punctures. As Tony said: "By the time the eighth happened we were absolutely shattered. We changed the tyre and decided to have a rest, just for five minutes at the side of the road, even though we knew Stuart would be mad with us afterwards. As I passed the other rear wheel I kicked the tyre in disgust and the damned thing went down! There was only one thing to do, we lay down and nearly went hysterical with laughing".

I got my way on the cars, which were Escorts, as strong though as light as we could make them. The mechanics had a think about our troubles in Australia, and recommended a push-rod engine for simplicity instead of the Twin-Cams. Castrol were our oil-company sponsors, and had worked out how they were going to mix aviation petrol with the local garage's jungle juice in any particular country, but we didn't want any repetition of the valve-burning tragedies of the London-Sydney Marathon. Peter Ashcroft came up with a nicely-tuned 1,800 cc engine, and we used virtually standard Escort cylinder-heads. The theory, never tested, was that we could change a head very quickly in an emergency, or that the mechanics could even by another one (or we could) in the many countries where Escorts were sold.

Though the event was a lot longer — in miles and in days — than the first Marathon, there wasn't to be as much sheer endurance because of the regular night stops, although that didn't stop us getting tired. Some of the mechanics, though, were shattered even before the

121

beginning, when both Timo and Hannu insisted on axle-ratio changes the day before the cars left for Wembley!

Stuart, being Stuart, had tried to link all his cars with newspapers or other associated publicity interests, and my Escort was sponsored by the *Shoot Football Weekly*. This time I couldn't have Ove Andersson with me because he had left the team, and Stuart teamed me up with Alec Poole from Ireland. Alec had been the third man in Paddy Hopkirk's Marathon BMC 1800, when they finished second to Andrew Cowan, but I had not even been in a car with him before we drove off to the start.

I don't consider my World Cup performance as anything very memorable. The atmosphere in my car was nothing like so relaxed as it had been two years earlier. Alec's driving style didn't suit me at all, which meant that I wasn't able to get as much 'off duty' rest as I should have done. Ove and I had been so compatible, so much like peas in the same pod, and drove so similarly that there was never a minute's worry, and we took turns at the driving without worrying about the section ahead. With Alec there was none of this.

Because the event was far too long for every driver to practise everything, I had had to skip the look-see around Eruope, so we were on borrowed pace notes until the start of the South American section. This helped me to blot my copybook on the second Prime, in Jugoslavia, where in conditions of mist and rain I managed to roll the car and we finished up in a ditch. Fortunately, Terry Hunter and Geoff Mabbs came along in their Porsche and helped us get the car back on its wheels. We had been hard at it, on pace notes at the time, and Alec called a mistake over the inter-com, which I couldn't know until I arrived at a bad left instead of the fast left he had called. A recce, which no-one completed from London to Mexico, might have helped. To crown it all, most of the petrol drained from the tank when it was on its roof, and we had to go back to the start of the Prime in our own time to get some more!

Add to this the fact that most of the European Primes were cleanable, and it is obvious that I was not at all happy to arrive in Lisbon down in 16th place with all five other works Escorts in front of me. Ford were also desperately unhappy by then, anyway, for some of us had run into a very serious axle problem. It wasn't the diffs. that were giving trouble, the axle tubes were actually breaking. We had the big new Atlas axles, which might have been man enough for the job under a 3-litre Capri, but were fracturing under the World Cup driving conditions.

On my car this wasn't helped because I had played 'wall-of-death' all round the edge of a corner in Italy, but after the Alpine Prime one axle tube broke completely away from the diff. casing, and only the half-shaft and wheel was holding the thing together. We struggled on for hours, it seemed, losing a lot of oil, before we got to a Ford (actually British Vita) service crew. Nobby took all of six hours to take the axle out, get it welded in a local engineering shop, and put the whole thing back together in the car. We then had to make a colossally high average across France to Spain and Portugal (getting the axle welded up three more times on the way) and we found that the same thing had happened to Tony Fall's car.

Quite suddenly, Clark-the-tester was faced with another job. Like many of the entrants, I was all set to fly home from Lisbon and get some work done in the two weeks while the cars were on a ship to Rio. Idleness in the middle of a rally isn't my idea of fun — that boat trip across the Indian Ocean was quite enough for one lifetime. As it happened I was faced with days of testing at Bagshot in another car, driving harder than ever in heavier conditions and jumping as high as we dared.

Bill Meade, Mick Jones and I had sat down in Lisbon before we flew home and pondered the problem. There wasn't time to consider any elegant changes to the axles, and there was no question of changing them because they had been marked with radio-active paint by the organisers at the start. Whatever we devised would have to be something we could fix, by strapping or welding, to axles already in place. We would have to get this done after the rally cars had been re-started in Rio. To save time any lash-up job we developed should be capable of being fitted without taking the axles out of the car.

It was all done in a tearing hurry, but the results were satisfactory. Between us we developed a dural bridge-piece which fitted inside the rear cover of the diff, with the cover bolted on top of it, and a couple of U-clamps to hold the piece to the axle.

The happy ending to the story is that our bolt-on goodie worked and worked well. Moreover, we still had a modified version of the same thing, slimmed down and refined, on every works Escort we built until recently.

My own South American rally lasted just a couple of days and two

123

Primes. We had just come out of the Rio Grande Prime, in Uruguay, and Alec Poole was driving. I was kneeling on the passenger seat, with my back to the windscreen, rummaging in the back of the car for a sweeetie or something, when all of a sudden there was an almighty crash, my backside hit the dashboard, my ankle twisted under me, and when I eventually managed to look round I found the Escort well-and-truly rammed up the back of a defenceless VW Beetle!

I believe Alec had been looking round to see what I was up to, and ran up the back of the Beetle without seeing it wandering about in the road. A silly accident, not even at very high speed, but that was the end of our World Cup Rally.

It was only a poor consolation to know that the axle bridge-piece helped Hannu to his big win, with Rauno's Escort third, Timo's fifth and Tony Fall's sixth.

There has been one other marathon-type event — the 1974 World Cup Rally, which went to Munich via the Sahara desert and Kano. The route looked interesting, and I'm all for a real endurance challenge, but the organisation was in a fairly average shambles and the factories would have nothing to do with it. It was announced very late, and the route was even later. There was just no way that a sensible team manager could commit so much money — it meant dropping so many other events, and we couldn't be sure it would actually happen! The fuel crisis of 1973/74 didn't help, either.

Ford were right to stay away. Press coverage was tiny, and most people have forgotten about it already, all of which proves that you need more than just an idea and a slick promotion. You can't just name a day and expect people to patronise your event.

Times have changed, and so have team budgets. Right now I'm not sure we will see any more of the really long-distance events, though it was once nice to hear of projects like the Alaska-Cape Horn, or an event through Asia. Like Stuart Turner, I really would like to tackle a 'Round the World' event, just once before I'm too old. Would it be possible? You'd have to ask the Russians about that.

Without any more marathons, we will have to fall back on the Safari for our greatest motoring adventures. I enjoy the Safari, political troubles or not, and I adore the country. Goo and I travelled to Africa for the first time in 1967 for my Safari debut, and have been in love with the place ever since. If ever there was a place that I could call a second home, Kenya is it. The Safari, whether in Kenya only, or in all three countries, has always been the sort of rally I relish, though I haven't a single good result to show for this.

Safaris are long enough, tough enough and varied enough for any professional driver to approve. There is still that element of local knowledge and experience needed to tip the balance, and in spite of huge efforts in the past at the time I am writing this a European driver has only won once, and I'm happy that it was Hannu Mikkola, and that the car he used was an Escort RS1600.

For my first three Safaris I have used a Lotus-Cortina, a Twin-Cam and, in 1973, an RS1600, and each time the car let me down because of the tremendous structural battering it received. To those who say that I should have been going slower and trying to conserve the cars I can only say that you don't win rallies, even Safaris, by setting out to go slower than other people.

The first time, in a Lotus-Cortina with Gilbert Staepelaere, was unfortunate, to say the least. Ford had already won the Safari with a Cortina GT, but speeds had risen so much since that the bodyshell simply cracked up under the strain; rallying for hours in the bush, quite literally without rear shock absorbers, was an experience I don't want to repeat.

Four years later we did little better in a Twin-Cam, but as that was the year when the Escorts were outpaced by the big Datsuns I don't think we would have won anyway. The Twin-Cam engine was on its way out by 1971, and we still worried about its reliability when drinking inferior petrol, so the cars were somewhat de-tuned to keep engines in one piece.

A year later, the team cars turned up with good, strong 1800 BDAs, and of course it was Hannu's car which won. My turn for a bit of glory came in 1973. After the big win in 1972 it was obvious that we would have to turn up in strength, and the Escorts had 2-litre aluminium BDAs with well over 200 bhp. They were all new cars — the notorious 'XPUs', one of which was to be stolen from Andy Dawson early in 1975 — and we were out to repeat the success.

That year's Safari only used roads and tracks in Kenya and Tanzania, for it was already impossible to get any sense out of the Ugandan regime, who kept their borders well and truly closed, even to a rally. This, incidentally, was in contrast to what happened on the first two marathons; on the London-Sydney event Indian and Pakistani border guards actually passed civil words with each other after years of conflict, while on the London-Mexico two Central American countries actually guaranteed not to be fighting when the rally cars crossed their borders!

Ford had no trouble in leading the 1973 Safari right from the start, for conditions were mainly dry and dusty. Bushmanship and pushing out of mud holes and rivers wasn't going to make much difference to *this* Safari, so we were out to show that where driving methods were important the Europeans could beat anybody.

We led and led easily. On this sort of going, with the Safari gear ratios in our ZF boxes, the Escorts could pull a really high gear, and not even the big Datsuns could keep up. I started at number 2, and drove into the stadium at Dar-es-Salaam completely alone — a wonderful experience. The car was running very sweetly and we didn't take any risks, yet by the time we got back to Nairobi for the half-way halt we had more than half-an-hour's lead. The locals couldn't believe it, and quite a few of the competitors didn't want to believe it, either.

But later, as on the Marathon, we ran out of luck. Not long into the second leg, first the steering rack let go, then the exhaust pipe came loose, and finally the alternator wiring burned out. All after a copybook run when we were driving to orders and massacring the field! All five works Escorts were destined to retire that year; Hannu's car also broke its steering rack, and Timo had a monumental shunt which destroyed the car.

There's no mystery about the Safari any more. The European drivers know enough to win, every time their cars stay in one piece and the weather plays fair. The weather is the big problem. Not many team managers are willing to risk a huge budget on a rally where a sudden rain storm can cause chaos. In 1974, one flood and one impassable section cut off most competitors for hours. If your car is stuck at the wrong side of this sort of thing, how do you start to explain to the managing director afterwards? I would tackle the Safari every time, just ask me and see how quickly I accept! But it would be nice to know we were tackling an event not subject to meteorological roulette.

Driving a car on events like the Safari, or endurance events where service support might be a long way away, has to be a different and 'softer' technique. On the Safari, too, the target average speeds are so high that there really isn't any time for service, anyway, which means that any time out for repairs means more penalties in the final results. There's no future in driving flat-out at all the obstacles, though it does mean, for me, a conscious effort to drive in a different way.

One has to try to pick a path through the hazards (not at all easy at those speeds, I can tell you) and to float over the bumps. The car has to be kept in a straight line much longer than usual, and every effort has to be made to give the structure an easy time. When it comes to impossible weather conditions and blocked tracks, there's no substitute for local knowledge in knowing which sort of bush can safely be driven through, and where the big elephant holes might be, but there's no local expertise which helps on the faster stuff.

What is interesting is that in events like the RAC Rally and the Thousand Lakes, the mechanics know that Hannu Mikkola has usually driven his cars harder than anyone else, given a rougher passage, and dealt out more damage. Yet Hannu. the lucky devil, won the Safari in 1972.

But if nothing else, the Safari introduced me to two other things — the use of two-way radio communication in team cars (and for the mechanics), and flying a private plane.

The two-way radio story is quite simple and logical. Distances on the Safari are high, and we couldn't afford a huge fleet of service cars to be around every other corner. It was easy to understand that even without a bit of bad luck we could find ourselves in trouble, and Stuart would be out of touch with his cars on the Safari for hours. Eventually he hit on the idea of using a spotter plane to keep up with the team cars, and keep radio contact between himself and all his people. It might sound like an excuse for spending even more money, but its value to us was immense. When the steering on my car broke apart, north of Nairobi, we were able to let Stuart know of the problem; he scooted off to find us a replacement part from the nearest service car, and by the time we had the rally car stripped out he was back to drop a bag of spares from the plane.

Radios, of course, won the 1974 RAC Rally for Ford, and might have made things a lot easier for me in 1972 if we had used them then. Going into North Yorkshire on the last morning of the 1974 rally, both Timo and I realised that our Escort clutches were worn out, and that full power was producing severe slip, even in top gear. Murphy's Law made sure that all the mechanics had dispersed before we found out, but both Henry Liddon and Tony Mason used their radios to alert the service crews. Stuart heard the cries for help first, and started to collect his Granadas from the hills. It is interesting that Mick Jones, who was in the one car not called up, heard him from a site high up in the forests, and arrived down in Pickering first.

It was all a bit touch-and-go, as Timo so nearly ran out of time, but we both survived the crisis in the end. Of the radio's value there is no doubt. Without them Timo would have lost the rally, and neither of us would have finished.

I was so impressed by this rescue that I was tempted to have the system fitted in my cars for the 1975 season — even for the one-night British events — but eventually decided against it. It might have been an amusing goodie, and a chat with Norman Masters might have helped him to keep awake at times, but it wasn't really justified. On most British events my service car follows me around like a faithful sheepdog, and when it isn't actually tending to all our needs it is usually on the way to somewhere else. With such a restricted radio range, and with such a regular personal service, the installation simply wasn't justified.

My own love of flying came about through the Safari trips. Getting round from place to place was so much more pleasant in a light plane. We learned this because Bill Parkinson, who is one of Vic Preston's directors in Nairobi, also has a fleet of planes he charters to tourists (and rally drivers). He used to take us up, and helped a lot with Ford movements on the Safari. Naturally he supplied Stuart's supervision planes.

Once flying was in the blood, I began to take lessons, and qualified from my local flying club near Leicester. By this time I was deeply involved in the Esso-backed rallying programme, the new garage business, and Ford forums all over the country, so I really began to need my own wings. It was fairly logical to turn to Bill Parkinson and Dave Leonard for advice, and they supplied my first new Cessna 172. Now that I have a bit of land around the house in the country there is room for a landing strip. I have very few neighbours within a mile of the house, yet when I applied for permission to establish the strip someone else protested — you would think I was going to set up a flying school instead of using the land as a take-off area two or three times a week.

I got my permission, the windsock is erect, and I now have a hangar at one corner of the buildings. In fact my new Cessna (a 182) now

The Ford Taunus on the 1967 Monte. This must have been the start because Jim and I are still smiling; the car turned out to be a cross between a camel and a London taxi. (Photo Junior)

Only another 10,000 miles to go. Ove Andersson and I leave Westminster Bridge with the Lotus-Cortina with which we so nearly won the London-Sydney Marathon in 1968. (Daily Express)

Rosemary Smith and I grapple for the same Guards Trophy at the half-way stage of the London-Sydney Marathon in Bombay. Ove and I did a deal there – he took the money and I kept the trophy. (Daily Express)

All crossed-up, but still under control, the Calypso Racing Lotus-Cortina at Silverstone's Copse Corner in 1967.

A happy occasion. Proud parents with baby Matthew in 1970.

Stuart Turner seems to be happier handling rally cars than he does Matthew Clark!

Jim and I on the way to victory in the 1968 Circuit with 'XOO'. Paddy Hopkirk's Mini-Cooper S had already passed through, which explains the exciting tyre marks!

On the Circuit again in 1968, in a full-blooded sideways slide; Jim isn't even looking, and I can't say I blame him.

XOO 262F was a splendid Escort. Jim and I had already won the 1968 Circuit with it, and here we are on the way to another victory in the Scottish in the same year. (Foster and Skeffington)

Testing sump guards for the new Escort Twin-Cam in 1968. It made a good publicity shot for Ford, too, but I've had Escorts higher than that since then. (Ford)

One of the ferocious four-wheel-drive Capris which made Stan and I work so hard during a busy rallycrossing winter. (Maureen Magee)

Pauli Toivonen, Goo and I after the 1969 Acropolis. Pauli's Porsche beat my Escort Twin-Cam into second place after a tree had jumped out and savaged the nearside of the car; we photographed it from its better side thereafter!

My only outing in the prototype Ford GT70 on the French *Ronde Cevenole* in 1971. What a car this might have been, if only we'd had the time to develop it. (Photos Rhone-Azur)

Under all that advertising is my World Cup Rally Escort, already rather crumpled on the quaysid at Lisbon. After my co-driver Alec Poole had shunted it out of the event in Uruguay it looked eve the worse for wear.

This American Air Force officer said I could sample his plane if he could go out in my Escort Twin-Cam in Greece in 1968. I kept my part of the bargain, but he wouldn't let me loose with the Phantom!

Two of these 6-litre turbocharged Ford diesels powered the Fairy Huntsman cruisers which the Ford Offshore Powerboat team used in the *Daily Telegraph* Round-Britain race in 1969. I drove one with Peter Twiss and finished fourth, while my old rival Timo Makinen was the winner in Pascoe Watson's 'Avenger Too'. (Ford)

A different sort of sideways. Peter Twiss and I in the Fairy Huntsman 'FordSport', which we drove into fourth place in the 1969 *Daily Telegraph* Round-Britain race. (Ford)

Left-hand down a bit! Jim and I in the 'Old Gold' Escort RS, the original 'Esso' car. RSs don't lift wheels quite as far as that any more.

lives at the bottom of the garden next to my own cars and the powerboat. I really do appreciate my toys!

It is quite amazing that I should love Africa so much when it has brought me so little luck. I have yet to finish well up in the Safari, and when I went out there in 1973 for a holiday before the RAC Rally I returned with a very weird African tummy bug that ruined everything. I spent a lot of money to find some sunshine and to get fit only to come back not very brown and feeling like death warmed up. So that win on the 1975 Total Rally, in South Africa, made a nice change.

To win the really long and tough events, where driving flat-out is not as important as having the right car and enough support, there is also the problem of living in a confined space for days on end with the same man. The co-driver is the chap who can make or mar any performance, and that is what my next chapter is all about.

Chapter 7

On co-drivers

THERE ARE NOT many sports where two people are involved (no, we'll leave out all indoor games from this discussion — Stuart Turner would approve, I'm sure) but rallying is one of them. It really doesn't matter how much of a hero is the nut who sits behind the wheel, or how good is his car. Without someone who is competent enough to tell him which way to turn, someone who can do all the worrying, planning, thinking and the paperwork, someone who gets on with him (*very* important, that) . . . well, most of us would never win a thing.

Motor racing is easy. You get into a car, drive like a maniac for a given distance, win if you're good enough, get out of the car and it's all over. No fussing over time schedules, navigation, service, petrol supplies — in fact I sometimes wonder why I didn't take up motor racing when it was offered.

Rallying is a team game. That's not a diplomatic remark made to make Jim feel better after all these years, but a fact. Neither of us, without the other, could do our job properly. It's always very easy to look at the antics of another car, and know whether there is an effective team inside it.

In about 15 years of serious rallying I've learned a lot about co-drivers. The most important lesson of all is that it is essential to have a regular man, and to stick with him through thick and thin. I started with Jim Porter in 1960, and we still turn out together unless something serious makes it impossible. Without giving offence to anyone else, or even having to make any explanations, I can also say

146

that I have never truly been at ease with anyone else.

The most recent of my alternative co-drivers, Tony Mason, knows exactly what I mean, and I know he can sense it, even after four years of driving together from time to time. I can say it, even of a man with whom I have done four RAC Rallies (and notched up a first, two seconds and a seventh in them, too — not a bad track record come to think of it), and I know he understands. In his own words: "... you really have to be on the ball all the time you are with him. He can be very demanding indeed when things aren't going too well, wanting to know all the details of what he needs to know all the time, and rather intolerant if any minor mistakes are made in navigation or procedure . . . He doesn't speak very clearly on a stage, even with intercom, and I often have difficulty hearing what he wants. That's probably because I don't live with him all the time. If I rallied with him all the time like Jim then I would *know* his next requirement. Roger is rather particular who he goes with actually, and he doesn't tolerate fools at all . . ." This is taken from a press interview, which I think sums it all up very well.

You have to get used to a man, someone who has to spend a great part of your working life with you, and if you don't get on in the close confines of a car it doesn't matter how competent he is, you will never make it together. Someone once said that a driver-co-driver relationship was as close as man-mistress, and I don't think I would argue with that at all.

Put in those terms, Jim and I nearly qualify for a Darby and Joan medal. We get on so well, and have always got on so well, that it is quite startling when something happens to disturb us. After all these years we trust each other so implicitly that the thought of mistakes never really occurs to us, all of which makes the misunderstanding on the 1974 Burmah Rally the more unbelievable!

Jim will not mind me making a point of this, I'm sure. On the Burmah, we had had a very close fight with Billy Coleman in his Escort, lost some time messing about with experimental tyres at first, but then pulled out enough to beat him again — just. The only thing was that in making sure we had won on the stages, Jim completely missed a point in the regulations which said we could be late on the road everywhere *except* the final control. So we 'won' the Burmah on the stages, but finished 41st in the results. Jim was so upset about this that when we settled down to this book he wanted me to round it off

147

on July 31st 1974 — the month before the incident!

I came back from Scotland with Graham Robson, who just couldn't understand why I was taking it so calmly. "I would be spitting mad", he said, "so why aren't you?". My answer to that was: "What about the times when I've gone off the road, or chosen the wrong tyres for most of a rally?"

There's also a moral to be drawn from the Burmah incident. Once it was clear that we had boobed, and that we had driven our hearts out for nothing, we accepted the situation. Not many people will do that. There is a breed of co-driver, quite common in Britain and *very* common in Europe, who regard the published provisional results sheet as merely the start of negotiations. They seem to relish trying to 'talk their way up the lists', and I sometimes think they would be better employed as courtroom lawyers. Mind you, if organisers draw up their regulations so badly that there's scope for this sort of sharp practice, should we always blame them?

It was a good thing that Jim and I got used to each other before the works drives came along. We found out all about our respective abilities, habits, likes and dislikes, in one-night events. It helps if any relationship can survive one night in a car, but when you have to extend that to two nights or three, the nit-picking problems really begin to show.

Jim knows that I am idle. He also knows that when I'm not actually driving I like to rest, or even sleep. He also knows that I only like to drive when I absolutely have to, which also means that he's going to have to do a lot of driving himself. After a rest halt, with no competitive driving to face straight away, there's usually a concerted rush for the reclining seat on the passenger's side of the car, and a few nasty scenes from me if he gets there first!

So over the years we have evolved this completely satsifactory system, which sounds quite brutal in print — I drive when I have to, and Jim does everything else! He looks after all manner of administration if the factory haven't already done it, and he even tells me when and where to turn up at places. It might sound completely callous, but I hold the view that a driver's job (a really top-class driver's job anyway) is to drive a rally car as quickly, safely and effectively as he can. Nothing else, and I mean nothing, should get in his mental and physical way of ensuring this.

When Jim and I are rallying together, Jim knows that my jobs are all connected with driving, with pacing myself and with keeping the car in top-class condition. It means that although he can order me when and where to re-fuel, in all other respects the well-being of the car is my problem. I am the one who is supposed to know how it is prepared, where the spares are kept and what it should sound like.

What it should sound like? Yes — when you have lived with an Escort as long as I have, it is possible to identify every little squeak, tap and groan. It's my job to listen for the noises and feel for the changes. Jim does know — because he's a very intelligent co-driver, and because he's probably experienced it all — how a healthy gearbox should rattle, and how a tired limited-slip should creak, but it's my job to fix it or organise assistance if anything goes wrong.

One thing I don't trust in a co-driver is ambition, by which I mean an ambition to get out of that seat and finish up in the driving seat. Jim never had this problem, and I call it a problem because people who suffer from itchy feet can't always keep their minds on the job. In any case, if you have a competent driver in the left-hand seat he might cotton on to the mistakes you are making, and might even be able to sort things out better himself. I once saw a devoted married couple, both of whom were good drivers, in a production car trial. The problem was that they ran a driving school, and their car had two sets of pedals and two steering wheels . . . the results were genuinely side-splitting to watch!

Incidentally, for all the co-drivers who think they will be top-class drivers there are very few who actually prove it. Most of them, like Henry Liddon and John Davenport, are too blind to do anything about it even if they had the driving urge. Only Vic Elford, as far as I can recall, made it in both seats, though I have a shrewd idea that Vic never intended to make co-driving his profession, and that he was only using his BMC rides as a way of getting himself known.

A lot of people seem to think that I have only rallied with Jim Porter and Tony Mason, which is flattering to them, but omits several others. It was only when I started to concentrate on this book that I realised just how many other partners there have been. John Sprinzel once dedicated a rallying book to the 'tolerant heroes who have sat next to me', and I know what he meant. The co-driver's chair is the ideal place to find out about my abilities and my faults.

But how's this for a list? Brian Melia, Graham Robson, Robin Edwardes, Gilbert Staepelaere, Jim Peters, Ove Andersson, Clement

Freud, Alec Poole, Geraint Phillips, Henry Liddon, Hamish Cardno, Stuart Pegg — plus, of course, Jim and Tony. All these chaps have been alongside in factory Fords. In other works cars you can add Bob Aston, Brian Culcheth, Richard Martin-Hurst and Johnstone Syer.

Nice men, all of them, though quite a few of them have only been with me on a single event. Sometimes they officiated because Jim was not available, sometimes because we thought that a two-driver team was needed for a very long event, and sometimes because Ford thought that a bit of good publicity — showing a competent press-man the ropes at close quarters — was appropriate.

There are a few people, of course, whom I would never take in a car with me (these gentlemen have even been in the same team from time to time, but 'no names, no libel actions'), and possibly once or twice I wish I had had more choice in the matter. I've never had a female co-driver; what a pity — there must be a few compensations, and in any case they're usually a lot lighter than the hefty men I have to cart around. It's easier and cheaper to exchange a co-driver for someone else 50 pounds lighter than to develop ten more horsepower into the engine and the result is about the same!

I can honestly say that at no time have I accepted anyone in the car against my personal better judgment. The day I was forced to do it would be the day I decided to leave Ford. Every single 'one-off' partnership was a good idea at the time, and many of them worked out extremely well.

If there's one thing that must develop between driver and co-driver it is a feeling of absolute trust. Jim and I have this, and have had it for many years; Tony Mason and I could have developed it if he had had time to devote all his thoughts to the job (instead of having to worry about team administration, too) and if he was to be my regular man.

But what is absolute trust? It's not just knowing that your co-driver's knowledge of regulations, rally-craft, back-up arrangements and the route is perfect. It's knowing that he is thoroughly on top of his job, that he knows what is going to happen just as surely as you do. How can I describe this? If we were thundering up a 20,000 ft hill-climb somewhere in the middle of Russia, with mountain on one side and fresh-air on the other, and Jim instructed me to turn sharp left into thin air, I probably would.

At the instant of going over the edge I would probably wonder what was going to happen next, but I wouldn't doubt him for a minute.

There would be a road or a track just out of sight — Jim said so! That's what absolute trust is about, and it works both ways; if I turned over the edge without an instruction, I doubt if Jim would say much, though he might raise one eyebrow at me as I did it.

It should take a lot to get a good co-driver excited. I've sometimes seen Jim excited-cross, but I don't believe I've seen him excited-pleased. Like me, Jim doesn't like a lot of pomp and circumstance, and some of the prizegiving ceremonies just curl us both up. The first time I had to march in to a Scottish Rally prizegiving behind a piper in full ceremonial dress my face was the colour of his kilt, and Jim was all for turning tail and going round the back way.

Calmness, preparedness and absolute faith in his own abilities are important. It helps if he can be right all of the time, but at least (and Stuart will know what I mean) if wrong he should go wrong in style!

There must be something in the fact that many top-flight co-drivers also make very good rally organisers, whereas top drivers rarely bother. It's all something to do with organisation and methods, of being able to administer things, to make an event simple yet challenging, to make sense out of very complicated situations.

I was tremendously proud for Jim when he was co-opted to the Organising Committee of the RAC Rally in 1972, to give it the contribution of an up-to-date competitor which it was so sorely lacking. Before Jim arrived there was usually at least one thundering row at the finish about stupid things like wrongly-arrowed special stages. Since he arrived I don't think there have been any.

Jim is now the most important functional cog in the rally's machinery, and he has missed the last four RAC Rallies as a competitor. Incidentally, just to shout down those who say that this must be a help to me, where rally roads are concerned I have a memory like a sieve, and even if Jim told me all the stages in advance I don't think it would help. I doubt if there would be any help in foreknowledge of the route for anyone except those planning service — and anyway it doesn't happen.

Having a really good co-driver is a great help to drivers like me who can't be bothered to do recces. In my first year at Ford, Brian Melia often used to do a preliminary survey for the entire team, which would then save a lot of effort when he joined me for some personal practice. In recent years, where it has been possible to make and use pace notes, Jim has usually made the initial set, and I only arrive at

151

the very last minute to make corrections, or even to upgrade them where I think he has been too cautious.

By now it will be quite clear that pre-rally preparation is not my scene. Norman Masters and Jim often look after formalities at scrutineering for me, and I never get involved with the service car's pre-rally planning — that is another of Jim's tasks.

On a rally like the Manx, where the stages have been made public some time earlier so that pace notes are a definite advantage, Jim has often travelled out to the Isle of Man a few days ahead of me, and has completed the pace notes even before I reach the Island. Jim knows my pace and driving style so well by now that he can usually make extraordinarily accurate notes, even when driving alone in a slow old hire car. My own Manx practice has often consisted of a run through all the stages with Jim reading his notes, and occasionally altering the emphasis of a particular bend. That would be all I would have time for, because often I have to drag myself away from business at the last minute, and I just know that Jim would have done a very competent job for me. I spent a few more concentrated days on the Island in 1975, but it was really the improvements in the car which helped me.

I tackled the Manx in 1974 with the usual 'Esso' Escort, and we were beaten (or rather the Escort was beaten) by a couple of Porsche Carreras. It wasn't lack of practice that beat me — just 300 bhp of good, thorough, German engineering and a lot more traction. They said that the final run over the mountain section of the TT circuit would be very fast, and it was — over 100 mph average I'm told. The Porsches won by so much that I wondered why I had come along at all. Why should I praise Porsches? Well, I do sell them, don't I?

Of course I prefer my rallying to be without pace notes, or rather any sort of rallying where nobody has foreknowledge of the route. Any fool (no, not any fool — you have to be competent and quite brave to go *that* fast in a Porsche) with a lot of power and a lot of practice should be able to score. But that way leads to rally successes by cheque book.

Personally, I would like to see all practising and all pace notes banned, but I admit that I can't think of a way to police this. Keeping a route secret is very difficult, especially in Britain where the foresters are kind and open-minded fellows, and in any case most International events refuse to try. The RAC Rally is an exception. Snap checks for the possession of pace notes rarely work anyway — just about the only way to pick them up off a naughty co-driver's knee would be to stop the car at a hairpin in the middle of a special stage.

Peter Browning's marshals carried out casual checks in the middle of the Eppynt stages on the last two Tours of Britain but found nothing. They were really very polite about it, and camouflaged it all by asking about stage times, but we knew . . . and they knew we knew.

Mind you, they had good reason to look. An awful lot of people had guessed that the Eppynt ranges were to be used and had been practising. A look at the registers of local hotels for the previous weekends would have been very revealing.

If there was no call for pace notes, there would be very little call for driver-to-co-driver intercoms. That's yet another item of expense a young driver could do without. Looking back at the days in Reliants and Rovers where we didn't have such luxuries, it really is quite amazing how a co-driver kept his voice for a long event. Don't forget, too, that cars could be a lot noisier in those days, as there were no strict decibel limits.

Gunnar Palm introduced Jim and I to a pair of Scandinavian helmets which we wore for years. Their attraction was that they had very comfortable fittings and everything, plus chin-cup microphones. If you see pictures of me wearing a helmet held in place by the cup, that is also what I can talk through.

They work perfectly, and I much prefer them to any combination of booms and throat mikes that I have been shown. Both can get knocked aside, bent, or come loose in the heat of the moment, but the chin mikes seem to be bomb-proof. We needed new helmets at the start of 1975 to comply with RAC requirements, but the chin cup feature remains. God Bless Gunnar, even though he does eat dog biscuits at times.

The question of which co-drivers I like and which I wouldn't like is all a matter of my personal opinion. Sheer competence, or even brilliance, isn't enough. I couldn't live with a cheat, or anybody who tried to bend the rules. The people who read regulations with the care of a company lawyer would soon get under my skin, and I don't think I could tolerate anyone who was rude to marshals or organisers. The important word, as I have stressed already, is trust.

I have had to admire some of my partners for their particular skills. With Jim, of course, nothing surprises me about him any more. It works both ways, of course. If I had put my car way off the road, and

153

needed a lot of effort and 'push' to get me back in the swing, I doubt if Jim would get quite as enthusiastic, or verbally get out the big whip as much as a young man. Jim's view is that I've been off the road before, that I would know what was now wanted, and let me get on with it without any prompting. Some of the bright, keen, new co-drivers I have seen in other cars seem to see their jobs as being professional morale-raisers and cheer-leaders — sometimes I think they do it to convince their drivers of a talent that is not there in the first place.

Of course there's much to be said for a co-driver always wanting to win, but if I had to put up with someone who was always saying "faster" I would be heavily tempted to offer him the steering wheel and then go off for a sleep in the back seat.

I don't know, perhaps after all this time the in-car atmosphere in our Escorts may be getting too relaxed. I promise you, hand-on-heart, that there have been occasions on long stages in a tough rally when I have caught Jim in the act of nodding off! I'm always very busy in a rally car (I need the driver's window partly open to keep some fresh air entry and keep the temperature down), but on stages it is my co-driver's job to look ahead and spot the arrows. Sometimes I have missed the warnings, flicked a look sideways, and found Jim in the act of dozing off. This doesn't happen on one-nighters, or on short, sharp, sections, but there have been instances on long stages like Dovey or in North Yorkshire where the old man has quite definitely started to dream!

Jim's excuse is that once I am into a stage, there is nothing much for him to do. However, we do have this convention that his job is to look out for special hazards, warning signs and things. As to arrows — this might even be an eye-opener for some organisers who think their layouts are perfect. At the speeds we see nowaday, and the driving knife-edge balancing tricks we have to use, the driver is much too busy to pick up the *direction* of arrows, even though his distant vision should pick up the flashes of orange or red.

The co-driver must pick up the direction and severity, and tell me over the inter-com as soon as he is sure. But he must be sure. It's not good for concentration if you hear something like: "Arrows left . . . no, hang on . . . er right . . . er". I haven't time to re-focus — he must do it for me. It goes without saying that if the driver looks like cleaning a particular stage the co-driver must tell him. If it's touch-and-go there might be that extra bit of effort to make it sure, and if it looks comfortably possible he will want to back off to preserve the car. But once again — care! A co-driver must know the stage and be certain of its length before saying this. Never, ever, believe the organisers' stage lengths (the RAC are among the worst offenders!).

A co-driver can't do a lot on the stages themselves, but he can do a lot before and afterwards. I expect Jim to keep a careful check on the times, and whether or not we agree with official clocks. I expect him to keep records of the time we put up on stages, which could be valuable for future use. I also know that he will be noting weather conditions, the tyres we used, and anything special that might be valuable in the future.

Pace notes are not allowed in forests, and much as I like driving on pace notes I agree that this is a great leveller. Over the years, of course, it really is amazing how certain stretches of road become familiar. Things like the riverside stretches in Keilder, the familiar sections in Dalby, Cropton and Pickering — there's no way one can legislate against this. There was one particular blind-brow corner on the Lindisfarne, in the Keilder forests, where a lot of people went off — the usual thing, a fire-break which should have the road down it but doesn't. We had no notes, but Jim still knew enough to warn me from previous experience; I slowed down and there was no danger.

You also get used to receiving intercom comments like: "Caution board coming, blind brow, fresh-air right — CARE!" and sure enough (in the Weldh Penmachno stages) it happens. Incidentally, it really is a long way down at that point.

There really is no substitute for that sort of experience, and I don't mean cheating. I have no sympathy for people who cheat to gain an advantage, and if I thought for one minute that Jim or any of my casual co-drives were operating beyond the regulations I would put a stop to it.

The atmosphere in my rally car is usually pretty relaxed. I nearly said quiet, but everybody who knows about RS1600 and RS1800 rally cars wouldn't believe it. Even with all the extra silencing we need now, there's a lot of commotion, and it's almost like driving a Formula One car at times. We let the engine do the talking, and the gearbox, and the axle . . .

The intercom sometimes comes in useful for Jim to take the load off me. If I'm thrashing on, and suddenly there's a ford or a water splash, I just bark out one word: "Wipers". There is a wiper switch on his side as well as mine.

Incidentally, that apart, the extra instrumentation is very limited. The inside of my rally car looks nearly standard around the facia area. Jim has a navigation light and the usual Halda Tripmasters but that's all. In the early days of Escorts we had a panic bar screwed to the floor so that a frightened co-driver could use his braking foot against it instead of damaging the floor!

The co-driver usually has a comfortable seat. I have my favourite Billover design (I think Boreham have a couple of them) which Norman guards like his own underpants, and which is transferred from car to car. The passenger's chair is a perfectly normal FordSport recliner, very comfortable for snoozing, though normally only I get the chance for that.

I expect Jim to plan my tyre and fuel needs on any rally. He knows what tyres I like for what particular surfaces, he keeps records of surfaces in any speed test I'm likely to have to tackle, and he always plans where and how many tyres I will have at a service point. If we arrive at the start of something I don't know, something that looks like the Sahara desert, and Jim asks for racing tyres, I believe him. There are times, but not many, when Jim will turn to me and say something like: "This is so-and-so stage. Last year on the such-and-such you used seven-inch M & S and didn't like them. You said they were too wide, and you could have been quicker on the six-inch. It's even drier weather this year and I think we still need seven-inchers. What do you think?"

Tyre choice is critical, and we don't often get it wrong. Fuel needs are easier, but we usually ask Norman to carry jerrybags on the service car so that I don't have to look for roadside supplies. Jim likes me to carry as little fuel as possible on a stage, against which we have to balance problems of surge, and the thought that one day Norman is going to miss a service point on a tight schedule.

Jim, of course, plans the service schedule entirely. It doesn't matter whether it is the most insignificent event, or a full team effort, Jim tells me where he is laying on service. He has the whole pattern of the event in his mind, and I have nothing. To me it doesn't matter whether it is breakfast time or Bank Holiday Monday. I concentrate on what's in front of me; tactics and driving, as I immediately see them, are mine and strategy and planning are his.

Smoking — thank God neither of us do. In a car I think it would irritate us very much. Rallying may be fun, and may be exciting, but it is also serious and dangerous. Anything that puts a driver's hair on edge spoils his performance. Smoking would get up my nose — literally.

I remember David Stone talking about his RAC Rally with Eric Carlsson (in 1962, when they won in the Saab). David wore his rally jacket and started to swelter because Eric's Saab had the heater full on. He took his jacket off and still sweltered. He thought he would open the passenger window a bit and cracked it open. Eric closed it and grunted. David tried once again, and thought he had opened the window without Eric seeing him. Eric's massive hand came across the car, clamped on David's wrist: "I like warm car. Ve will have warm car!" That was that — Eric had his warm car and won the rally.

Anything a driver needs to keep his performance up to scratch should be indulged. If he like to drive in his Y-fronts — fine. If he insists on all the windows being down — fine. He must have his way. Personally I like a cold car with the heater off when I'm on stages. We both wear flameproof overalls, which are warm anyway, and when I'm driving I generate a lot of energy. Poor Jim — he has to wear a rally jacket, but I know he understands.

There have been times when Jim has been away and I have had to recruit a new man. There have also been occasions when I needed Henry Taylor or Stuart to advise me. One of the most famous occasions was when Clement Freud and I tackled the SMILE Rally in Finland. The event wasn't important, but the get-together was. It was a simple little snow rally in the forests, and the importance was that the *Daily Telegraph* were sponsoring two Escorts in the World Cup Rally (for Timo and Hannu) and wanted pre-rally publicity. Clement would co-drive, and wrote about it afterwards.

Before the start, the show-biz streak showed, and Clement did his thing for the *Daily Telegraph* and the media. Once we got going he got down to the serious business of mentally holding my hand, and we had a whale of a time. We must have done, for we finished fifth without pace notes. Later, in the *Telegraph Magazine,* he wrote:

"There was an overall Jekyll and Hyde pattern of the night. A relaxed, amiable drive down a main road, talking of this and that, the cost of beer, the quality of Midlands birds. Then a wait and then, after the Finnish language countdown, the searing, gut-clutching race over packed snow and ice. The car bounced upon snowbanks and slithered

157

accurately through a chicane of frozen gorse bushes, and after one stage Clark turned to me and said: 'It's a bit of a circus act, really'.''

The passengers I have enjoyed having along have all been calm, relaxed and competent. I think we all know the other very accomplished people who are never relaxed and very rarely calm — they are not for me. I don't mind the ones who get a bit excitable and enthusiastic, but when it comes to arguing with marshals, losing tempers, and such things — no thank you.

I think I must be quite calm in a rally car, because I've never found anyone who came with me the first time and threatened to jump out on the first stages. It's a pleasure to go along with people like Henry Liddon, who are so quiet, so polite, and so obviously in touch with everything that is happening around them. It helps that people like Henry have been with Timo, Rauno and most of the other Finns, so that nothing I get up to in a car surprises them.

The journalists, and there have been several in my rally cars, have usually started by being tense and a bit over-anxious to please, but have usually ended up as relaxed and easy going as I hope I am. Hamish Cardno saw me win the Granite City in 1971, then watched me going low-flying in 'Old Gold' in the Snowman. Gerry Phillips thought he had everything sewn-up on the Welsh one year (local knowledge, or something), so naturally we took a wrong slot on Eppynt.

The two guys I took with me on Shell 4000 rallies in Canada were usually too busy to be frightened. Both Robin Edwardes and Jim Peters were that peculiar breed of North American co-driver — programmed to be computing humans who could read a map — and believe me, in most events over there they didn't find time for anything else. Now that really is a stupid way to go rallying. When split-second timing and secret checks get into an event, the driver skills are non-existent. I won the 1967 Shell because I was quicker than everybody else on a few stages — for the rest of the time any competent, obedient, taxi driver could have done the job.

Really good co-drivers are few and far between. Remember the song: ''Once you have found him, never let him go''. I did and I haven't. The problem for many people at this moment is that the good co-drivers are all getting old together. OK, so they don't have to have the fine skills of a fast driver, but in the end the long-distance, odd-hours strain gets through, and they wilt. Rally times are hard, and young partners are hard to find. The way to bring them on, as any

158

team manager will tell you, is to give them plenty of experience.

There is the old problem. To the question: "How do I get into a works team?", you say, "Get experience and success internationally". "How do I do that?" "Get into a works team!" There must be a way round it somehow.

Chapter 8

I do it this way

ANYONE WHO has read this far will know that this is no book of instruction. Anyway, I see there is a rash of new rallying 'How to . . .' books on the market already, and against wily old experts like my boss, Stuart Turner, I don't think I could compete. Since I see he has also stolen at least half of my funny stories and quite a few of my pictures, there wouldn't be much point, but it would be quite wrong to dismiss the driving part of this story as incidental. This, therefore, is the only chapter where I discuss driving, preparation, and allied details in depth.

I have to admit that I am not a very analytical driver in a rally car, so I have no fears about giving away hard-won trade secrets to the young and inexperienced drivers — they will still need to be brave and accomplished before they start to beat everybody. The fact is that much of my driving, my methods, my preparation, and my approach to rallying is very simple, almost instinctive.

If you want to read reams of theory about this and that — anything from tyres to gearing — you will have to approach the Finns. I certainly wouldn't put myself in the same bracket as people like Timo and Rauno. They spend so much time theorising that I'm convinced they worry about their rallying, and would be good material for a psychiatrist's couch. It's all very convincing — the Finns are great theorists, and I've sat in on many a discussion — but they can then go outside and drive in a completely different way! The infuriating thing is that they seem to be just as quick whichever method is used.

In everything I tackle in motor sport, my aim is to be prepared, to be healthy enough, to know what I am trying to achieve, and to try to be relaxed. Anyone else who can follow that, and also be a gifted driver, should soon be chalking up big wins — assuming, that is, that he has chosen a good car and has built it properly.

Split the operation down into three main factors — driver, car and crew — and rallying is not as complex as it first appears. Nowadays, of course, an important fourth factor is usually the sponsor — the man or company who picks up the tab and for whom, if you are honest, you should be performing.

I don't think it is necessary for me to talk about relations with a sponsor, or how to set about finding one. Stuart Turner has already spelt this out in *The Way to Win* and I can do no better. Don't forget, though, that there are professional organisations which go in for preparing sponsorship presentations, and if you find a good one half your troubles are over. The important thing to remember is that, having picked up your sponsorship, you should not pocket the cheque and rally off over the horizon, never to be seen again. There are not many sponsors in the business who will hand over sizeable sums of money and not want anything in return, and any driver worth his cheque should be ready to get involved in publicity and marketing activities, even if they do sound bizarre, childish and unnecessary. If they *are* childish the publicity manager will get the sack, not you.

I have already spelt out my requirements from a co-driver, but I must add that however easy-going I may look most times, I subscribe to a rather ruthless dictum; if you can't get on with other people in your team, ditch them. Sentiment has no place in a rallying team. Harmony and all-round agreement are vital, and there will be moments of stress when this is tested to the limit. Try not to discover your co-driver's temperament when he is pushing you out of a snowdrift or a Welsh bog, but if you don't like it, don't take him again. Try not to discover your mechanic's dislike of lying on his back on a dark wet night under your car, but if he won't do the job the car won't do *its* job, so find another crew.

Generally speaking, rally mechanics are the salt of the earth. I have been involved with Ford for so long that I have become thoroughly spoiled. Norman Masters and I have grown up with the Escorts, and there really isn't anything else we need to learn about each other. It's got to the stage that we even talk in shorthand gestures. If there is time, and if the car is running well, I may roll into a service point and

161

hardly speak at all. Norman will come up to the car and raise his eyebrows. I will merely look at him, and pull down my bottom eyelid. Nothing said, nothing needed — in our language this just means "Have a Look".

There's a big difference between bad temper and recognisable temperament. Norman doesn't say much anyway, but Ford's famous competition foreman Mick Jones is something else. There have been times when I've seen Mick and his buddy Ken Wiltshire working away under a car, and the language pouring out would be hot enough to boil a kettle. It's no place to take a sensitive girl-friend, or the local vicar, to watch — but it's also nothing to get worried about. People like that have a reputation for car-bodging and repair that any team envies.

I sometimes think there ought to be one rally every year where mechanics drive and drivers provide service, with no cheating allowed. I'm not at all sure who would come out of it best, but I have an idea the mechanics are more versatile than we think.

Be sure to have the sort of mechanic who can't be shocked by *anything*. Years ago, in the Ford team, this was essential. With the Cortinas, we went through a period when axle changes, half-shaft swops and gearbox rebuilds were common occasions. A Ford service camp at the side of the road was always a busy place, but not for the squeamish. I recall one occasion on the Scottish a couple of years ago when I thought I heard odd noises from my car's Atlas axle. Mick Jones and the boys had the complete diff. out for inspection in a matter of minutes, found nothing, and attempted to put it back. By then the casing had cooled down and contracted that important little bit — I don't know if you've ever seen a precision instrument like a limited-slip diff, with its crownwheel and pinion persuaded back into a tight fit with a copper hammer, but I have.

The double clutch change in a Yorkshire garage on the 1974 RAC Rally is something that people often mention when praising works mechanics, but on that occasion they had it easy. After all, it was daylight, and they had the luxury of a warm workshop with a ramp to help them. A mechanic really comes into his own when he has to make major repairs at the side of the road, at night, when it is snowing, and when *any* time taken is too much because the schedule is so tight.

Some of the things achieved are nothing short of miraculous. Diff.

changes in less than 20 minutes, Bullet gearboxes swopped in the same time, bent steering racks toothpicked out in no time at all — this is fact, not fiction.

Improvising is usually more difficult than swopping major items. When Timo's Escort suffered broken engine mountings in Finland the mechanics patched him up with engine supports carved out of hard wood. I once saw David Seigle-Morris' Lotus-Cortina front wing patched up with a metal Pernod advertising sign on the Alpine. Baling wire, fence posts and even mechanics' braces and belts have all been invaluable from time to time.

Commercial service managers just wouldn't believe the speed at which top mechanics can repair things, nor the things that sometimes get done to keep a car going. On the World Cup Rally to Mexico, what do you do if your petrol-injection Triumph holes a piston with no chance of a change? You disconnect the injector nozzle from that cylinder, add a long tube to it, and direct it safely to the side of the car.

If your Imp needs a gearbox change, the engine has to come out first, and there isn't time to complete the job before the car goes into *Parc Ferme,* how do you cope? You do as much as possible, calmly put the engine in the back seat and push the car into the *Parc,* then complete the job the next morning.

Drivers, too, can be resourceful, like Zasada, in an Escort, on the World Cup Rally. His car ruined a front strut on the very long Peruvian Prime, and when he reached Ford Peru's emergency service a few miles further on, what did he do? He pinched a complete strut, brake and all, from the mechanic's own Escort. What's clever about that? Only that Zasada's car had Twin-Cam disc-brake suspension, and the mechanic's car was a drum-braked 1100. Why not?

The funny stories illustrate what can be achieved. I hope you get mechanics who are as resourceful. If you do, you deserve to do well. If not, I hope at least they are cheerful. It helps if they hero-worship you, and no amount of cash will buy loyalty like that.

A really good service crew, and here I'm talking about gilding the lily, should also be good cooks, although there are limits; when Citroen were really commited to their European rallying they used to have special cars (we would call them supervision cars now, I suppose) whose sole purpose was to be at service points early enough to set up trestle tables with cloths, French bread, pate, and even wine for their works team. On the other hand, the BMC team from Abingdon used to be famous for their fried sausages, their Chicken Supreme and their sandwiches — in the end it was diverting as much time as rebuilding the cars, and Stuart started to frown on it all.

But seriously, rally drivers will always appreciate something to eat or drink when they make a stop. I know that road time schedules are a lot easier nowadays, but it is not at all unusual for the crew to spend too much time at a service point, and have no time to feed at the control hotels before clocking out again.

I am fairly easy-going when it comes to rally eating. My belief is that 'little and often' works well for me. It's a big temptation, sometimes, to get into a rest halt where the hotel has really tried to make a good meal, sit down in front of some delicious steak or poached salmon (yes, at Machynlleth on an RAC Rally), then feel all bloated and sluggish.

No driver ever won a big event by eating his way round the country, but very few get anywhere by starving themselves. All this talk about needing to be hungry to 'tiger' doesn't work for me. I have to keep eating nourishing bits and pieces because a driver who is *really* trying expends a surprising amount of energy. I'm usually thirsty at the end of strenuous stages, so Norman always has the kettle boiling for coffee, and there is usually orange juice nearby. No Cokes or fizzy drinks, though — they make me . . . sorry vicar.

Lightweight snacks — cheese, biscuits, that sort of thing — all go down well, but I don't go in for instant energy like glucose tablets. I tried them once, and tried to be analytical about the effects, but there seemed to be no discernible effect. I went back to my nibbles, which have done awful things to my figure but keep me happy.

Drivers sweat a lot, and that liquid has to be replaced — during a long hot rally like the Safari I consume gallons of the stuff, so that I'm tired of it before the end, but it's the only way to keep cool.

Incidentally, on hot events there's really no substitute for a quick dip in a bath or even a swim to freshen up. I've done it at odd minutes on the Safari, if we know the water is clean, or in Greece on the Acropolis. It helps if you take your clothes off!

Dog biscuits? Yes, I thought we would have to mention those. I promise that it wasn't me who ate them, in spite of what Stuart has said so often. Mick Jones and Norman say the whole thing started on the World Cup Rally, where we were all eating like gannets everywhere. Apparently Hannu and Gunnar Palm, who were running ahead of the rest of us, would descend on a Ford service point like a cloud of locusts and clear the decks, without thinking of us. Norman decided to put a stop to this, and put out a delicately arranged plate of dig biscuits at the next point. He swears that Gunnar actually ate them *and* asked for more; he liked the black ones best of all.

One final point about mechanics. Never take them for granted, and never forget their feelings. Mechanics *are* people, and very skilled people at that. It might be our job to play the hero, and twirl the steering wheel, but that doesn't allow any of us to act like little tin gods. A mechanic's road schedule should be as gentle as possible, and he should get just as much opportunity as the driver for rest, a meal, and sleep.

Car preparation is not something I am very well qualified to discuss. I haven't had to maintain my personal rally cars since 1965, though Brian Gillibrand looked after the Alpine-Renault we ran on behalf of the British importers a few years ago. The Ford set-up is so professional and their standards are so high that I think I can comment on what I like to see in my cars.

As far as any of my Escorts are concerned, the preparation secret is simplicity. Ideally, I would like to see rally cars which could win with no extra fittings at all, but that isn't likely to happen. The more extra bits and pieces are installed, the more there is to go wrong at a critical moment.

Allied to this, it helps to have a car that's easy to drive. I class a really hot Escort as being very easy, and something like a Porsche or an Alpine as difficult. By really easy I mean a car with which you can take outrageous liberties, get well wound up, all sideways and ridiculously out of shape, and *still* have a fighting chance of coming out at the other side of the corner in one piece.

There's a world of difference between driving a car briskly and driving it really flat-out. Quite a lot of people can drive fast enough to win Restricted events, and perhaps Nationals on their own territory, but not many can win anywhere. That is where cars like the Escort have really helped the clubmen. Properly set up (and that means listening to what Boreham recommends, rather than rushing off with fancy ideas of your own) any idiot can drive one quickly — come to think of it quite a lot of such people have won important events in them, too! Like the Minis of the 1960s, I really don't know what club rallying would do without its Escorts — if some of the brave young men who throw them around had to try something else that needed precision, then we might find out who really are the good drivers!

My particular fad on cockpit equipment is that there should be as little extra equipment as possible. Timo Makinen tends to have all manner of fancy switches — to cut out this, turn over that, render such and such inoperative — and he once insisted on an alternator charge cut-out switch so that he could save a bit of engine power and make the fan belts stay in one piece that little time longer. I don't have hang-ups like that. Have four extra lamps at the front, a set of clocks, a map light for Jim and of course the essential Tripmaster, by all means, but after that I'm ready for the road.

When it's allowed I even do without the petrol gauge — we make do with a sight gauge on the tank. I have *two* big warning lights — one for oil pressure and one for ignition — big enough for them to shine out even in bright sunlight.

The rev-counter I use is chronometric — the one with the jerky needle and a tell-tale — but frankly I don't have much time to look at it. When we are driving hard in the forests, and getting really nasty with the car, there simply isn't time to look. Anyone who knows his car gets used to the sound of the engine and changes gear literally by ear. In the latest Escorts we tend to change up at about 8,500 rpm, though it's safe to 9,500 rpm, and in top gear we just hang on to whatever we can get. On Bramham, the first stage in the 1974 RAC Rally, all the team cars pulled well over 9,000 rpm in top, and when we pulled in for service soon afterwards Peter Ashcroft nearly had a fit! He was all for washing his hands of the whole affair and writing us off as lunatics. None of us had fingers slim enough to reach the re-set buttons behind the facia; Mick Jones is the expert!

Very occasionally a works-built engine (actually they are Brian Hart-built) lets go, but on the whole they are amazingly reliable. A gasket on a few events and a crankshaft pulley in the Isle of Man are the only failures which spring to mind.

The only piping or wiring we duplicate on the cars are for fuel pumps, and we have a spare coil handy. It's not so much because we don't need back-up systems, but because of the philosophy of winning; unless we are on a long-distance rally, *any* breakdown on a stage usually means a maximum penalty and the loss of all hope. Repairing a failed coil or a fuel pump is quick and easy, but anything else — forget it, and wait for the service crew to tow you out!

166

On seats and safety belts, find something that suits and stick to them. I've already said that my driving seat follows me from car to car, and until it falls to pieces I am happy with it. Don't be tricked into paying huge sums of money for seats that might not fit your bottom. Use what is best, and don't be ashamed of it. Mike Sutcliffe once supplied Triumph with a seat from a delivery van that he said he liked, so they trimmed it in appropriate colours and fitted it. Why be over-proud?

I have safety belts, full-harness, but surprisingly a lot lighter and cheaper than most. I know that the car is very safe, and I don't intend to have accidents if it can be helped, but good efficient belts are essential. Never skimp these details.

I have strong views on helmets. My own is a fairly conventional open-face design, very strong, very comfortable, and with a visor in case of broken screens, but with no gimmicks. The intercom system is built-in, with the microphone in the chin-cup, and there is stowage space behind me where it lives between stages. I don't believe in the full-face 'flower-pot' helmets for rallying in closed cars. For starters they give me a touch of claustrophobia, which is unsettling, and there are practical disadvantages such as weight, inertia and the difficulty in breathing. I get a hemmed-in feeling, with a lot of condensation. The breathing problem is important, for any rally driver who is trying hard is also working hard, which means heavy breathing and a lot of water vapour moving about. The other thing that affects me when I wear a full-face helmet is that I can see too much of it, which distracts me; an open-face helmet is invisible, apart from the peak when I am using it.

Incidentally, this view of mine doesn't apply to open cars. I have a 'flower-pot' for powerboat racing, which is essential in order to keep dry, and if I wear goggle straps inside it means the goggles can't be whipped off by a big wave!

I have no magic formula on clothes. Flameproof overalls may look poofy, but there may be occasions when there is a fire, and I need protection. In any case, some sort of overall is essential in a rally car — they're comfortable, they're useful, and on the occasions when I have to help with work on the car they're quite invaluable.

To complete the outfit, there is the question of gloves and shoes. Some of the young tigers invest in super professional looking racing shoes, which don't help at all if you have to get out in the mud and sand of special stages; I prefer a pair of comfortable, worn out, expendable old casuals — the more disreputable the better. When Tony Mason and I won the RAC Rally in 1972, K Shoes advertised that we used their products to do it (Tony worked for K Shoes at the time) but if they had seen the ruined old slip-ons I was using they might not have been so proud!

I have no preferences over gloves except that they should fit properly and should breathe. The lightweight ones wear out very quickly, usually by becoming worn or torn in the palms — I went through two pairs on the 1974 RAC Rally, which shows just how hard a rally driver works at his job. If I remember I usually ring up John Hopwood for a few new pairs, but I have often had to wander round to the accessory caravan at the start of an event and buy on the spot. More than once it's needed a loudspeaker appeal just before the 'off' to fit me up for the next night!

Incidentally, on seat coverings, I must mention how comfortable the covers provided by the Woolmark people were when we used them on the London-Sydney Marathon. Much too expensive for everyday use, and not very practical because they get dirty too easily, but very soft and sleep-inducing.

Other equipment in my car always includes chewing gum and sweeties. I suffer from a dry mouth because of all the effort, and a chew in moments of peace helps. But I never chew anything on stages. On arriving at the start of a stage the gum or the sweetie has to go — I don't want the possibility of swallowing at the wrong moment, or getting gum stuck in any accident.

I tend to carry very little extra clothing in a car. It helps if you assume the car isn't going to break down, and that your service car will always find you anyway — let them carry the baggage instead. Jim and I usually have a Lombard bag each, with a change of clothing, a toothbrush and shaver and possibly a change of shoes to something decent. That and the inevitable rally jacket is as much as I ever need.

Preparing for rallies has never been a problem to me; I just don't do anything about it. I don't have any particular regime, or sequence of preparation, because I find that I am most relaxed if I don't try to organise anything special. On the other hand, I do try to go off to the start without any big domestic or business worries overhanging. If there's anything I can put off from consideration before the start I do so. I live sensibly before an event, but that's all.

I never, ever descend to taking stimulants. Even on the marathons and Safaris there is usually enough happening in or around the rally car to keep me interested when I should be awake; when I should be resting, I sleep. On the Marathon, Ove Andersson and I tried to do about twelve-hour sessions on the long run to Bombay, and when off duty I reckoned to be resting or sleeping most of the time.

With that sort of approach no-one who is at all mentally fresh should ever need to resort to pills, and it would make me happy if they could be banned altogether. There is no excuse — if an idle chap like me can manage then surely any of the young bloods should be able to do the same?

I'm one of the lucky few who doesn't have to drive really hard on public roads for a few miles before stages to get into the right mood. That sort of behaviour is anti-social, and almost by definition you are driving where there's most likely to be congestion and conflicting traffic. People who believe they have to warm up in this way should learn otherwise.

It *is* difficult to 'switch on' or 'switch off' between stages and public roads, but this is something I have had to learn. I try to have a few minutes' rest in the passenger seat on the way to the next stage. On arrival I can usually get out, walk round the car a couple of times, kick the tyres, see that everything is still working, shake my head, jump in and go.

Experience will tell you a lot about pre-stage tactics. It is sometimes comical to get to the first stage on important events and find all the seeded crews hiding round corners to make sure they don't have to tackle a stage first! There are many reasons for this. I like someone else to 'warm up' the marshals, to make sure they work off their nervousness and timing errors on somebody else, and to let someone else find the occasional badly-placed arrow and fly off the road so that the rest of us can be warned!

On really strange stages, there is no harm at all in listening very carefully to the engine note of the first cars to disappear into the distance (it's surprising just how much you can learn from that). Climb up on the roof of the car if a lot of the stage is in view (airfields and open scrubland stages, for instance), sniff the air, smell and listen. There's always something to be learned. The tip of your nose will warn of frost. I can usually smell fog, too, and we all have that inexplicable sixth sense about danger.

Treat anything strange with suspicion. Behave like a nervous animal and learn as much as possible; there's never any harm in asking the marshals what sort of stage they have. Many of them are happy to boast about something, and you might discover something valuable.

Get your co-driver to read out target times, but don't believe anything you are told about length. Nobody sticks to the letter of the rules, nowadays, and almost every stage we tackle is stretched way above the theoretical length. If your co-driver *thinks* he knows a stage don't listen to him; if he *really* knows it, listen to *everything*.

When it comes to analysing my driving methods, and trying to pass on a few tips, I have great problems. My driving is fairly instinctive, and anyway I am not very good at boasting about things. In this respect I have to fall back on what co-drivers have said about me and I hope they will not bring on the blushes too much.

Jim Porter thinks that perhaps the reasons I have won so many events is that I try consistently harder than most other people. That certainly applies on short, sharp stage rallies where every effort should go into the sprints from start to finish. I certainly don't rely on local knowledge, which some of the local heroes tend to do. Over the last few years, while making a comprehensive tour of the country on my Esso programme, I have often found problems in beating a local Scottish driver in Scotland, a Yorkshireman on the Mintex Dales, or an Irishman on the Circuit, but bring the same people back to strange territories and the story is usually very different. Incidentally, although I say that I like to run through stages that already have wheelmarks on the road to follow, Jim insists I am quicker without them!

No top rally driver has a completely unique approach to driving. Jim has been with them all and confirms this: "Roger and Ove Andersson are very similar in style and speed, and Timo is not a lot different, though I think he lacks in mechanical sympathy. Hannu may occasionally be a little bit quicker, but he tends to charge up to his corners, stand on his brakes at the last minute, and not be as far sideways as the others — but nothing picks out Roger from the rest."

Tony Mason — I never can stop him talking, he's so enthusiastic about everything — goes into a lot more detail:

"Roger's approach is not different, but he is very relaxed. He's very confident, something quite amazing that rubs off on a co-driver. He is very calm, and his precision is notable. You go into a corner, or over a blind brow, and I might be convinced there's no way in hell that a car will do what it has to do to stay on the road, but with perfect timing and precise control he always does.

"I've no doubt at all that this is due to accurate placing. On a rally where there are 'Mickey Mouse' stages, which everybody else hates, Roger loves them because he can try very hard and apply all his driving skills. The first time I started a rally with him, I just couldn't believe the speeds we were achieving. On the first corner he was driving on three wheels round a corner that he couldn't possibly have known. He was completely sideways, couldn't see where he was going, and I thought he must have misinterpreted one of the arrows. There was a gate we had to get through, he twitched the car and it went through straight . . . then I realised it was all a question of car control, and after the next corner I stopped worrying. It was then easy to sit back and watch the calmness and control that goes into driving a rally car this quickly.''

It goes without saying that the way an Escort, or any similar front-engine-rear-drive car, is set up suits my driving style. Many years ago I used to drive very sideways, but that was often a function of the way the cars behaved. Now that we all have a limited-slip diff. the rear wheels sit down that much better, they're driving so much more of the time, and the cars are much more likely to be pointing straight up the road.

There's no merit at all in being sideways after a corner, but in many cases a sideways entry gives more balance and more transient control in case of emergencies. I would far rather arrive at a tightening situation with a car already well set-up than in one that was about to understeer itself off into the pine trees! The racing driver's approach never works for long on a rally — unless you are a millionaire with the fastest Stratos or Porsche in the world, where 'point and squirt' will win all the money for you.

I don't dislike any particular road or track surface, though like any driver I hate the thought of black ice or other hazards that can't be seen. Any rally driving is good for training and experience, though I would not willingly go back to road rallying again.

People who still say that road rallying is necessary for training just don't understand. Usually they don't know any different, and many of them haven't even done any serious stage rallying! It's coming to something when a quick man can be belting down a road on a selective

171

and actually meet a police car coming the other way. No thanks. Not any more.

"How should I start rallying?" is a regular question fired at me at Ford forums or during other public appearances. There's no easy answer, because every individual case has differences. Someone might have to buy an old 850 Mini, do all the work himself, and keep stopping because the money has gone. Another bloke could be lucky and find a new RS1800 or RS2000 with a mechanic and workshop to look after him. My usual answer is to do as much motor sport as possible, any sort that's legal, to become master of the car and to learn how to handle it.

Driving tests, for instance, give one good example. I'm on a special stage and over-shoot a junction, perhaps shoot off into a firebreak. I can stop the car safely, get into reverse without breaking the gearbox, back out into the road, and be off again without straining anything. That sort of calm comes from driving tests. If I need to make a neat handbrake turn, I know how to do it, and I don't finish up in the trees or the ditch after a glorious failure.

Autocross is very good because it trains a driver to go over bumps and humps very fast. The thing that stands out in my mind is that autocross teaches bravery, and to *really* learn about balance when sliding around. It also teaches that you can't turn a car if the front wheels are off the ground!

Autocross is also good for teaching a driver to get used to other cars around him. That shouldn't happen on a rally stage unless he is either much faster or much slower than the nearest opposition, but there are times when even I get down among the middle runners, and there are right and wrong ways to get past them on a stage. I may be very lucky in that most people would rather let me go off in front of them than be caught in mid-stage, but it does happen. On the 20-plus miles of Dalby South I caught and passed three cars in the 1974 RAC Rally — two were very good about it but one was an absolute pig.

I simply don't understand how anyone can hate being passed. It must be quite obvious that they are holding up the quicker man, throwing rocks and mud at his screen and lights, and it usually means they are a bit slower, too. I *know* that a car which has been passed is often sucked onwards very profitably indeed — it is always easier to follow at a respectable distance, and the extra warning of blind bends is a great help.

Tyres are things people get very het-up about, and once again the Finns are great theorisers about the subject. Tyres are quite obviously the vital link between engine and road, but it is surprising how much change in tyre equipment produces relatively little effect on performance.

Dunlop's present M & S treads are very good for us, but they don't last long. If I'm really trying hard a rear wheel tread life of 15 miles is about average!

On rim widths, it took an awful lot of guess work on the Escorts before we finally settled on the best system. You could say now that we are 'all at sixes and sevens', because that is our stable choice of Minilite rim widths.

Generally speaking we use the seven-inch rims on hard surfaces with hard make-up. A surface with a lot of rock and stones keyed in can be very grippy, and I can leave black tyre marks across them. With that sort of grip I can use big rims with the extra-wide tyre (which has the extra band round the middle). Almost anywhere else, where it is wet, loose, or generally boggy, we use six-inch rims and the standard tyre.

One Scandinavian theory that works, and works well, is to fit very narrow tyres for soft snow and deep mud. On this sort of stuff we need to be able to dig through, try to find some grip down under, and even use the sides of the tyres to get some traction. The other big advantage is that there is so much more steering control — so much more 'feel' and precision, with the steered wheels 'talking' so much more.

We try not to run with different width rims, even when this is allowed, but remember here that I am talking about a conventional well-balanced machine. Wider rear tyres and rims might work, probably do work, for an Alpine, Porsche or Stratos, but they very rarely do the trick for an Escort or a Firenza.

Incidentally, I'm not even convinced about having very wide tyres if they lead to wide tracks. Escorts, Asconas and things are tending to get very wide with all their wheel-arch extensions and things, and in some forests anything which makes the car that much more bulky is bad news. The ideal for me would be an old original Escort without bulgy arches, but with the grip and handling of a 1976 car.

On lights I have long been used to using just the standard Rallye Sport set-up on the front of the Escort. That means two big lights high up, even above the level of the headlamps, and a couple more way down at the bottom of the bracket. We used to go in for two spots and two fogs, but now I prefer to have four big fat powerful long-range driving lamps. The cars are so quick that we really need all the range we can get, and I haven't believed in lights for fast fog driving for years. Any fool can try to drive fast in fog, but I don't think many of us can see that well; in a proper fog, lights don't really help, and I haven't found any that are that much better than dipped headlamps.

Ray Wood of Lucas used to complain that rally drivers were using too many lights, and that they would get the overall effect with fewer but more powerful lenses He obviously hadn't driven a car at the speeds we have to face; you just cannot have too much light on a rally car. Switch on six big iodines in front of an Escort and it is as if the sun had come up, yet at speeds up to 100 mph even that isn't enough at times.

When we go to Africa for the Safari, we sometimes have extra lamps mounted on top of the front wings. This isn't because they give better vision in dust, but because they are that much farther away from the mud splashes. African mud can be very clingy and can bake itself hard on to a hot lens, and they might just be spared in a big head-on shunt with a wild animal. Even in a roll there will be a good chance of having some lights left — either the wing-top lamp will survive or the front lights will still be there. Another advantage of a scuttle lamp is that the co-driver can lean around the screen pillar and give the lens a clean.

Years ago, when I had Minis, I used to like the movable spotlamps on the roof that were so popular. They were quite illegal for on-road use, but they had a certain charm on stages, and I used to work my roof lamp personally and drive with only one hand. That way I could point the lamp where I needed it, but it made gear-changing very interesting! In the end we dropped the method, even though it wasn't illegal in the forests, because I thought I was spending more time driving the lamp than the car!

Having said all this, I must say that I prefer daylight rallying. Any driver who thinks deeply about his rallying, and worries in case he is not completely in control, should want to see everything. It doesn't matter how good one's lights are, there is still a lot of darkness around wherein lies the unknown.

A good driver uses all his senses — sight, sound, smell, touch and taste — and in a properly organised rally car nothing should be strange. The question of good vision means that it ought to be possible to glimpse the TV helicopter before its engine noise worries you, that oil leak on to the exhaust should be an obvious smell before you see the pressure falling off, and an odd vibration through the gear lever will always tell a story — is the engine mounting OK, or are the selector bushes breaking up?

When it comes to tactics, I can only explain my own approach to rallying. It helps to have one of the best cars in the business, and be blessed with such a good co-driver and team backing, of course. As I have said more than once already, I am essentially idle and slow in my movements, so I rely on Jim's calculations and my own native cunning to go as slowly as I dare. 'Slowly' is a relative description, of course, but I can't honestly see any point in thrashing the car to win by a distance when the odd minute or so is quite enough.

I can look back over my wins, and point to many victories by small margins on events where I had been leading by much more at half-distance. Like most drivers, I have a natural pace when everything is comfortable and safe, and I like to plod along like that. Sometimes there is even time to get an eye-corner view of the spectators, some of whom still contrive to look horrified, so even though I'm driving below my quickest, it must still look good enough!

I take a long time to warm up in the car, so any event with a lot of starts and stops means that we have to work harder. It's nothing to find us trailing down in third or fourth place at first, before the adrenalin really starts to flow. Tony Fall summed it up very well not long ago when he said: ''If you're in a forest at dead of night, and it's all going wrong for you, the tendency is to slow down. If you slow down the car won't be set-up right and will tend to understeer more. An accident is that much more likely. A professional has to keep going all the time, tail out and ready for anything, but a clubman is mentally only able to do it for half a dozen stages, then he flags off. The clubmen are all good on one-nighters, but look at them on an RAC Rally. Roger and I are just getting into our strides by the second night — all the young lads are getting tired and flying off into the trees''.

I rely on Jim completely for tactical information. If Jim tells me I have a 30-second lead, or am trailing by that much, I believe him. In this respect I let Jim drive me, and guide me on my pace. At times he judges it very well but there have been times when that judgment has been damned fine. Without the regulations nonsense on the 1974 Burmah we would have won by just one second, which to Jim was enough, but was pretty damned close. Even on the RAC Rally in 1972, with Tony Mason, when we reached half-way no further ahead than at the finish, we knew what the gap was at any time.

For a clubman, it is essential to know who the rivals are, and to make sure you know their times. Let them know your times, too, and add seconds if you want to confuse the issue, but they might have done the same, and a third co-driver might know the truth about each of you . . . it gets so complicated that you meet yourself coming back at times. Incidentally, that's one big advantage of hanging back slightly on a stage rally — you can often get a report on rival times from the control caravan at the end of the stages, and be much more in the picture than them.

The only snag about playing it cool and relaxed is that stages could be cancelled. This has worked both ways for me. There was a Jim Clark Memorial event a few years ago where one stage was cancelled after I had put up a very good time on it, and the recalculations put me just a couple of seconds in front of Andrew Cowan's car. On the Mintex Dales in 1974, the only one I competed in an RS2000, a cancelled stage gave me the win after all — my car had actually broken down in it, and I had a cancelled maximum penalty to laugh off at the prizegiving!

After all this advice a good clubman will soon start beating me, so I really have to wind up the chapter with a warning about interviews. Over the years I think I've improved — I hope I've improved — but I still find the public-relations side one of the hardest to carry out properly.

Forums, rally schools and other such public appearances are all very easy, because I'm among people who understand motor sport, and know basically what this exhilarating business is all about. But there are two basic type of interviewers; those who are genuine enthusiasts, and are interested in what you might have to say, and the other breed — the 'back-room boozers', the gad-flys, and the all-purpose TV personalities. Answering sensible questions is one thing, and as a works driver it's part of my job to do it well, but the sort of thing that really floors me is to have a microphone thrust into the car with the fatuous questions: ''How do you feel now that . . .'', or "What do you think of your chances now . . .", or even "What's it been like out there?" How do you answer such a dead-end question without sounding boastful or as stupid as the questioner?

I have been told that I interview badly, and in my quieter moments I worry about this. Analysing why, I think it is because I have to apply myself very thoroughly to the job in hand, and most of the time I know that the interviewers don't do so themselves. Face me up to a man who is genuinely interested in the event, or even genuinely interested in me, and I will help him to get a story. Give me a parasite and I will probably ignore him — that, or spray him with champagne.

But remember, if you are lucky, a lot of your performance, both the driving and the public speaking, may be on behalf of a sponsor — and that is what the next chapter is all about.

Chapter 9

The Esso years

IN 1971, QUITE a few people were ready to say that old Clark was finished. I wasn't doing many rallies, and I wasn't winning, either. A professional who isn't winning always has his critics, and when his car is breaking that makes it even more difficult. I hadn't finished a rally since the previous Circuit of Ireland, which we *had* won, and the new RS1600s were giving trouble. The GT70 which we had designed for ourselves didn't work, and to crown it all Stuart Turner was still in his 'Finns are Kings' phase.

I was depressed and bored, in fact I hadn't felt so depressed since the early 1960s, when nobody wanted me for their factory teams. I was bored, quite frankly, because I was getting to be out of practice. We hadn't been looking forward to the most active year anyway, but the nine-week Ford factory strike in the spring had made everything worse. Boreham's competitions budgets were slashed, entire events were cut out of the schedule, and for a time it looked as if we might be out of work completely. At that time I came very near to leaving Ford; there were offers from other teams in Europe, some waving lots of money around, and I was tempted. However, I didn't get too involved with their offers.

The outlook for 1972 was grim. The worldwide programme was cut to the bone, and it looked as if I was being squeezed out. I wasn't entered for the Monte (Stuart wanted Hannu and myself to drive the ice-notes recce cars instead!) and I wasn't being asked to do the Safari.

It was my professional pride that was hurt. Stuart is the most analytical of men, but this time I just couldn't agree with his judgment. I wasn't prepared to face a year of idleness, but Stuart wasn't prepared to give me much work. We discussed things, we bargained, we even had a row or two. Finally, I had a minor brainwave — if Ford wouldn't give me enough work I'd better go out and find my own.

During 1971, when I'd been particularly slack, I had done several British events for Cal Withers (Withers of Winsford, the car breakers, who had a very active rallying team). Jim and I had taken an RS1600 on the Hackle in July and had won it, then Henry Liddon had come with me on the Manx in the same old car and we had won again. Now, if I could get a car from the factory, I would get back into 'match-practice' by doing as many of the important British events as possible. Stuart agreed. Boreham would provide an Escort — a brand-new car, with every up-to-date tweak on it — a mechanic (Norman Masters) and some backing for a British season. It was up to me to go out and find what else was needed to balance my finances.

I had already decided to tackle the RAC Championship — a much more important series than ever before — and I needed a sponsor for whom all this British publicity was ideal. As soon as the 'knockers' got to know about my intentions there were lots of snide remarks about Clark going 'pot-hunting'. In fact, I'm convinced the reverse has happened. Without wishing to be big-headed, I'm sure that my factory-backed entry did a lot to raise the status of these rallies, and the standards are now very high. You could even rank a Jim Clark or a Manx with the local French Internationals we all used to admire so much a few years ago.

Stuart was a bit half-hearted at first, but before long he became very enthusiastic; it's history now that I won a lot of events in the Championship. At first it was very easy to stay ahead of the field, but by 1974 standards were appreciably higher. Whereas I could win easing up in 1972, in 1974 I had to keep my mind on the job and press on to the very end. Any messing about with experiments like coil-spring rear suspension (the Lindisfarne in 1973) or tyre changing (the Burmah in 1974) and I found myself behind the leaders.

I didn't have the trouble I had expected in finding a sponsor. I was lucky, I suppose, that my name helped, and I landed the very first sponsorship deal that I tried! Is this unique?

The rallying grapevine, active as always at our level, whispered that Esso were keen to get back into rallying after years of involvement only in motor racing. They had a premium oil, Uniflo, which needed publicity, and they were looking for a way of doing this through production cars. Their motor racing outlet was Graham Hill (with his Brabhams, Shadows and things) but they had no rallying links, so I got on the phone to their competitions man, Jeff Edwards, and within a matter of days the deal was done.

We worked out a simple and all-embracing contract (which, as I have already mentioned, was to lead to all sorts of complications with Ford and their own sponsors!) and it meant that I would be doing a complete British rally season in a personal Esso-backed Escort which, as part of the publicity rub-off, would be painted to look like a Uniflo can. That was how the 'Old Gold' nickname came about (the 'Old' bit, incidentally, referred to the age of the car, not the colour!).

Although Stuart had promised me a completely new car, the deal had been fixed in a great hurry and as the new season was about to start there was no chance of a new Escort being built in time. Even without interruptions it takes about six weeks to produce a new rally car, and of course once the season had started Norman Masters would also be busy looking after whatever car we used in the interim.

This turned out to be a disgracefully old Escort which already had quite a history. Known officially as LVX 941J, it had been built up at the end of 1970 for a Ford France rally programme, and Jean-Francois Piot had driven it in at least ten French Internationals, usually with Jim as his co-driver (Jim had been running the Ford France competitions department for some time, at Stuart's behest). Ironically the car had originally carried BP sponsorship and livery, and now, as a tired old workhorse, it was to run in the colours of the rival Esso concern.

It had been shunted several times — usually by going straight on into a mountainside — and I soon discovered it was rather a horrid old car. It was a bit ragged round the edges, and I have an idea the body wasn't all that square, either. Norman says that between the four events we did with it on the Esso programme he used to hide it away around the back of the Boreham workshops so that nobody else could see it. "It was patched, it was cracked and it was tatty — not at all the sort of car I could be proud of!"

Not that we had any choice because Ford were short of spare cars at that time (and since — a tremendous amount of trouble was caused when a works car was stolen in Wales in January 1975!). But as

180

usual, Norman performed miracles, and once it had been sprayed up to at least look beautiful superficially the rally circus soon christened it 'Old Gold', or sometimes 'The Golden Oldie'.

I mustn't be too rude about the car, anyway, because it won several rallies for me, and as I write this it is still around the British rally scene. Also, I have to admit that the first time I used it I managed to shunt it again. It wasn't just any old shunt, either, but a really thorough one, an object lesson on how not to make friends and influence people.

Jim was still slaving away in France so I had Hamish Cardno beside me for my first rally in Esso colours; as Hamish at that time was an assistant editor on *Motor* magazine we thought a bit of rallying from the hot seat would be instructive for one and all. The event was the Snowman, organised in the north of Scotland, and because of the likely weather conditions (winter up there meant almost certain snow and ice) there was no ban on the use of studded tyres on the special stages.

We set off in fine style and were really tramping along. Good studs on fresh snow (we were running at the front of the field) gave us really tremendous grip on the forestry tracks, and with about 250 pins in each tread our Dunlops were giving us splendid traction.

All was well until we reached the seventh stage near Invergarry, and this is how Hamish described what happened next in his *Motor* column:

"Just under two miles into the stage there was a bridge with no parapet, which we negotiated without drama, then accelerated hard through a series of fast open bends. The last one was a right-hander, deeply rutted on the inside, and followed by a left kink, then a 50-yard straight.

We were using all the road, Clark was swinging the car about in his normal fashion, and we were doing about 55-60 mph as we came out of the right-hander.

But we didn't go left. Funny I thought, the car's heading for the edge (the road was built up and there was a steep slope on the left with trees about 15ft down). Then we were over the edge and the whole world was upside-down. Then a crash. Then a series of bumps and bangs as the car settled back on its wheels, between the trees."

The car had taken the steering wheel clean out of my hands, turned of its own accord, and flown off into the trees. You'd probably expect Hamish to say something like "Do you always do this sort of thing to

181

strange co-drivers?'', but by the time we had stopped moving the only thing we could utter was, ''Crikey, that was quick'', then get out and see where we were. I was all for carrying on, but as we had finished up about 20ft down the embankment and were stuck between some trees it wasn't going to be as easy as that. The next morning it took a tractor and a lot of heaving to get the car back on to the stage, and it wasn't until then that I realised how it had happened.

The whole thing was caused by a puncture. There was a gash in the front tyre's sidewall, which must have been caused when I clipped a rock on the inside of the previous corner. The tyre had deflated quickly, mis-shaped itself, then suddenly flown off the rim due to the weight of the studs, wrapped itself round the front suspension and strut and caused that wheel to lock. The lesson from that Snowman rally was 'Never have high-speed punctures on studded tyres!'.

After a start like that things could only improve, and I was very happy with our good fortune during the rest of the 1972 season and the following year. I think it is in order to boast just a little by quoting the results — we had nine wins and a second in 1972, and ten wins and a second in 1973.

'Old Gold' became a successful car for me, even though it was tired. We won three events together early in 1972, including the Welsh International, then we retired it to Boreham in favour of the new car. It had to be used again for a couple of events in the autumn (winning those, too) and when it was finally pensioned off I bought it. Not that the 'old nail' was finished, by any means; Vic 'Junior' Preston used it more than once, and eventually I sold it to Donald Heggie. The last I heard was that Donald had re-sold it, a year older but with a new shell — *and* for more money than he had paid me. Lucky devil!

The really famous Esso car, which got the magazines talking, was my second car — LVX 942J. This was the long-awaited new machine, which wasn't actually a runner until May and did its first rally — the Scottish — in June. One often finds this sort of delay, even in a works team (perhaps I should say *especially* in a works team) because there's always something more pressingly urgent, so that the all-new projects usually suffer. Hands up anybody who has just mentioned the GT70?

Although the car was new, its registration number originally graced one of the 1971 Safari Twin-Cams, which was later scrapped.

182

Norman had taken many frequently interrupted working weeks to build up the new car, but he had done the job with very great care. The specification was very much the same as that of 'Old Gold' but one thing we changed was the colour scheme.

Even though 'Old Gold' was absolutely true to Esso's advertising requirements the results looked pretty awful on a car, particularly when it became good and dirty. It also photographed very badly, and since part of the publicity is to make the sponsor's name obvious we had to do something about that. The compromise, and a very famous compromise, too, was to spray the car white with just a broad blue band carrying the 'Esso' signwriting inside it.

I must make a few things clear about the Esso link-up, as there was much ill-informed comment in the press while we were campaigning the car. The Ford factory had little to do with the programme, which was entirely my own choice, even though the car was kept at Boreham and maintained by a Boreham mechanic. Esso, for their part, took little functional part in the programme, either. My agreement with them was that I should take part in the RAC Rally Championship series, but they very rarely attended the events to give me any service.

The lubricants in my care were all standard Esso oils, even in the engine, which invariably gave a power output as good as or better than any other rally Escort; it would have been quite pointless having Uniflo support for a car that was using a non-standard brew. It wasn't just a case of being told by Esso that the oils were standard when they supplied them — sometimes we had engines that were oil-burners and Norman had to use oil which he bought at Esso stations. I changed the engine oil at Narborough more than once from bulk supplies in my own workshops.

It was always a rather low-key relationship, too. Occasionally I would find my face alongside Graham Hill's in Esso adverts, but only rarely was I asked to put in public appearances, and thank goodness the company never went in for much of the 'pretty girls, give-away badges, special-uniforms' razzamatazz, which I would have hated.

Esso's marketing people made a good job of the first contract, and we produced the results they needed, so when it became re-negotiation time it seemed reasonable that all my activities should carry the same banner, so Stan's Group One racing cars (the Alfa Romeos) and my Formula Three powerboat all got the same treatment. The upshot was that Esso had first call on my services for events in Britain which they specified.

That worked very well, but almost too well as far as Stuart and Boreham were concerned. We had not foreseen any complications when I started on this personal programme, and neither had Ford, but when Ford began looking for individual event sponsors, or their own fuel company backers (Shell) thought they had first call on my services, we found ourselves in a complicated little knot.

The fuel company clash of interests came about because Shell backed Ford *as a team* in their rallying. This meant that if there was to be a team entry in Britain, and I was supposed to be in it, then I was supposed to be in another Shell-backed Escort. Obviously this wasn't on, which explains why I was usually a rather obvious-looking outsider in events like the RAC Rally or the Scottish, when the Finns turned up in Shell-backed cars.

Even that wasn't an insuperable hitch, until we came to the Tour of Britain in 1974, which of course I won from Gerry Marshall, both of us in identical factory-entered RS2000s. Somehow, and don't ask me how it had happened because we fell over the same problem the year before with 3-litre Capris, my Esso contract didn't cover the Tour of Britain, so Stuart entered team cars without any particular livery involved, and after the finish I found myself in the middle of a very gentlemanly but politically significant dispute.

In spite of the enormous rows that tend to develop in Grand Prix racing, most people in motor sport are very gentlemanly and civilised, and it never reached the stage of anyone suing anyone else over my services and successes. But we've learned that in future there must never be such an obvious clash of interest between myself and the rest of the team. Perhaps if a little more interest had been shown right at the start, in the winter of 1971, this would never have happened.

There was still some embarrassment to Ford, even when the oil company business was settled. When I rallied out of Great Britain (which effectively meant Safaris and odd-balls like the Hong-Kong and Total events) my cars could have any backing that Stuart had fixed, but in Britain, if he wanted to arrange individual one-off sponsorship for something like the RAC Rally, there was still a conflict.

I sympathise deeply with Tony Mason, who had to rush around London in the autumn to fix an individual sponsor for the RAC Rally. He would get heavily involved with some interested party, and even get over the hurdle of money. Then the conversation would go something like this:

"Fine, we'll sponsor the team, then. That means Roger Clark and who else?".

"Sorry, you can't have Roger. He's tied up to Esso. But you can have the rest of the team."

"Who are the drivers?"

"Well, there's Timo Makinen, and Hannu Mikkola . . ."

"But that's no good to us for advertising. Everybody knows Roger Clark, but I don't know about the others."

"But Timo won the last RAC Rally, and Hannu has won the Safari and the World Cup Rally . . ."

"But I can't even pronouce their names. I certainly don't know how to spell them. Where do they come from?"

Tony would even have to say that, much as he would like to be in one of these sponsored cars, he would actually be with *me* on the event!

It is heresy to have to say this, but there always seem to be problems where sponsors are concerned, which I suppose is quite understandable, bearing in mind that they have their advertising and publicity priorities, whereas we have our competitive worries.

At least my own deal with Esso was directly connected with motoring and engineering, but I'm not at all sure that some sponsoring companies ever get their money's worth out of their involvement. When money was plentiful much of sponsorship was purely for 'good fellowship' and to foster happy feelings towards their product, but now that times are harder almost any sponsor needs a direct spin-off from his exposure. For instance, it wouldn't be any good at all for a company which specialises in horses or hiking getting involved with a rally car — unless they were sure they could gain converts this way!

Some of Stuart's advertising and sponsorship deals for RAC Rallies must surely have been for purely prestige reasons, or to use the cars as mobile hoardings. On the 1970 RAC Rally we all carried newspaper livery (mine was from the *Daily Express)* which was very cheeky as the *Daily Mirror* were sponsoring the event. A year later all the cars looked like Embassy cigarette packets. Team cars have also looked like Milk Marketing Board tankers or Colibri cigarette lighter packets, too. Not much of an engineering connection there.

The blue Esso car, or 'LVX' as it was known, was really quite remarkable. It won so many events for us that I thought it worth listing them in a special index to show just how much hard work a modern rally car will accept.

In all the time I used it, we only had one bodyshell change, and that was because Yours Truly rolled it at — of all places — Boreham, while we were doing film work in connection with Esso's 'Our Man Clark'. The second bodyshell was new for the 1972 RAC Rally, and it carried right on, including three more Internationals, until my third Esso car was built at the end of 1973.

The high spot of that first Esso year was naturally the RAC Rally. The RAC, of course, is the rally that everyone wants to win, foreigners as well as British drivers. It is now the most popular rally in the world, and both the quality *and* quantity of the entry reflects this.

Ever since Jack Kemsley first directed the 'route to the woods' Scandinavians have tended to dominate the results, and we all began to think that a British driver simply couldn't win his own event, ever again. Gerry Burgess, in a works Mark 2 Zephyr (yes, it was that long ago!) was the last Briton to win, in 1959, and even then it was after snow-blocked roads, protests, and a lot of aggro.

By 1972 I was beginning to wonder if we could ever get our own rally back, and whether I could ever do it personally. I hadn't shone in previous years (sixth in 1969 was my best score to date), and we knew the Escort was a bit of a flounderer on snow. Snow on the RAC? Yes — it's rather like fish and chips, or ham and eggs — the one wouldn't be complete without the other.

In 1972 everything worked in our favour. From mid-year we had the lusty 2-litre RS engine, with lots of power and reliability. I had been working away in British forests since January, and I was really feeling match-fit; incidentally, Stuart now takes the credit for me doing the British Championship series, though it was originally my idea just to keep myself busy. What does matter is that by the autumn I was absolutely in the swing of forestry-stage driving, and I needed no preparation at all for the RAC Rally, having scored four wins from five events during the previous two months. In 1971 I had tackled only one event, the Manx, in the three-month run-up to the big event.

My rapport with Norman Masters had continued to build up throughout the season, and in his crafty way he was encouraging me to try harder and harder. Every time we achieved something new in testing, or won another National, Norman would say: "This year we're going to win the RAC Championship and the RAC Rally." After a time this sort of thing got through to me, and I even started to believe the propaganda.

That stupid roll-over when filming was a blessing in disguise, because at least it meant that we had a completely fresh car for the RAC Rally. 'Old Gold' did its stuff for us in the intervening weeks.

Getting to the start of the RAC, and being named favourite by the newshounds of the national press, was nothing new; I had seemed to be somebody's favourite every year from about 1966, when I had led from the start and then leaned a Lotus-Cortina against a tree.

I was too busy to worry much about the pre-rally build-up, especially as there was this new-fangled and unproven fuel-injection system on 'LVX' to worry about, but the thought did cross my mind that it would be nice to have a troublefree run for a change.

Everything seemed to fall into place beautifully. It was Jim's first year as a rally organiser, it was the first RAC to start and finish in York, and for the first time in years there wasn't any snow. The Escorts were very fast and the team was strong. In my Esso colours I was on my own, but with full factory service. We also had a huge quantity of Dunlop M & S stage tyres, which seemed to make so much difference to grip and traction.

What followed was almost like a dream, a fairy tale. Timo and Hannu's cars both dropped out on the first day in Wales, and by midnight mine was the only works Escort still running. I was desperately sorry for the Finns, but it was a godsend for me because for the next three days I had complete personal service from the most dedicated and skilful team of mechanics in the business.

It was a horribly wet and misty rally, but thank goodness there wasn't any snow. The new Escort needed virtually no work at all, and there was never a time when we were going slower than we had hoped. The previous year's winner was Stig Blomqvist, in his Saab 96, so he started first, and as I was running at number 4 we were fighting away for the lead all week; it was very cosy and exciting!

The trouble with rallying is that stages are fairly short, so that the seeded drivers rarely see each other on a stage. It can get very lonely at times, really lonely and discouraging, so it was very stimulating to be running so close to Stig and his Saab. We both tried to hang around and tackle stages after each other, in the best professional style, but by asking marshals and having a good spy network we always knew how far ahead or behind we were on time. It was a straight battle between the two of us; we led him out of Wales, and after his car assaulted a park bench on the Sutton Park stage there was really no danger, and throughout the second half, from York up into Scotland and back again, I was driving to orders.

Barring accidents we wouldn't lose, but that accident damned nearly tripped me up after all. It was all over; we had stopped being heroes, had clocked in to the last time control at Newby Bridge, and were pottering back towards Skipton and the finish. Then it happened.

We were cruising down the main road near Settle, trying to keep down to the 40 mph maximum average. We had no service cars tucked in behind, not even a supervision or press car. Suddenly there was a screech, a grinding noise, a lot of squealing and the car felt very odd. After all that time it had broken! We pulled straight into a lay-by to have a look-see. Fortunately it was still daylight, and mercifully we were not pushed for time, because that poor car had disgraced itself by destroying a front wheel bearing. Were we carrying a spare? Of course not. Would the service cars have any on board? Yes, but we didn't know when they would appear.

While Tony sat down dejectedly to work out averages from where we had stopped to the finish at York, I started to strip out the hub, knowing that the mechanics could complete the job as soon as they arrived.

But it wasn't a mechanic who saved us. Round the corner, looking more like a Fairy Godmother than ever he has before or since, came Andrew Cowan in his *Scotsman*-sponsored RS1600, which had already retired. Almost before he knew what was happening I had commandeered his Escort, and when the mechanics finally arrived they completed the swop in no time at all.

That was the end of the drama for us, but what a news story for the daily press correspondents. They were all stuck in York, and not at all sure my car would make it in time. It looked like being a sensational finish.

When finally we did arrive, the finishing ramp at York was complete bedlam. There were flash-bulbs popping off, TV interviewers rushing around, Goo struggling to get up to the top to greet me and one of the biggest bottles of champagne I'd ever seen waiting for the celebration.

Everybody at Ford was delighted, but no-one could have been more thrilled than I was. I had broken my run of bad luck, and I had proved to myself that a Briton *could* beat the Scandinavians on his own territory. It was incredibly important that I should have done well, almost a command performance in a way, and it was the final proof. For years there had been that wretched comparison with the Finns and Swedes which we couldn't overcome — it was as difficult as proving that a European driver could win the Safari. We proved it, and proved it without qualification. Apart from Timo and Hannu, none of the important Finns or Swedes retired, and those who finished had healthy cars; behind me, there were nine of them to complete the top ten.

It was the biggest boost I could have had, because it meant that no longer would I have to try to prove anything to myself, to my sponsors, or even to the rallying public. But I hadn't had to work as hard for a long time; the mental and physical control necessary had been immense.

By winning, we broke all sorts of records. I was the first Briton to win the rally since 1959 (Gerry Burgess); it was the first Ford win since 1966 (Bengt Soderstrom); it was the first win by a British car since 1966 (Bengt Soderstrom); and it broke a sequence of front-wheel-drive winning cars which stretched to 1968 (Saab, Lancia, Lancia, Saab).

We spent most of that winter sitting back and planning for 1973. As the record books show, 'LVX' went on to win a further nine events in ten starts (on the Manx the poor old thing retired with a deranged engine crankshaft pulley). Part of this splendid record was all a matter of confidence. After that RAC win (and after leading the Safari at Easter by more than half-an-hour) I felt that I could achieve anything, and I jolly nearly did.

Unlike 1972, when I changed cars and co-drivers quite a bit, 1973 was all consistency. In a dozen events I had Jim alongside me the whole time, apart from the RAC Rally itself, where he was once again the most important cog in the organising machine.

We seemed to be winning events just about every month, and people were relieved when Stuart sent me out to Africa to tackle the Safari at Easter-time. The press were at their wits ends, trying to find something new to say about us, and by using our middle names they even came up with the 'Albert and Arnold Show'!

189

We ended that season by selling off 'LVX' to Adrian Boyd (who shunted it the first time out!) and took a completely new Esso car — OOO 96M — on the RAC Rally. By my old standards I would have been delighted to finish second overall on the RAC Rally — which is what happened — but after the previous year only another win would have made me satisfied. But whereas in 1972 everything had gone right, in 1973 quite a lot went wrong. The car was good, new and tight, and the final development of the 2-litre engine, large Weber carbs and all, had made it the quickest Escort ever, at least according to Boreham.

I had taken a couple of weeks away from business worries early in November, and flew out to Africa with Goo to get a rest and some sun, then I came back just before the start feeling lousy with some awful African tummy-bug. Once again, it was good copy for newsmen, but definitely bad news for me.

I was shivering, aching and occasionally seeing double by the time the rally started. I wasn't at all certain that I could get round to the finish, and I didn't even know if I was infectious or not! It wasn't a rally any of us were likely to forget, anyway, because the oil crisis had just struck, and a lot of stupidly biassed radio and TV reporters were asking why the RAC Rally should be allowed to take place when the country was likely to be so short of oil? If only they'd bothered to ask if Government approval had been given (it had), or they'd bothered to work out what a tiny proportion of our total fuel consumption the rally represented . . . but that's one reason why often I cannot respect what the national or media pressmen are saying.

John Teall, who is a sort of unofficial rally doctor (he's a completely qualified medic, but the RAC Rally don't list a doctor among their officials) kept having a look at me, and it was really quite amazing that before the half-way halt I had started to feel a bit better. There was no improving on my very poor and shaky start, though, and I had to struggle very hard to get up into the top three places before the last morning. Nobody was going to catch Timo's Milk Marketing Board team Escort, though Markku Alen was making frantic efforts to catch up again after collecting a maximum on Sutton Park in the first afternoon.

The irony of it all was that although I gradually came out of my African 'flu, or whatever it was, I must have been infectious after all, and poor Tony caught all my symptoms and discomforts. OOO 96M wasn't a very happy car that week. When we got back to the finish Tony was probably in a worse state than I had been at the start. He had to be bad — when an extrovert like Tony starts dodging press interviews there must be something seriously amiss.

After that the fuel crisis, petrol shortages, Government bans, and a very leisurely RAC Motor Sport Division attitude to our rallying meant that all the professionals were out of work for the rest of the winter. What looked like being a very full season when we planned it back in October had turned into a real hotch-potch by the spring.

I had now won the RAC's National Rally Championship for the second time in succession and was looking forward to trying for a hat-trick, but there were going to be two big handicaps in 1974, even with a full programme, and the rallying ban just made these worse.

First of all, Stuart wanted to encourage the use of the RS2000 in British rallying. For months we had been talking about building up a 2000 for me to use in British rallies, but it didn't happen until the winter of 1973/74. Boreham finally managed to throw together a car which was really an RS1600 with a tuned single-cam RS2000 engine that was struggling to push out more than 160 bhp.

At first I was faced with the possibility of using this car fairly regularly, but just one run in the Mintex Dales was sufficient to convince me that there was just no way I could win with it. It was all very well saying that I ought to be competitive with the clubmen in their 230 bhp BDA-engined cars, but it didn't happen. When I pointed that poor little car down the long straights of the Yorkshire stages, and waited for the speed to build up in top, and waited, and waited, I knew we had to be losing.

The irony was that we didn't lose the Dales — we actually won by just a couple of seconds — but if one particular fast stage hadn't been cancelled we would not have made it. But that was the limit. I wasn't interested in losing rallies just to publicise the RS2000. I never sat in the car again, and I can't say I'm sorry. It really is very interesting that everbody tries to afford an RS1600 or RS1800 if they can — winning is more important than saving money!

The other factor was that I had now decided to keep away from Ireland. I have very pleasant memories of Ireland – as anyone who had won the Circuit three times would have — but the political situation which existed there frightened me. I had friends and Ford contacts in Ireland, all of whom advised me to stay away. I don't think it was

191

being over-boastful, but if ever there was the likelihood of a rallying name being attacked on an event like the Circuit, the Galway or the Donegal, they figured it might be me.

I know all about the theory that sport makes ambassadors of us all, but the sort of people who were terrorising Northern Ireland probably didn't agree. I was scared, really scared of the consequences, and so I resolved to stay away.

All this meant that my rallying season didn't begin until May with the Welsh International, and blow me if 'OOO' didn't let me down with a blown cylinder-head gasket soon after the start. After that I was always struggling in my search for championship points. Billy Coleman had a flying start with successes in his own Irish events, which we never made up. There were wins later, of course — in the Jim Clark and the Lindisfarne — but then a third place behind two very fast Porsches in the Manx and a disappointing seventh in the RAC Rally (my personal standards in that event are now very high) put the lid on it. What with Norman shunting the car after scrutineering for the Dukeries and the regulations snarl-up in the Burmah . . . it was quite a season.

I didn't have any better luck when Ford sent me off to South Africa to tackle the Total Rally with Tony Mason. Our car was one that had been re-imported from Australia, re-prepared in a hurry, and sent out to South Africa before us. There was no question of practising, and when we got in the car everything went wrong. Tony had trouble with the navigation (he hadn't done an African event before) then the car started to give trouble. The mileage recorder wasn't working, which meant that Tony had enormous problems, we lost a dust-sealing plug from the clutch housing, then the clutch itself filled up with mud and refused to disengage, and before long reverse gear had disappeared. It was a pantomime, a whole chapter of bizarre incidents. Every time I overshot a junction (which happened quite often, because of the useless mileage recorder) Tony had to jump out of the car and try to heave it backwards, then on one occasion he slipped, fell down, and the front wheel ran over his foot.

There was nothing for it; in spite of the 10,000-mile flight and all the effort we were forced to retire. Even finding a hotel in the wilds of Africa was a real pantomime at that time of night (it was 4 am) so when eventually we collapsed in our room and I asked Tony, ''What do you think of the show so far?'' he could only reply, ''Rubbish!''

The bright spot of a very confused 1974 season was the Tour of Britain. This was only the second Tour, and it was to prove a much more successful one for me and the factory than the first had been. The event was limited to Group One saloons, to coincide with the RAC Saloon Car Championship, so in 1973 we had decided to go along with a set of 3-litre Capris, but my run had been spoiled at Oulton Park when the car had an ignition failure and finished the race at the side of the track.

Before the 1974 event, I sat down with Peter Ashcroft, who by this time had taken over the day-to-day management of Boreham from Stuart, to discuss the possibilities. The question wasn't whether or not we should enter, but what cars we should use. The Capris hadn't been fast enough on the circuits in 1973, but what other choice did we have, I asked? Peter replied that because it was a Group One event, the only suitable cars were the 3-litre Capri (with about 170 bhp, he thought) or the Escort RS2000 (with about 135 bhp in its latest twin-carb form).

Once I knew this I didn't hesitate. In its original guise, with only one Weber carburettor, the RS2000 wasn't fast enough, but with the latest German set-up there was more chance. There wasn't going to be a lot of difference in straight-line performance between the two cars, and because of the Escort's handling, small size and light weight, it just had to be more suitable.

Ralph Broad's 2-litre Triumph Dolomite Sprints were claiming over 160 bhp, which ought to have made them quicker than the RS2000s, but they were a bit heavier and would still have to lick me on the special stages where agility and cunning mattered most; all the British Leyland cars except one were driven by circuit specialists. Brian Culcheth had the other, but I wasn't too worried about that.

Stuart Turner pulled one of his notable deals out of the hat, and when he heard that James Hunt would be driving a Vauxhall (which meant no car for Gerry Marshall) he invited Marshall to drive for Ford!

Now Gerry is a well-known circuit racer, with a lot of Vauxhall Firenza successes and quite a reputation behind him. He also enjoys a much bigger physical frame than me, which meant that our car would start with a weight advantage anyway. There was no attempt to impose any sort of team driving orders, and it probably wouldn't have worked anyway, because once in those Escorts we both 'grew horns'.

193

We had identical new cars, identically set up, identically tuned and even painted the same, with consecutive registration numbers. It was all going to be a bit close, though I had had quite a lot of track racing experience whereas Gerry had never done a rally at all.

The thought of special stages, driving flat-out over roads unknown to him, was making him very twitchy, and Stuart asked me to take a day at Bagshot to show him the ropes. It was my usual circus act, in a practice car, and I think Gerry was soon reassured about the way to control an Escort, but he joined that illustrious band of drivers who have been to Bagshot on test and have finished up by rolling the car! At least it shows how hard he was trying, but I'm glad I wasn't in the car at the time.

I was expecting to do well on the Tour. The racing would be fun, and I thought we might just manage to surprise the Dolomites, while on the list of special stages there were several that people were not supposed to have seen before. Unknown stuff aways appeals to me, but unfortunately nearly all the stages were sniffed out somehow, and though there were heavy penalties on people caught practising I know that a lot of pace notes were prepared.

Some of the press went into raptures over the way Gerry took to an Escort, but my view was that if he could drive a Vauxhall he ought to be able to drive an Escort in his sleep. The Escort has no vices, and I sometimes call it an 'idiot's car'; perhaps that's why I have won so often in it.

It was incredibly close right through the weekend, and after we had driven nearly all the races bumper to bumper I'm told Peter Ashcroft had grown a few grey hairs. But though it might have looked hairy from the grandstands, it was all very gentlemanly; there was never any bumping and boring, and not a mark on either car at the finish. In the dark Gerry and I were fastest of all bar none (and that included the big BMWs) but we were rarely more than a car's length apart.

Chrysler got into a real state about the regulations when it looked as if they might talk their way to the top with the Avengers, but in the end it was all between the RS2000s — my own car beating Gerry's by just 18 seconds to win. Oh yes, the racing drivers were second, third, fourth and fifth.

Working up the Esso programme had kept us all quite busy, but because I had been competing at home there had been more time left to enjoy myself with other pastimes. There was flying, of course, but that has been mainly valuable for business (there's really no other way when you are faced with a Ford forum in Middlesborough one night, in Cardiff the next, and a rally in Scotland the day afterwards), but purely for fun, and very extrovert fun at that, I had taken to powerboat racing.

Now if you think top-class rallying is expensive, you should take up powerboats. The wag who likened it to standing under a cold shower, fully dressed, and tearing up £5 notes had something. I became interested in 'messing about in boats' some years ago, and a passion for the high-speed stuff was really kindled when I was asked to crew a FordSport Fairey Huntsman in the *Daily Telegraph* Round-Britain Powerboat Race in 1969. Timo took the headlines when he drove Pascoe Watson's out-and-out racing boat to win, but Peter Twiss (the air-speed-record pilot) and I pushed around what was really a super-tuned touring boat to take fourth overall. Quite a bit later I bought a Formula Three powerboat of my own, and these days whenever spare weekends and a race coincide I'm usually out on the water with it.

There are classes for powerboats, just as there are in racing. A Formula Three craft can have three engines, with a total capacity of 4.1 litres (that's 250 cubic inches — a convenient American limit). My own has three engines, and is near the minimum hull length of 16 feet. The two big engines are 1,600 cc each (big American outboards) and connected to a foot throttle. The little fellow in the middle, only 850 cc, is just wound round to full throttle and ignored!

Racing a powerful boat like this is really not all that different from driving a rally car. There's a lot of throttle-control skill required — every time you jump out of the water the engines have to be killed — but all-in-all it's a question of balance with hands, feet, seat of the pants and vision.

Developing the handling is a lot simpler than doing the same for a rally car — after all you don't have to worry about going uphill or downhill — and the traction problem is a lot more consistent, but we have to make sure the trim is just right, the weight distribution is as it should be, and that the planing angle is good.

Breaking down is sometimes just an embarrassment, but it can also be expensive. I was thundering round the Isle of Wight in the Bollinger Trophy race in 1973, well screwed-up and doing something like 60 knots, when suddenly I started to get wet feet.

At first I thought it was a leak from the decking; it isn't easy to peer into the footwells, and the pedals are all hidden under the dashboard, but eventually I managed to look under and found a foot of water in the bottom of the boat. I wondered why we had started to slow up!

There was no time to think. I just swung the wheel hard to port, headed for the Isle of Wight, and ran the thing aground just as it sank. If I hadn't made the beach the whole thing, powerboat and me, would have gone straight down. It was a fatigue failure of the hull.

You don't carry insurance against that sort of risk, and without the handy beach it would have been a dead loss and the end of my powerboating.

On the credit side, the craft don't go out of date very quickly. In spite of the money spent, development in powerboat racing isn't all that intense, and compared with rallying the whole thing is rather lighthearted. When the Escort RS1600 got going it made the Twin-Cam out-of-date overnight, but with powerboats there is no such tendency; my own machine was still competitive after three years, just by keeping the engines in fine fettle.

Interspersed with my own Ford rallying programme, my garage was approached to run an Alpine-Renault for a year or so. When the first rumours got around, all the talk was of me leaving Ford to use my own Alpines, but the truth was a lot simpler than that.

Renault Ltd, in London, had always been vaguely interested in competitions, and in 1972 I was approached as a Renault dealer by Alan Dakers, their Director of Public Relations, to see if I was interested in Alpines. I'd been beaten by them more than once when conditions had suited them, and since the works cars were now capable of winning rough events like the Moroccan Rally it all looked very interesting.

But there was no way that I could drive the car (an ex-works Berlinette) because of my Ford loyalties, so for the first year at least we thought we would learn all about Alpines, let Brian Gillibrand prepare the car at my Hinckley place, and take it from there. We got Pat Moss-Carlsson to drive the car in the few events for which it was suitable, but quite frankly the whole operation was a bit of a disaster.

I expected Renault to provide a good, strong car for this sort of operation, but it turned out to be a tired old thing, and it had its problems. It was potentially excellent for rallies like the Circuit or the

Manx, but as supplied it wasn't strong enough for the forestry events. We didn't get much interest or encouragement from Renault, and it was extremely difficult to get spares from Alpine. All in all the programme went off at half-cock, and we were quite glad to drop out when Renault got themselves interested in their Renault 5 Challenge instead. The car went back to Acton, so if you see an ex-works Alpine-Renault in an exhibition or a dealer's showroom you can be almost certain it was ours.

After so many things going wrong in 1974, with events cancelled, crazy things happening, and everybody feeling the economic pinch, I was looking forward to a more settled time in 1975. I knew there would be a new Escort RS for me to use, and I knew that the Ford team, though slimmed down, was going to be as active as ever — everything had been planned. But I was too complacent, and I should have known better; for 1975, things were to turn out completely differently!

Chapter 10

Adventures with Cossack

MY DICTIONARY SAYS that the word 'cossack' derives from the Turkish 'quzzaq', meaning an adventurer, and since 1974, when I first met my sponsors and started rallying in their colours, I have often felt like one. Before then I was used to rallying in fairly quiet colours, but my bright red Mark 2 Escort is something else!

Cossack's link with Ford, and with me, is a classic case of intelligent advertising. I don't think there is anybody in the British rallying business now who doesn't know about our association, and I'm quite sure that everyone knows the product. It has all worked out very well; Cossack have helped me to carry on rallying with the very best of new Fords, and they have their product name in front of a whole new public. Isn't that what sporting sponsorship is all about?

Rivals and friends thought it was all a great joke at first (''Old man Clark's going poofy at last, then'' was one of many remarks), but Stuart Turner knew what he was doing, and so did the company.

Stuart rang me up one morning, mentioned the name and the product, and asked me if I was interested in doing a television commercial? It all sounded very strange at first, but once I had met the Reckitt and Colman people (who make the hair spray) and listened to their thoughts on motor sport and rallying, I was convinced.

There was a fee involved, sure, but I wasn't interested in just lending my name (and Ford's) as an advertising peg until I knew they were interested in me and my sport as well. What they had to tell me was very interesting.

Motor sport in general, and rallying in particular, they said, was now recognised as a top spectator sport, for real men doing brave things. They had launched Cossack, which was the original men's hair spray, in 1962, and although it was still a leading brand they felt it needed a face-lift. They had to convince men that it was OK to use hair spray (especially after hair creams had died the death so completely), and they thought a link with rallying would be a good thing. They also remembered that they had used me in some publicity shots for Cossack some years before, when I first used the product.

Then they flattered me by saying that they would only consider the top British driver in the best car, and that was me. Flattery, as they say, get's you anywhere — well it did with me, and the deal was done. Incidentally, I am not the only member of the family to use the stuff. The fact that it also works well for a girl, and that the kids have been known to spray Maxwell, my Old English Sheepdog, helps to increase consumption in my house . . .

Back in 1974 this was a very simple deal. Cossack would borrow me, and the Esso car, for filming at Bagshot, add in a few mug shots of Albert, and make a commercial. There would be a bit of 'voice over', as the professionals call it, and the job would be done. Easy, I thought. No problem — half-a-day should do it. I should have known better.

First of all there was the action photography. Peter Ashcroft sent Norman Masters down to Bagshot with 'OOO', and the filming people (Young and Rubicam) started work. First of all they wanted a lot of 'odd angle' shots of the car at speed, so I thrashed round and round the familiar track while cameramen kept popping out of the bushes and swinging from the trees to get new shots. I'm sure that if Bagshot's Joe had let them they would have dug a deep hole in the track and had me drive right over the cameras as well! If the sun went in, shooting stopped. If it rained, that was that for the day. If the car wasn't *quite* sideways enough then would I please do it again and flick the tail out a bit more? Could I find a big bump and wave a front wheel even higher next time? How high could I jump the car without damaging it? How high could I jump the car even if I *had* to damage it? Could we do a run with all the lights on? Just the headlights on? Just the fog lamps on? Now a shot or two from behind on that brow, and could you dab the brakes so that the stop lights flash? It seemed to go on for days, and that was just for the standard shots. By the time they finished there must have been enough film 'in the can' for a full-length motor club instructional film. But that was not all.

Next came the 'camera-on-car' sessions, and if I say that the camera was mounted everywhere, I mean *everywhere*. They had cameras inside the cockpit with floodlights, shooting up at me from the footwells, over my shoulder and through the screen, across the car from the other door window — everywhere. They even built a structure to mount the camera on the nose, and had a cameraman there with it; that must have been a very exciting ride! Looking where you are going at those speeds is busy enough, but having to look backwards, work the camera *and* hope that the car isn't going to have an accident must be quite something. There was a very brave man. I must say I was tempted to dive in close under a few trees to tweek him up a bit, but that would have been a bit sadistic.

All in all, we were at Bagshot for a week, and the original commercial ran for just 30 seconds; advertising agencies are that thorough. I was pretty bored with it all by the end of the week, but one of the most interesting parts was driving 'OOO' round Bagshot behind another car which had a cameraman in the boot. We didn't have an accident, but it would have been a complex one, recorded on film, if we had!

That was in the spring of 1974, before the rallying season had started, after which I became much too busy to worry about sponsors for a while. Even though I had a rather unsettled season, and there was the disagreement over the Tour of Britain entry, I was quite sure that Esso would renew their contract on good terms.

I met Jeff Edwards for talks in October, and again in November, with Ford sitting in on the discussions to sort out a 1975 programme. We had a new car coming up, Esso knew that Boreham would only be looking after Timo and myself, and that we would both be kept very busy. We had an agreement drawn up, all the fees agreed, and we even remembered to sort out such problems as the Tour of Britain. It all looked very neat and tidy, and I left Esso to prepare things for me to sign.

But it never happened. There didn't seem to be any hurry, but as Christmas arrived I thought that things had gone very quiet. It was obviously not directly connected, but I do remember that one day I heard news of the Burmah collapse on the car radio, and the very next day I had an apologetic phone call from Jeff Edwards. He was sorry, but top management had told him to close down all his support deals.

Esso were pulling in their horns, sponsorship was at the bottom of their priority list, and I had lost my backing.

You can guess how I felt. We had three years of rather remarkable success, having served up the string of wins that every sponsor needs — and now they had backed out.

It came at exactly the wrong time. Any good deal has to be fixed up at least three months before the start of a rallying programme, and here we were in January without a backer to our name. If ever there was a time to sit down calmly and look to the future this was it.

I had a rallying programme which started with the Mintex Dales in February, and there was no way I was going to cut it. Ford were very understanding about the situation, and guaranteed that my car and its service support would be ready whether I had a sponsor or not. We turned up at Selby Fork for the Mintex in OOO 96M, and there was only one major difference — the car had had a respray! It was pure, virginal white, with only a couple of Shell petrol decals to tell a story.

Ford announced the new Escort at the end of January, and started deliveries in March. They had a new RS — called an RS1800 — on show, but none actually to sell. The Advanced Vehicle Operations production line was closed down, because the Halewood factory needed the work, and it didn't look as if production-line cars would be ready before June.

Even so, we thought the new car could be homologated on the grounds of evolution — in other words it was mechanically like the RS1600, but simply wearing a new dress — and if that was so Norman could start building a new car for me right away. In the meantime, we would try out a few tweaks in the old-shape car.

Peter Ashcroft felt that we ought to be pushing the power output up again as 2-litre BDAs had been producing a dead-reliable 235 bhp in rally cars for a couple of seasons. Consequently, although my Mintex Dales car looked the same as before, it had a hotter engine than usual. There was really no problem in finding more power — we could get another 30 bhp just by changing the camshafts — but this moved the power and the torque up the range, and it didn't work. Even Brian Hart, who builds the engines, agrees that he loses out on reliability when doing this, and I found it made the car more difficut to drive, and it didn't *feel* quicker, anyway.

We could have lived with this difference in feel, but every time we pushed up the power we started blowing cylinder-head gaskets. It was really quite consistent — more power, then *phumff,* no gasket! This happened after just one stage on the Mintex, so we limped back to the start and started the party a day early.

The same thing happened on the Circuit of Ireland, but with a different car. For the Circuit, all on tarmac roads, Boreham built up a really smart tarmac-racer, which had once been used in a Ford Belgium saloon car racing programme. Apart from being quite low, and having a very clever coil-spring rear suspension, the engine was a full-race, fuel-injected, big-valve-head, all-happening device which pushed out something like 280 bhp. It gave all the signs of being a good car, even though the suspension was a bit hard for Ireland's rough tarmac, but after leading the event at the end of the first ten stages a head gasket let go again! There was no cooling fan, and by the time we had struggled through crowds of spectators to our next service point the engine had fried itself.

So that was the end of our Circuit, but at least we thought we had pinned down the problem. Highly-tuned BDAs generate colossal compression pressures, of course, but that wasn't the cause of the trouble. There are also high temperatures, and we discovered that the special 2-litre liners, which were steel, were expanding more than the light-alloy cylinder block. This pushed them up that important little bit, and broke the gasket seal between the block and the head. I'm told that this is exactly the headache Coventry Climax found with their 1½-litre racing V-8 in 1961, but we've cured it in a different way. Now, instead of using steel liners, we apply a chrome coating direct to the aluminium. I suppose this means that we could try out the higher tunes of BDA again, but I still find them harder to drive, and the car just isn't as flexible as I like.

Meanwhile, Tony Mason and I had been looking around for a new sponsor. It wasn't that we wanted jam on our bread and butter — the sort of rallying we do nowadays is so expensive that *any* support from a sponsor is much appreciated. I know that we could have carried on with some sort of programme and a virgin white car, but other activities would have had to be chopped out. People without the success record of the Escort and me would probably have been struggling at this point, but I can honestly say that having lost one sponsor, and decided who we would like to co-operate with instead, we made one phone call and were fixed up.

Both Tony Mason and I knew that Cossack had been very keen to sponsor my RAC Rally car the previous year, and I had already been told that the TV commercial was well-received, so it was an obvious link. I won't say that Reckitt and Colman jumped at the deal — they are much too commercially shrewd in their dealings — but it seemed to make a lot of sense, and we soon fixed up the details.

Like my previous links, Cossack were now to support my rallying in Great Britain, with the accent on the RAC Rally Championship and all the home Internationals; it was to be both personal and with Ford, so there could be no mix-ups.

All this was being negotiated as my new car became ready, but we really didn't think it was wise to rush the announcement for the Granite City. So that's the answer to people who thought that nobody wanted me any more — we were waiting to launch the tie-up on the Welsh!

One of the busiest outside contractors used by Boreham is the little paint shop a couple of miles away which gets the job of doing all the new sponsors' paint jobs. Whether it's blue-and-white for the Milk Marketing Board, orange stripes for the *Evening Standard,* a perfectly ghastly brown for the Colibri Lighters cars, or a vivid bright red for my own car, it's always the same shop which does the job. Some cars get new paint so often that they must end up weighing a lot more.

Ford Styling, at Dunton, had their own ideas about RS1800s, which explains the layout of the new screw-on wheel-arch extensions. The frontal dam and the bootlid spoiler are both functional, especially for race cars, and the result is a car quite distinct from any of the other Escorts.

But when we came to paint the new rally car we had problems. Peter Ashcroft tried to get some artwork, transfers and schemes from Cossack, but time was so short (isn't it always short when you're preparing a rally car?) that in the end Tony Mason had to rush out, buy a big spray can of Cossack, throw it into the car, and ask the paint shop to 'do a car like the can'. It was a fine job, in double-quick time, and the fiery steed painted on the bonnet was done by a craftsman's steady hand.

In the meantime, we had been settling the specification of the new car. There wasn't a lot of basic development to be done, as there had been with the first Twin-Cams, because we had the same basic floor pan, front suspension, engine and transmission as before, so we only had to worry about the new body.

With my car, HHJ 700N (and I hope that this will be as famous a number one day as any of my earlier cars), Boreham tried an experiment. Instead of starting from a shell specially modified and built up in Maurice Gomm's workshops, they did this one themselves. The RS1800 uses a heavy-duty bodyshell anway, and is supposed to be a lot stronger than the original car. Boreham tried to keep the specification as simple as possible and left out one or two of the original 'rally' stiffening pieces.

My car was first on the road, followed by two more for Billy Coleman and Russell Brookes. All three did the same series of events during 1975, and each soon showed some tell-tale crease marks around the screen pillar/door shut lines. We don't have a Mark 2 Lotus-Cortina problem, but there's no doubt that the bodies as built show a slight tendency to bend a bit around the scuttle; this means that although you can just about get away without any expensive additions at first, the shells will not last quite as long as they once did. It also proves that we must have got the engineering of the last Mark 1 Escorts down to a fine art.

Perhaps one long-term answer is to look closely again at the layout and mounting of our full roll-cages. Properly and carefully mounted, there's no doubt that they can add quite a lot to the stiffness of the structure, and perhaps we can gain something there in the future.

There is a feeling that over the years the Escort became far too special, too clever anyway for the British type of rallying programme which I do now. With the new cars the modifications are fewer, for example the facia layout is much nearer to standard, we use basically standard wiring looms, and we don't even modify the wings in the same way as before. The new wheel-arch extensions are bolted on, but not in the way the styling department intended.

When I stepped into the new car in Aberdeen, before the start of the Granite City, I almost had to be introduced to it, for apart from being fitted into the seat, safety belts and controls when it was still on stands at Boreham, I knew very little about it. The shell was originally left-hand drive, and had been meant for Timo, but it had been converted for me when my own body failed to be delivered in time.

I had already driven another Escort Mark 2, so I knew that it would go, stop and handle much as before. The only real difference, and it made quite an impression on me, was the visibility. It was a case of the same ride with a different view.

Although ride and response are much the same, the rear-suspension changes have made the car feel nicer. It seems more refined — if you could ever call a rorty rally car that — and the bigger windows make it more pleasant to drive. At night there is little change except that the lights are arranged slightly differently, and of course the much bigger screen helps. I happen to like the new styling and the paint job very much, and I have some rather smart new overalls and jacket to match.

The new Escort started its career for me in the same way as the first one did, and I hope it's an omen. Reliability has been good, and we haven't turned up any awful snags. That's the advantage of using a proven mechanical package.

The Granite City was too short to prove a lot, except that I am lazy until I see that other people are beating me! I must have been half-asleep early on; at the end of the morning I was somewhere down in ninth place, so I had to shake a leg after lunch and pull it back.

The Welsh was to be different. There would be enough hard work to sort out the good cars from the bad, there would be enough endurance to wear out the drivers as well, and there would be more than the usual number of cars to fight. We all thought the car would be good enough to win, but I wanted to get the measure of the Lancia Stratos, which the media were playing up so hard. It was quite reasonable that they should do so, if only because talking about the same successful Fords must get boring after a time, but on its record the Stratos didn't seem to have much chance.

There were three of the new Escorts in the list, all built by Boreham, though mine was the only true works car, and they were all as quick as each other. Russell Brookes, who has made the change from Mexicos and RS2000s very quickly, beat me on several of the early stages, but later on he had a roll and mechanical trouble. Billy Coleman appeared to be having more trouble inside the car than under it, and I wasn't surprised that he didn't always look very cheerful. Sometimes he was going very well, and sometimes he was surprisingly slow. The car was just as good as mine, so it must have been something else.

The Lancia soon broke. I felt very sorry for The Chequered Flag, who ran the car. Their mechanics had had to learn all about rallying, all about new drivers *and* all about a complicated little car. Even though a works car did so well on the 1974 RAC Rally, this particular

205

one didn't seem to like the rough roads and it soon broke, but when it was going it was very quick — I must say I would like all that power and traction under my Escort!

We won the Welsh rather comfortably, even though the published times made it look close. Jim knew exactly what was coming, and where we could pull out a lead. It helped that none of the top crews kept secrets from each other, so we could all compare times, and Jim could almost programme me to go faster if he thought I needed to, all of which must sound very carefully controlled. The only shock was when I had a rear brake seize on in the middle of a stage, and I had to drag a leg for a few miles before I found the next Granada service car. The rally was good, but there was a huge delay after the finish, and I was forced to leave for Bagshot to play at TV personalities again, this time as an instructor.

I think we were all looking forward to the Scottish. It was the first chance we had had to try the new car on some really fast stages — believe me, some of those stages in Galloway and Moray are flat-out for *miles* — and Ford had also entered Timo in his new Escort 2. This meant that all four of the Boreham-built Escort 2 RS1800s would be in the same rally for the first time.

The first thing that surprised us — and the press — was how quickly we were getting through tyres. Dunlop's special M & S tyre is very effective on rocky stages, but after about 12 miles of dry and flinty going we were having to change the rears. It's not that the Escort is particularly hard on tyres (though with 240 bhp on tap they have a difficult time) and we certainly don't change them just to give our mechanics something to do, but at the sort of speeds we do we can really tell the difference between new and worn rubber.

It's all a question of square corners. The tread as a whole doesn't disappear, but hard cornering, rocks and flints soon chip away at the blocks, and in no time at all it feels as if we are driving along on a series of pimples. An average driver would look at a discarded tyre and wonder what all the fuss was about, but if he came for a drive with me through a stage he would soon find out.

We also had these phenomenal speeds. Now I'm as happy to go quickly as the next man, and even after years in the business there's still a lot of sheer gut-twisting excitement in it, but on the Scottish the pace was exceptional. We don't alter axle ratios on rally cars, nowadays, and by pulling 9,000 rpm in fifth gear on the ZF gearbox we could expect to see more than 115 mph. That's quick enough for most people even on surfaced roads, but in the forests it feels even quicker!

There were several stretches which were dubbed 'Stratos auto-bahns', where we came over a brow and saw the track disappearing into the distance, a couple of miles away, without a throttle-lifting curve in sight. At that sort of pace the trees buzz by at a fair old rate, and it doesn't need much imagination to think what might happen if we had a sudden failure.

Incidentally, that doesn't mean that the tracks are smooth and flat, either. Some are quite rough, which means that the car is bouncing up and down, jumping over brows, sliding in a full drift through long open curves, and having to be pointed through the unexplained wiggles that all forestry tracks seem to have. I'm told that the sight and sound of a rally car in full cry down one of these tree-lined sections is quite something; it's very interesting from my view, too!

It's on these sections that I wish the racing fanatics could be educated. The talk about Silverstone's Woodcote Corner (before they put the chicane in) being amongst the most demanding in the world — fine, but if it had a few rocks and a 'yump' right across the middle I'd be even more impressed.

No wonder that we seem to get through fuel pretty quickly on an event like this. We base our judgment on 10 mpg over stages and about 15-18 mpg on the road, though it's usually a bit better than that. In spite of these stages, we think we could even go *down* slightly on gearing (I rarely need more than 100 mph in a rally car) but that would make the car even more of a pain on the road, and bottom gear would be just about useless.

The Scottish, of course, was very satisfying for us. We pulled out a fairly comfortable lead which Jim then controlled, and once again the car was almost completely reliable. Norman changed front struts at half-distance, but that was purely as a precaution; they must still have been good, because Russell Brookes used them on his car after that! Timo had some trouble with brakes on his car, but blamed a poor engine for his slower times. As for the Stratos, it battered itself to pieces again; I was sorry to see this, but not surprised.

On paper, 1975 might not have looked too busy for me, but I soon found out that sponsorship and publicity was going to take up more of my time. Just jumping into a rally car and driving fast isn't enough any more. Personal appearances and 'show business' matters a lot, too.

I had a week at Bagshot with Dickie Davies and an ITV film crew. The idea was that Dickie should live in a car with me and learn how to be a rally driver. Dickie's performance was a revelation to me. I expected him to put on a competent professional show for his World of Sport programme, but I hadn't realised just how keen he is on motor sport. He hadn't ever been in a car with me before, and I expected he'd be a bit frightened at first, but although like most people it took him a few corners to settle in, after that we had a lot of fun. He was genuinely interested in making a go of the week, and that made me all the more relaxed to be with him.

The week's filming produced a 20-minute taster on World of Sport for the Scottish, after which they filmed the rally itself. It would have been quite a squelch if we hadn't won, but in the event everyone was pleased. It was interesting to note that the word Cossack was avoided during the week's training, but it had to get a lot of exposure during the rally itself; with that sort of paint job it couldn't miss!

But when it comes to film work, give me that sort of thing any time. Recently I have been updating the original TV commercial, and there may be more, but the studio work really was interminable. The film crew take such care, with so many different shots and so many repeats, that it's not surprising how polished the end product is.

It was all a bit different this time. In 1974 I didn't have to do much 'into camera' work with the preparation, but now I was being asked to play-act as well as drive. One whole day, when I might have been selling cars or building the new boat, was taken up in the studio for a couple of two-second shots. There was one short sequence, I promise you, which I repeated 68 times before the director gave in. I know it was that many, because I asked him afterwards.

In between shots, I suddenly thought about the differences between motor sport and advertising. In spite of what jealous rivals might think, the Ford involvement in motor sport is now very low-key, and we have to cut all sorts of corners to get a sensible programme. With no spare cars, and only a few mechanics, we almost feel like the poor relations in rallying. The fact that we have the best and most reliable car is ironic. Advertising and film-making, on the other hand, still seems to operate on a large scale. There I was, in the studio, with at least a dozen technicians, cameramen, make-up artists and directors

I'm making a splash on the 1972 RAC Rally with Tony Mason and 'LVX' although we're not on a stage because I'm not wearing my skid-lid. (Colin Taylor)

Ken Wiltshire busily wiring up 'the office'. This was one of Timo's cars – I like mine to be more simply equipped if possible. (Ford)

Rather a battered underside – the sump shield is OK but the chassis rails have suffered. The five-speed ZF gearbox is a very tight fit. (Ford)

We use the less-vulnerable single-piece propshaft on our Escorts. Note the big bridge-piece which we developed during the World Cup Rally, complete with a diff-case skid. (Ford)

Nearing the end of that fabulous RAC Rally in 1972, we round the well-known hairpin at Gubhill Farm, in the Forest of Ae, in South Scotland. (Colin Taylor)

After the hard work, the flashbulbs and the celebrations, with the help of a magnum of *Moet et Chandon* back at York.

Rally people can look elegant at times! The unlikely line-up of sartorial elegance includes Henry Liddon, Hannu Mikkola, John Davenport, Bill Barnett (for many years Ford's rally manager), Andrew Cowan, Timo Makinen, Yours Truly, and Tony Mason.

Making 'Our Man Clark' at Bagshot for Esso during 1972. The car in the foreground is the 'Old Gold' escort. (Mike Hughes)

The only time I rallied an RS2000 was on the 1974 Mintex Dales; we were at least 80 bhp underpowered and it was very hard work, though we just managed to win. I see that Castrol's Roger Willis is making his usual caustic comments to me with the aid of a public-address mike! (Ford)

Two ways to tackle a corner at Cadwell Park. Gerry Marshall follows me during our enjoyable thrash on the 1974 Avon Motor Tour of Britain. (Ford)

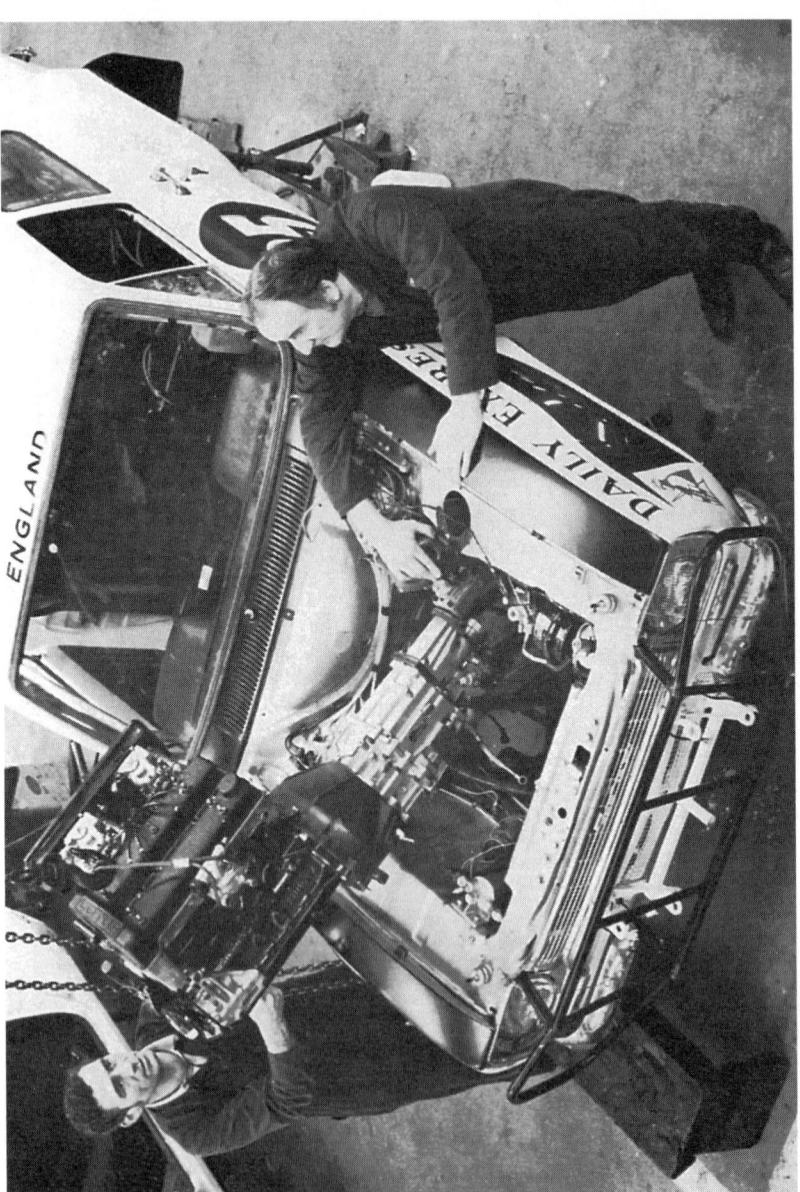

Peter Ashcroft watches as Norman Masters, my long-suffering but so talented and dedicated Ford mechanic, hoists one of Boreham's engines into one of our Escorts at Boreham. So much of what I have been able to achieve has been due to Norman's

Lower the rolling resistance and you go quicker, but not for long; the crunch was about to come. This was on Eppynt during the 1975 Welsh, our first Cossack outing. (Colin Taylor)

Working hard on the 1975 Scottish. In wide . . .

turn in . . .

correct with opposite lock . . .

tighten again with left lock . . .

clip the apex . . .

more left lock to tighten line . . .

opposite lock again to check tail . . .

. . and on in a cloud of dust.

The expression on my face tells everything, even if it is a waste of good champagne. It happened in the Isle of Man in 1975,

Matthew, standing half in the car, now has a younger brother, Oliver. Proud dad and enthusiastic sons turn up for a press test day with the Cossack Escort. (Coventry Evening Telegraph)

Whipping off my helmet and ducking inside the winner's garland after the 1975 Manx Rally gave me an un-Cossack-like hair style (sorry, Mr. Sponsor!), but wearing the greenery that day was a very comfortable feeling. (Ford)

. . . just think of it, Old Man Clark being looked after by make-up girls!

A sponsor's attention to detail even comes across in the car's paint job. On my newest Cossack car — the third such Escort — the decoration has been changed so that there's a broad black band running along the sides, which points to the brand name even better than before. It's all a question of what photographs well and what photographs splendidly.

But why three Cossack cars? My original car, which made its debut on the Granite City, completed the 1975 forestry events, then got itself involved in a lot of filming, testing, development, and trips to Norway and Finland to test the latest in Dunlop snow tyres. For the RAC Rally, which completes my 'story so far', I had a brand new car (LAR 800P), while for the Manx International I had a third machine. The Manx car was special because it was what we call a 'tarmac Escort'. The differences were basically in the suspension, and a few more horsepower in the engine department, and were all part of a rather frustrating 1975 tarmac programme.

When Peter Ashcroft and I sorted out our 1975 programme it centred on the RAC Rally Championship, but would also include trips to the Circuit of Antibes in France, the San Remo in Italy, and the Tour de Corse in Corsica. There would also be one long-distance trip to South Africa for the Total Rally, which Tony Mason and I had ploughed through in 1974.

Peter wanted to continue tarmac suspension development with the Escort and he sent me out to do the Circuit of Antibes with Jim in a new car (KHK 983N). We had quite a bit of practice, which I didn't enjoy in spite of the splendid weather, but we were soon forced to retire from the rally when the front suspension collapsed on one rather nasty fresh-air corner, high in the French Alps, and nearly sent Jim and I sky-diving without parachutes.

The breakage was bad enough, but apart from that I was quite convinced that the roadholding on lowered suspension and racing tyres was not good enough. We had to get into a serious testing programme, and fast.

Already there have been two phases. First of all, Tom Walkinshaw and I spent hours and hours at Cadwell Park and on the Boreham testing circuit, re-assessing the suspension settings, ride heights, dampers and tyres. Nothing fundamental was changed — in other words we still have MacPherson front struts and a cart-sprung rear — but in detail we made great improvements. As a result of this work Timo's Tour de France car was very rapid indeed on the circuits (he was leading until the engine blew), and I certainly felt a lot happier than ever before in the high-speed environment of the Isle of Man stages.

But we didn't let it rest there. The next phase was another programme to see how close the forest-spec cars could be brought to the new tarmac settings — and that was what Timo's last-minute entry in a Scottish club event was all about. The new Escorts for the RAC Rally had a compromise set-up, and it is now possible to make very quick changes from the latest forestry settings to the latest tarmac settings — and this includes fitting or discarding the front compression strut that is so much a part of the tarmac settings.

I seem to have gone into this in some detail, not to boast about how clever we all are, but to show that being a works driver is not just a matter of turning up at the start and driving off in a car someone else has built. At our level, a lot of thought, analysis and patient development goes in to making a good car even better.

In the middle of all this testing, I took the original Cossack car to Scotland for the Jim Clark Rally, hit a sheep very hard on one of the Otterburn stages, and proved to myself yet again that there are many very good reasons why I should never be first on the road! It was one of those instances where the first car through was almost bound to startle the sheep and their lambs — muggins thought he could get away with it, and didn't. If only the shunt hadn't occurred in Otterburn I could have carried on, but with a shattered radiator and more than 20 miles of stages before I could get to Norman Masters and his 'Grandad' service car I was lost.

After that it was a relief to go off to South Africa and meet a new co-driver (Stuart Pegg), in yet another RS1800 rally car, this time built locally by Ford South Africa, and to win the Total Rally after my disastrous showing in 1974. Not that it was easy. The locally-built car was fine — it was close to a Boreham build anyway — but all the locals knew their own stages, and I was struggling to get ahead until the last day.

That was a big win, but it couldn't possibly have been as satisfying as our performance on the Manx. I said earlier that you couldn't really expect an Escort to beat a competently-driven Porsche Carrera, but this time we did! No wonder I looked so delighted when I was pictured spraying the crowd with champagne at the prizegiving.

We prepared well, but we didn't do much practice — just a day and a half in the Island before the Burmah, and Jim preparing the original notes and updating our existing set. Our crashed Antibes car was repaired, given the Clark-Walkinshaw suspension, painted in Cossack colours, and — our secret weapon — fitted with some rather fine new Dunlop racing slicks.

The new car was a revelation and we won against all expectations. It wasn't much more powerful than in 1974 (a reliable 240 bhp instead of 235 bhp, without losing any mid-range torque), but the suspension was a joy, and the Dunlop tyres were just fantastic. I don't think I've ever been accused before of jumping out of a car at a service point with a broad grin on my face and enthusing about anything — Norman will confirm that — but on the Manx I did it several times.

There comes a time when you have to prove something to yourself and the public, and on the island in 1975 I think I did. I know I hadn't worked so hard in a rally car for a long time, but after the first few stages when I found I had the edge on the Porsches there was no holding back; the 'welly' went right down for the rest of the event, and I finally proved my point. But I still reckon that I could go even faster in a Porsche — if I did perhaps even Jim would get mildly animated.

If Antibes had shown just how badly the Escort still handled on tarmac, the Manx had cheered us up quite a lot, and Timo's performance in the Tour de France did the same, so we were all looking for success on the San Remo in October. But we didn't get it — San Remo was a disaster.

What happened was that our Dunlop tyre supplies never arrived — the truck having broken down in France — and we started the event knowing there were no spares of any kind. Timo and I didn't even have complete sets of rubber on the starting ramp — Timo rolled down the ramp on three wet racing tyres and one Kleber we had scrounged, while I started with four racing slicks, hand-cut to make them legal on the road, with a Kleber spare which we had bought. We had ten wheels and tyres between us, so once Timo and I had more than two punctures we would be out. As it transpired it was a rough start and Timo's car punctured almost at once, so that was that — we went back to the pub, changed and flew home to tackle the Lindisfarne instead! It was a bit of a shambles, something which ought never to have happened, and Dunlop were mortified. But at least it meant we had even better service than usual on the RAC Rally, with the most fascinating results.

The second half of my British season was really a chase for the 1975 RAC Rally Championship. Because of my poor start to the season, I had to win more or less everything to stand a chance of catching Billy Coleman's car, and when I collected the sheep on the Jim Clark things looked black. But after a win on the Burmah (no trouble with regulations and lateness this time), another on the Manx and one more on the Lindisfarne, it all hinged on the RAC Rally. I had to finish better than seventh to beat Billy, and with the sort of entry we faced that wasn't going to be easy.

For me, the RAC Rally was a disaster. Funny, isn't it — I can finish second overall in Europe's most important event and consider it a disaster, but as I've already indicated on the RAC I have standards — I won in 1972, I could have won in 1973, and I should have won again in 1975. There's no doubt about this — I could have won and I ought to have won, Timo being in my way or not!

The good news was the new tyres — yet another quick development with Dunlop — and the bad news was my new car. The team had a set of new Escorts which afterwards were to be rebuilt for the 1976 season. As usual, there wasn't enough time to do the job in a leisurely fashion, and I arrived at scrutineering in York without ever having sat in the car. I took it out to try the new suspension settings and the new tyres on the Friday morning, and the rally started a day later. Something to be ashamed of? I don't think so. We had no reason to suspect any problems, and I challenge any rally team (or Formula One team, for that matter) to have their cars ready a long time before an important event. The theory behind the new tyres, which proved themselves so dramatically on the event, was that our cars were now fast enough and precisely-enough developed to deserve a racing type of tyre. I had been impressed with the rallycross-racer type of rubber for some time, and in less than two months we got together with Dunlop and further redeveloped this rubber so that on hard forestry stages it was much superior — two or three seconds a mile — to the faithful M & S knobblies.

We made the rather astounding discovery that tread pattern was less important than a soft compound where traction on 'hard loose' surfaces was concerned. Basically we now use racing slicks with the heavy-section sidewalls (to eliminate punctures) and a thick tread hand-cut to make the tyre legal on the open road and to provide some water drainage. The compound is one of the softest we can find, and it really seems to mould itself around the slight undulations of forestry stages.

The pattern doesn't seem to make a lot of difference; the secret is to have a lot of rubber on the ground and a compound which is good and sticky. It feels very stable, as a racing tyre should, it makes the car even more precise to drive, and incidentally it gives a life at least four times that of a good old M & S in the same conditions! So the process has turned full circle. Originally rally cars used cross-ply tyres, then radials, and after that radials with an M & S type of tread. Now we are back to race patterns and cross-ply construction again.

I think I had all my season's bad luck collected together on the rally itself. By the time I had reached the Lake District on the third day I was thoroughly browned-off with all the failures, and I told one reporter ''Eight lives gone, now'', which meant that if I was a cat there wasn't much hope of finishing.

Sure, I finished second overall (that makes the four-year record first, second, seventh, and second again), and Timo only had a margin of one minute after 72 stages — but I should have won.

Time and again something on the car let go, and it really was a miracle that Tony Mason and I managed to struggle back to York after all. Norman had built the car and simply couldn't understand what was going on. Most of the failures were in the suspension, which tells me that perhaps we still have something to learn, but others were pure Acts of God.

How about this for a list of dramas — siezed rear handbrake calipers, broken (and I mean snapped) rear shock absorber and front strut on the same bump, another strut failure later in the day, a clutch fixing bolt breaking in half and being punched out through the bell-housing, gearbox selectors coming adrift and leaving me with only first and fifth for three stages, and finally another rear shock absorber, which also carried away the handbrake cable and other details. Each and every one occurred in a stage, and I reckon they must have cost me around seven minutes overall. Now remember that gap behind Timo and you'll understand why I was so very disappointed!

229

The only consolation was that I had won the RAC Rally Championship after all. Even though Billy finished well up, my second was good enough to clinch it on points, and that made it three times in four years.

Incidentally, even though my car really disgraced itself, it could be rebuilt, whereas Ari Vatanen's works Escort would never be the same again — it went off into the trees of Clipstone when flat-out in fifth (over 110 mph) and was only good for the scrap merchant.

In the last couple of years, rallying has moved into the realms of show business. The promotional build-up to top performers has intensified, and the flat-out motoring is only a part of a total sponsored commitment. I look at the way motor racing has developed, particularly in North America, and wonder if rallying eventually will match it. Those of us who compete have no doubts about the spectator interest, and I'm sure the new sponsors have caught on to the same viewpoint.

Even in Scotland, where most of the rallying was a long way from centres of population, the crowds were phenomenal. On that first day in 1975 there seemed to be people hanging from every tree to watch, and when I tell you that the organisers had taken the trouble to get a public-address system into the middle of one stage you can see how things have changed.

In 1960 I had a Renault Dauphine which handled like a boxful of wet fish and could hardly drag itself along. I used radial-ply tyres when I could afford them, and didn't expect to get a mention in the local paper unless I did something really spectacular. There were no spectators — often there were not even enough marshals — and the whole business was very secretive. Often we didn't carry numbers in case people should realise there was a rally in the district! We've come a long way since then. What changes will we see in the future? Will I stop entering an Escort, and have a 'Cossack Special' instead? How much of the sport will be motoring, and how much will be show business? I wonder!

Chapter 11

What next?

I HAVE A bit of a problem. The end of this book is being written at the close of the 1975 season, but whatever I write cannot be read until at least the spring of 1976. We have already had a very successful first season with our Mark 2 Escorts, and we know what improvements should now be made. But 'What next?' means what we have in mind now and by 1976 everything could have changed.

In a previous chapter I described in some detail my early relationship with Stuart Turner at Ford, so it's nice to know that he still wants me in his team, however slimmed down it might be. What Stuart did at the end of 1974, faced with budget cuts and knowing that he could only afford to keep two of his contracted drivers for 1975, three of whom were famous Finns called Makinen, Mikkola and Alen, needed guts.

I don't think there is any doubt that for 1976, and probably 1977 too, Ford's rally cars will be the very latest in 2-litre Escorts. I think you can forget any wistful rumours that have been flying around about revived GT70s; even if Ford in South Africa does decide to make a few, I don't think we would decide to use them over here. Talk about trying to make a racehorse out of a camel . . . it's a daunting prospect.

And of the future? We know that four-wheel drive doesn't work in a racing car, and I proved to myself that it doesn't work very well for rallycross. I'm absolutely convinced that it has no future in rallying, either, even if the regulations allowed it.

For the moment the future at Ford lies with conventional, front-engine-rear-drive motor cars, and in spite of everything that theoretically hampers it I'm also quite sure there are some improvements still to come. Quite a few more will have been developed before my book reaches the bookstalls.

At the moment I can't see an alternative Ford to the Escorts, certainly not in the current British/German range, but I'm very interested to get a close look at the new front-wheel-drive Fiesta, which will be pouring out of Ford's new Spanish factory as well as from the German and British plants, before the end of 1976. The 'Bobcat', as it has been code-named during its development, will be smaller and lighter than any other Ford, and it could prove to be an advance on the Escort as a rally car. If it is, and if we could squeeze a full-house 2-litre BDA engine into it, and if we could get the power down to the ground, and if we could make it handle, and if . . . but there are nearly as many 'ifs' with a front-wheel-drive car as there are with mid-engined Specials.

Had I been writing this book just five years earlier, I would possibly have been full of enthusiasm for a mid-engined car. Five years ago we had the new GT70 to occupy us, and we were quite sure it could become a Porsche and Alpine-Renault-beater, but it didn't happen. So why did the cars not succeed?

The entire GT70 project began in Monte Carlo after the 1970 rally. It was Ford's first Monte under Stuart Turner, who had tried to match the Porsche/Alpine challenge with a set of real 'ice-racer' Escort Twin-Cams. I have no complaints about those cars, about how they were serviced, or about the ice-notes information we were given. The plain fact was that neither Timo, Hannu nor myself could get anywhere near the mid-engined cars. The best we could manage was fifth (me) and seventh (Timo), after Hannu had dropped out with a jammed gearbox.

We weren't just losing seconds, either. Ake Andersson's Porsche took 90 seconds off me on the Burzet loop and Larrousse's car could take half-a-minute out of us on every passage of the Turini. I finished the rally a total of nine minutes (on 16 stages) behind the leader. My highest stage placing was second, once, when everything went right, but usually we were struggling to get into the top six.

Stuart and I were due to fly back from Nice on the same aeroplane, and after take-off we tried to analyse what had gone wrong. We soon decided that nothing had gone wrong, we simply needed more advanced cars to win. Using the theory 'If you can't beat 'em, join

232

'em' we said: "OK, let's work out what we need to produce a competitive rally car. Then, and only then, let's see how it could be made''.

Using the classic formula of scrap paper and soft pencils, we started to sketch away, and by the time we reached London we knew what we needed; it was up to Stuart to get someone else to agree. We wanted a mid-engined car, to use as many Ford parts as already existed, and it was to be a pure competition car. If the rules said that a minimum production run was necessary — well, that wasn't our problem that day. At first we were only interested in the first two or three cars, and we would use them as prototypes until we proved something.

You could only get approval for that sort of scheme in a company as committed as Ford, and probably only a Stuart Turner could have talked his way to getting it. When you consider that the germ of the idea came before the World Cup Rally, in which something like £100,000 was tied up, it was a miracle. After we had won the World Cup, of course, I think Walter Hayes would have approved almost anything!

Stuart got Len Bailey to design the car. Len was retained by Ford, and had had much to do with the GT40s and the Ford 3-litre sports-racing prototypes, but he had never designed a rally car. Len still does a lot of work for Boreham, and much of it is successful, but I think it was asking too much of him to design a car to win rallies at a time when he knew very little about them.

It didn't help that Ford were anxious at that time to promote their integrated European image, so that the first cars were given the German V-6 engines in 2.6-litre form. It was a very odd size indeed when it came to competition classes, and even the Germans didn't know an awful lot about their engine's potential.

The team drivers were invited to be closely involved in the parts that affected them, which really meant pedal layouts, instruments, switches and seating, and we thought we had done a job until we came to drive the first cars. After that we had to withstand a lot of ribbing, because one of the first things we asked to be changed was the facia layout!

The first car took a long time to build (with the World Cup Rally imminent we had other things to worry about) but by the end of the year it was nearly ready to run, and we needed something to cheer us up after that disastrous RAC Rally when all the team cars went out with broken transmissions. Somehow, the secrecy had been well-kept right up to the end; nobody knew anything about the project until then, only a few discreet words having leaked out to keep the opposition guessing.

The GT70's reception when it was announced in January 1971 was very favourable. One car was finished and another three started — all with chassis built by Maurice Gomm's workshops in Old Woking — and we were looking forward to some good sport during the summer, but two things made a nonsense of the project. One was the nine-week Ford strike, which hit us immediately after the car was announced, and the other was even more basic — the new car was a pig! As completed, it handled very badly, and there was obviously a lot to be done to make a proper rally car out of it.

The basic difficulty we had early that year was that the strike caused financial chaos, and everybody's budgets were slashed to the bone. Boreham more or less stopped rallying for months, and it meant that there was very little money to spare for advanced projects like GT70. If Ford were to justify themselves in competitions they had to win right then, not later, and the GT70 had to take a back seat.

The car didn't do an event until September, when I was asked to try the third prototype on the French *Ronde Cevenole* — a sort of racing rally in the south of France, where a single long special stage or circuit was used, with a 'pit stop' control every time round. I didn't need a navigator, because I knew the circuit well, and the regulations allowed me to drive alone. But against things like the hottest Alpines and the CG-Simca prototypes the car still wasn't competitive, and eventually I retired after a couple of push-rods in the German V-6 engine had broken, and one of the suspension members had pulled away from the chassis.

Apart from the gearbox, which was a ZF in unit with the axle (the same as the GT40 used), most of the mechanical parts were Ford, including the engine, steering and brakes, and all of them were covered by a lightweight glass-fibre coupe body that almost any little shop could have built in the numbers needed. The chassis was all straight lines, sheet steel and a few tubes, and again was something that could have been built adequately in small quantities by a company like Lola or Lotus, but not by Ford.

One item in the rather impossible brief to Len Bailey was that the car had to be strong enough to win rallies, and light enough to win races! It also had to be capable of accepting a whole range of different engines, including our 16-valve BDA.

The original thinking was that if the prototypes were successful, somehow, somewhere, in Ford we would build a small number to achieve homologation. It is just possible that the job could have been done at AVO (Advanced Vehicle Operations), which was opening up at Aveley, but really I doubt whether there was any way that the Ford system could have coped with such a specialised job. Ford was geared to building many thousands of the same sort of thing, and hundreds would probably have puzzled them. They certainly couldn't have coped with small numbers of a relatively complex little chassis, and they would also have had to farm out the glass-fibre body.

It hadn't proved a very successful project, right from the start, and the GT70 became one of those cars for which we couldn't raise a lot of interest. After the 1971 budget cuts the mechanics were feeling a bit depressed, and the mid-engined Ford was relegated to being one of those third-line priorities that could only be tackled when time permitted.

Gerry Birrell and I did quite a bit of development testing, he for circuit racing and myself at Bagshot for rough-road work. There's no doubt about it, the strength was there, but that meant weight (it was, after all, a platform-type chassis) which didn't do much for the performance. But the handling wasn't up to much to start with, and I had a lot of aggro with brakes on the *Ronde Cevenole*. We could have improved it, and we *would* have improved it, if the RS1600 hadn't been so good in most events. With no preoccupations with other cars, a couple of mechanics and just one driver ordered to make the damned thing work would have done the job; as it was, the GT70 was a camel, a real camel.

After a year we ditched it, and it never did a single event in Britain. Possibly it's one of the few blind alleys Stuart has been dragged up in the competitions business. Later, much later, one of the prototypes was given a BDA engine, which did great things for the handling, and later still the last three cars were shipped off to Ford in South Africa, who were threatening to make and sell a few more. I'll believe that when I see it.

It's interesting that Lancia's Stratos was hatched at about the same time, and that Lancia now seem to be winning everything with their works-built cars. But isn't it also interesting that they can't sell many to the public as road cars; as I write this I'm not at all convinced they've sold enough of them yet to guarantee homologation.

Times have changed so much since the GT70 was conceived that I can't see Ford ever trying anything similar again. Stuart and his men are still convinced that there's quite a long way to go with the Escort, if only they can find the time, and with only two of us in team cars this year, there ought to be the time.

I don't think we need to do anything about the handling, because the Escort is a very forgiving car. You can really get away with murder in an Escort, in fact I'd like to see a few of the British rallying heroes put into something vicious like a Porsche to experience the difference. Going downhill in an Escort, for instance, is really very restful. You can get the car way out of line, lock up the brakes, and make all sorts of brave manoeuvres, and after a bit of wrestling you can get it all back into shape for the next corner. Try that in a Porsche and you'd swop ends very smartly indeed.

Traction is another story. We are stuck with the limitations of a beam axle, and a rather heavy one at that, and of course there isn't as much weight over the back wheels as we could use. We have a very effective limited-slip diff, but there may still be ways of getting some more of that lovely power down on to the road. In forestry events, I don't stand to gain much from the coil-spring set-up with more precise axle control, for reasons already described, though on tarmac rallies the gain is probably there for the taking.

Personally, I am also convinced that we have nothing to gain from using larger wheels, either. The works team tried 15-inch wheels and new Dunlop tyres on the 1974 RAC Rally, and quite frankly I thought they were a failure. My 'off' in Dovey on the first night was a result of using them, and this probably cost me a certain place in the top three.

I believe in testing any new development thoroughly before we ever try it in a rally, and it's always advisable to try things out in a minor event before committing the team to changes in anything important. We were dragged into the 15-inch tyre situation by the over-enthusiasm of Timo and Hannu, who later also became unconvinced about the results.

A couple of years ago, more likely three, we were scratching our heads and wondering how we could improve the Escort's traction. We couldn't improve weight distribution because we were committed to

236

running Group Two cars, where most things have to be in the same places as designed. One theory was to try larger wheels, but it *was* only a theory. A 15-inch wheel sometimes has a larger contact patch than a 13-inch wheel, and since Timo and Hannu were always enthusing about the traction of their native Volvos and Saabs we thought we ought to give the idea a whirl.

In the middle of other tyre testing at Bagshot we put on a gash set of 15-inch Minilites and Dunlops, then carried out some simple traction testing. From these very rough trials we thought there was a chance of progress. We didn't change axle ratios, though there was an eight per cent difference, because in the loose an Escort is in wheelspin so much of the time that accurate gearing doesn't matter that much.

That was in 1973, but the next thing was that the Finns wanted higher gearing and more grip for the Thousand Lakes. They took out two Escorts for practice, with locally-made *cross-ply* tyres, and came back with the story that the big wheels were worth up to two seconds a kilometre. Once Timo gets a development idea firmly in his mind, and it looks promising, we all have to try it, even if it's to convince him that he's misguided, so the outcome was that we all sat down round a table to design a new Dunlop rally tyre. Jeremy Ferguson and his men at Dunlop were very helpful, and within weeks they produced a 15-inch cross-ply tyre with the M & S tread pattern.

In the meantime I was busy at Bagshot, doing back-to-back tests for traction and handling with all sorts of rubber. But I was beginning to have serious doubts, because every time I tried, the fastest tyre was the good old 13-inch M & S with its 6-inch rim width. Worse, the handling wasn't nearly as good on the 15-inch tyres, because the suspension hadn't been altered, and the larger-diameter wheels made the steering heavier. The car was unstable and the geometry was different, and the big thing that surprised us was that we didn't get any better traction, no matter what we tried.

Timo then arrived in England before the RAC Rally, tried the cars and got nearer to a competitive time with 15-inch wheels, although he still couldn't quite match it. But he wasn't dismayed: "I've tried big wheels on a rally and I *know* they work. Forget these tests, and don't trust Bagshot, they will be better on the RAC". I could only say, "OK, you've tried them in Finland, so we've got to be guided by you, or at least we've got to give the new tyres a fair chance".

So we agreed to start the whole team in the RAC Rally on 15-inch

237

wheels. We completed the first day, and went into the first night in Wales, and I must say I was never happy, whenever we needed knobblies. I certainly wasn't in contention for the lead, and I couldn't get to grips with the car at all. My accident in Dovey was caused because I arrived at one particular hairpin not as much in control as I should have been, purely due to the car's handling, and we went off into soft ground.

As soon as I could (which wasn't for hours because of the supply situation) I asked to go back on to my old tyres, and immediately I was the fastest Escort. The I went back on to 15-inch wheels to check, and was slower, before returning to 13-inch wheels for the rest of the rally; as soon as Timo and Henry saw the times they also changed back on to the old equipment, and they won the rally like that.

Incidentally, it is quite true that at one point a hurried service resulted in Timo's car doing several stages with big wheels on one side of the car and 13-inch wheels on the other; nobody noticed until Timo wandered round the car and found out for himself!

Although we had abandoned the big wheels well before half-way, to help the advertising people both Timo and I were asked to fit them again to drive from Flamingo Park to the finish at York.

After all the rigmarole the situation might have seemed confused, but as far as I was concerned I was completely convinced that this experiment was a loser. Stuart spent thousands of pounds on new wheels — I think it was £5,000 — there was a new mould from Dunlop for the tyres, and personally I don't want to see them again.

Another way to improve performance would be to lose some weight (I mean from the car — I think I would find it difficult to lose a lot, personally!) but we've been fighting a losing battle on this with Escorts for years. Every time we fit essential things like fire-extinguishing systems, full roll-cages and beefier gearboxes we seem to lose, and I am sure the new re-styled car hasn't helped matters, either.

Stuart has a theory that we can still save quite a lot of weight by using more exotic materials for our various special fittings. It's all a question of economics, of course. Two or three years ago there was a fairly quick turnover of works cars from Boreham — we would only do two or three rallies with a new car before it was sold off to some deserving private owner at a very reasonable price. But times are hard now, and in view of what we know about the Escort's built-in strength we will probably be using fewer new cars for much longer periods. As Stuart has pointed out, this could mean more costly things like roll-cages in exotic alloys, which would pay for themselves in time, and more attention to sump guards and things.

I would like to see improvements to our optional gearbox. The big ZF is still bomb-proof, but it changes like a truck, and if only we could get some time out of the change we would have faster cars. This is purely arithmetical — save a quarter of a second in 100 changes on a long stage, and you have a bonus of 25 more 'driving seconds' to push the car along. It would also mean that important extra time with both hands controlling the steering, though I tend to be a 'hand-on-gear-lever man all the time these days — one-handed steering at those speeds!

Engine power — well, I don't know. We knew there's still a lot of power inside the BDA, because the few competitive Formula Two engines prove it. Brian Hart has built screamers with up to 280 or 290 bhp from the same 1,977 cc block that we use to go rallying. I wouldn't like to have an engine exactly like that in my rally cars (up to 7,000 rpm we have more power and torque anyway), but this proves that there is more to come.

Perhaps we have been a bit lazy at Boreham since 1973 because the only time an Escort is occasionally beaten for pace is by a Porsche Carrera or a Lancia Stratos on tarmac rallies. We still have a very tractable unit, even though it produces nearly twice as much power as the standard product; often I don't bother to change down if I can get out of a corner at 5,000 rpm in the higher gear, even though we can use over 9,000 rpm, and the only way to get more steam will be to give away something on temperament. On the other hand, the new cars would be so much easier to drive if we could get even more mid-range torque without losing out anywhere else.

The sort of motor sport I intend to do in the future is not likely to change much. Though naturally I enjoyed the Tour of Britain (sorry, the Avon-*Motor* Tour, and now the Texaco Tour — we must never ignore the sponsors) I don't think I could ever become committed to circuit racing. From time to time I dabble in saloon racing (one of my last outings was in one of Stan's Uniflo Alfa Romeos in the TT) but I soon get bored with the same corners and the same situations turning up every other minute.

As far as rallying is concerned, nobody, not even with a lot of money, would ever tempt me to tackle road rallying again. The last event I did with any element of public-road speed would be the Mintex Dales that introduced me to Tony Mason, but I don't want to repeat the sensation, thank you. In spite of what the die-hards have to say (funnily enough, the ones who shout loudest don't seem to do much driving themselves) I don't see the value of open-road driving as a training to anything else, and there's such an element of danger to it now that I just don't want to know.

When I started my Esso programme back in 1972, a lot of people accused me of pot-hunting, and I must say that for a time it was very easy to win the Nationals. I still wouldn't like to stick my neck out and nominate a driver to take over where I leave off, but there are many more in a competitive fighting situation now than there were then.

One reason for this, I'm sure, is that there are so many more competitive cars about. In 1972, as we continued to improve the Escorts, my car was usually a lot quicker than any of the others, but that doesn't apply any more. First it was Clark & Simpson who got a 2-litre replicar, then Barry Lee, then others. Actually, in 1972, 'Old Gold' might have been the quickest Escort around, but it certainly wasn't the best. It was tired, loose and creaky, and that first bodyshell wasn't even square after all those shunts!

In the past Ford have tended to sell rally team cars when they were still fairly new, so as soon as the 2-litre aluminium engines were on stream at Boreham they began filtering down into the British rallying circus. But that isn't the whole story. Mick Jones told me, quite some time ago, that Boreham must have supplied at least 30 complete Mark 1 Escort rally car kits — that includes everything from a Brian Hart engine to the ZF gearbox, the Atlas axle, body items, Bilsteins, in fact everything that my RAC Rally Championship car had.

There has been nothing very special, nothing unique, no secret parts, and no underhand wizardry in Timo's cars or mine. There simply isn't any excuse any more for any private owner to complain of having an inferior car. No excuse, that is, if their cheque book will stand the strain. The going rate for a completely new, professionally-built Escort rally car, in 1975, is around £10,000.

Now that I think of it, this makes the prices people pay for Porsche Carreras look a lot more reasonable after all. But why shouldn't I put in a good word for Porsches anyway? After all, they help to pay the rent at my garage in Narborough!

People often ask me if I am bored with all this forestry rallying? Or will I soon give up because there is so much of the same sort of driving? The short, sharp, decisive answer is "No", and I don't have to make any compromises to convince myself. On the other hand, if I decide that I'm getting slower, past it, over the hill, call it what you like, then I will certainly stop. Just like that, without regrets, because there is no place in rallying for a second-best Clark.

I don't know for sure how I will know, though I suppose the results will tell me soon enough. Ian Appleyard once said that he knew it was time for him to stop when he started to notice the big drops over the edge and began to think about the danger — that probably sums it up.

I certainly will not carry on rallying just for the money. I don't even go rallying for the money today — I can think of better ways of turning over pound notes without getting so tired. There *is* good money to be made, by anyone who is good enough and dedicated enough, and I am very grateful for the rewards motor sport has brought me, but I have also enjoyed my rallying without any. When we lost the Esso Uniflo backing early in 1975, at very short notice, it meant that my own programme was quite seriously out of balance. There was just no way that we could make ends meet without alternative help. Even so I was quite content, temporarily, to carry on until some substitute could be found.

Rallying, like top-grade motor racing, or almost every other competitive sport, is something where success cannot be had without almost total dedication. People and teams have burst into rallying flourishing lots of money and the best in cars, but without enough talent to be sure of getting into the money. I am much more impressed by the impoverished private owners who scrape together some sort of a car and manage to appear; if they are good enough the successes, and the backing, will follow.

The one thing I sometimes regret is that I haven't done much in other than Ford cars in recent years. Quite frankly this is because Ford have usually had the best equipment, and I do like to leave the start with as much chance as anyone else! But there have been times when we have been beaten by Porsches, Alpines or Lancias, and I have wondered, just briefly, just how much easier it must be to have a go in a car with more traction.

The Alpine-Renault we prepared a couple of years back wasn't a particularly good car, especially because of the spares problem, but what really impressed me was the lightness, and the way most of the power got itself down on to the ground.

Four years ago, when I decided to do a lot more rallying at home, and was derided for becoming senile and a pot-hunter, what actually happened was that I was able to bring some much-needed new promotion to the sport, and the standard of events, cars and drivers has risen rapidly since then. Previously the *Motoring News* road-rallying series had definitely been the most significant contest, but now there's no doubt at all which one matters. The *Motoring News* is finished as an important series, and factory team managers now attach great importance to the RAC series; not only do they watch for outstanding performances, but they enter team cars of their own. The RAC series is now very highly regarded, and is almost as important to rallying as the French Internationals, which mean so much in that country.

The standard of driving is up, but I regret that I still cannot pick out any brave young blood who is sure to dominate forestry rallying in the next few years. I seem to have the most enjoyable fights with Billy Coleman and Russell Brookes, both of whom have cars identical to my Cossack machine. Billy goes very well indeed when his Irish donkey is awake and standing up, but there have been occasions when he has suddenly slowed down and stopped worrying me at all.

Russell Brookes is in a rather strange position. He is in one of the most successful rallying Fords, yet he works for British Leyland. Some clash of loyalties there, I would have thought. Russell is the Ford pilot who has given me the most trouble in 1975. Apart from these two, a surprising number of drivers have shone briefly, or had their day on one event (usually near their homes), but nobody else has emerged.

The Kleber Rally Scholarship has failed in its purpose, except that it has given publicity to deserving cases — both Chris Sclater and Jimmy Rae found themselves short of money before their seasons finished, and Andy Dawson actually ran out of competition parts for his free Datsun.

Tony Fall predicted great things for Tony Pond when he joined DOT, the Dealer Opel Team, but apart from a good win in the Avon-*Motor* Tour (in a Ford — what else?) he has no other successes to boast about so far, although it will be interesting to see what he makes of the Triumph TR7 now that he has joined Leyland for 1976.

Stuart Turner's opinion is that there is no single outstanding young driver at the moment but that, like Jody Scheckter in Grand Prix racing, there might be someone lurking around in autotests or autocross who could suddenly burst among us and make us all look slow.

What encourages me is that whereas ten years ago British rallying was a rather grubby, hole-in-corner game for disorganised crews, it is now big business. If you count the spectators who watch the major events it is quite clear that rallying is no longer a minority sport. The cars look good, the trade and industry is happy to be associated with them, and there is that exciting air of professionalism around.

The bigoted motoring writers who suggest that rallying is like a destruction derby with a small and declining number of friends, or who liken participants to football hooligans or vandals, are either joking in very bad taste or haven't even been to look. At least the rallying fraternity haven't descended to forming their own trade unions, like the racing crowd, and running events their own way (or they won't play) and we certainly don't stop work if it comes on to rain.

One famous pre-war racing driver said that he took up motor sport as it was the only exciting one he could find where the participants sat down all the time. It doesn't stop the whole business being highly exciting, demanding and satisfying.

Unless something desperate happens like petrol rationing, the mass-bankruptcy of the motor trade, or revolutionaries taking over the country, rallying is where I'll be. If I'm lucky I will still be winning. Perhaps going sideways *is* fastest after all!

Appendix 1

What goes into a winning Escort?

Engines

I thought it would be interesting to find out some accurate engine power figures for our Escorts, which Boreham have supplied. They warn me that there are minor differences in testing procedures — the Twin-Cam engines were tested by taking the drive through a gearbox, and with an open exhaust system, while the later engines were tested without the gearbox but with a car exhaust system in use.

The best 1,600 cc Twin-Cam we ever had produced about 150 bhp at 7,500 rpm.

The best 1,800 cc Twin-Cam produced about 175 bhp.

For 1971, the de-tuned 1,800 cc Twin-Cams used in the Safari produced only 155 bhp at 7,000 rpm.

The best 1,800 cc BDA engine (for Mikkola in the 1972 Olympic Rally) produced 206 bhp at 7,400 rpm.

The 1,800 cc BDA engine used to win the Safari in 1972 produced 203 bhp at 8,000 rpm.

The best 1,977 cc BDA rally engines we use produce 244 bhp at 8,000 rpm.

Transmissions

These are the alternative ratios for a Group Two Escort:

Gearboxes: Standard   1.00, 1.40, 2.01, 2.97 to 1
              Bullet   1.00, 1.28, 1.70, 2.30 to 1
              ZF Safari   1.00, 1.26, 1.76, 2.40, 3.85 to 1
              ZF normal 1.00, 1.14, 1.36, 1.80, 2.30 to 1

Axle ratios: 5.1 to 1 is normal. Alternatives are 5.3, 4.9, 4.6, 4.3,

4.1, and much higher ratios for touring Capris.

Brakes

Front discs are 10-inch diameter, ventilated.

Rear discs are 10-inch diameter.

Suspension

For rallying, the standard rear suspension is altered. Leaf springs are retained, but a twin, parallel-arm, radius-arm linkage is added to give complete axle movement control. There is no Panhard rod sideways location, except on the latest 'tarmac' cars.

Steering

A high-ratio rack, with 2.2 turns from lock to lock, is used (standard is 3 turns lock to lock).

Bodyshell

Apart from precautionary checks and seam-welding, rally cars also have a rear damper turret kit, oil tank supports, rear suspension radius arm supports, re-shaped gearbox tunnel to allow fitment of ZF gearboxes, re-shaped gearbox tunnel to allow fitment of ZF gearbox extension, front and rear wing 'eye-brow' extensions to give clearance for wide tyres, and many other details.

With eyebrows fitted, the car is approximately 5ft 6in wide.

Ground clearance

Surprisingly, this is only 6 inches, though somehow the cars look higher. The measurement is taken under the sump shield. Experience has shown that although the car could be raised higher, handling then suffers.

Weight

I said there were no secret lightening tricks. An average RS rally car in 1974 weighed 2,265 lb (1,027 kg). This is quite a lot heavier than the standard car, which weighed 1,920 lb (870 kg).

How long does it take to build one?

From a Gomm-prepared bodyshell, with all modifications completed, something like 250 to 260 man-hours.

However, this does not include the time taken to modify the bodyshell, paint the completed car, build the gearbox, build and power-test the engine, build and check the axle, and build other items like oil and petrol tanks and wiring looms.

Appendix 2

LVX 942J — a very special friend

At the start of my Esso rallying programme, we used the original 'Old Gold' Escort, while Norman Masters set about building me a completely new RS1600. This was the famous blue-and-white Esso car which brought me so much success.

Mechanically and structurally it was nearly identical with 'Old Gold', though we soon grafted a 2-litre engine into it. I used it almost continuously from June 1972 to October 1973. Here was its record during that time:

Date	Event	Crew	
June 1972	Scottish	Clark/Porter	2nd overall. Mikkola beat me narrowly in an identical Escort
June 1972	Jim Clark	Clark/Porter	1st overall. This was the first appearance of the 2-litre RS engine
Sept. 1972	Burmah	Clark/Porter	1st overall
Sept. 1972	Manx	Clark/Porter	1st overall
Oct. 1972	Lindisfarne	Clark/Porter	Retired — we lost a wheel on a stage, plus vital bits!
Oct. 1972	I took it round Boreham proving ground while making the Esso film, and succeeded in rolling it in front of the cameras.		

No, we didn't use that shot in 'Our Man Clark'! Norman Masters then rebuilt the car around a new bodyshell, and fitted the alloy-blocked 2-litre RS engine.

Nov. 1972	RAC	Clark/Mason	1st overall. We led all the way and beat Stig Blomqvist's Saab. (He had won in 1971)
Feb. 1973	Snowman	Clark/Porter	1st overall
Feb. 1973	Mintex Dales	Clark/Porter	1st overall. Broken distributor drive on a stage, subsequently cancelled!
April 1973	Granite City	Clark/Porter	1st overall
May 1973	Welsh	Clark/Porter	1st overall
June 1973	Scottish	Clark/Porter	1st overall. My fifth on the Scottish
June 1973	Jim Clark	Clark/Mason	1st overall
July 1973	Hackle	Clark/Porter	1st overall
Sept. 1973	Burmah	Clark/Porter	1st overall
Sept. 1973	Manx	Clark/Porter	Retired — detached engine crankshaft pulley

After this the car was retired as I was to have a new car for the 1973 RAC Rally (my 1974 Esso car — OOO 96M). LVX 942J was sold to Adrian Boyd, who entered it for the 1973 RAC Rally and promptly shortened the body by several inches by hitting a very solid bank!

Appendix 3

Roger Clark rallying record — 1961 to 1975

Date	Rally Grade	Event	Co-driver	Car	Result	Notes
1961						
Mar.	I	Circuit of Ireland	J. Porter	Renault Dauphine	51st Class 12th	First ever National or International
Nov.	I	RAC	J. Porter J. Oldham	850 Mini	52nd	
1962						
April	I	Circuit of Ireland	J. Porter	Mini-Cooper	4th Class 1st	First run in a Mini-Cooper (the original 2 ANR) Winner: P. Hopkirk
June	I	Scottish	R. Marriott	Mini-Cooper	Nowhere	2nd overall until late navigational error
Sept.	N	London	J. Porter	Mini-Cooper	14th	
Nov.	I	RAC	J. Porter	Mini-Cooper	Retired	

(In 1962 Clark and Porter also won their first big trophies — the East Midlands Association Rally Championship)

Date	Rally Grade	Event	Co-driver	Car	Result	Notes
1963						
Mar.	N	Express and Star	J. Porter	Mini-Cooper	Retired	Drive-shaft failure
April	N	Birmingham Post	J. Porter	Mini-Cooper	Retired	Lost transmission plug

April	I	Circuit of Ireland	J. Porter	Mini-Cooper	Retired	Clutch failure
April	I	Tulip Rally	J. Oldham	Mini-Cooper	Retired	First ever Continental event
June	I	Scottish	H. Patton	Mini-Cooper	2nd	Winner: A. Cowan
June	I	Coupe des Alpes	R. Aston	Reliant Sabre Six	6th GT Class 2nd	First ever works drive
Sept.	I	Liege-Sofia-Liege	B. Culcheth	Triumph TR4	Retired	Fractured exhaust, then seized gearbox
Nov.	I	RAC	J. Porter	Mini-Cooper	Retired	Gearbox failure
1964						
Jan.	N	Welsh	J. Porter	Mini-Cooper	Retired	Gearbox failure
Mar.	N	Express and Star	J. Porter	Cortina GT	3rd	First event in Cortina GT
Mar.	I	Circuit of Ireland	J. Porter	Cortina GT	Retired	Dynamo failure
May	I	Acropolis	R. Martin-Hurst	Rover 3-litre	9th	Semi-works drive — Clark co-driving
May	I	Scottish	J. Porter	Cortina GT	1st	First ever International win
June	I	Coupe des Alpes	J. Syer	Rover 2000	Retired	Axle failure
Sept.	N	Rally of the Vales	J. Porter	Cortina GT	20th	
Sept.	I	Liege-Sofia-Liege	B. Culcheth	Rover 2000	Retired	Engine (after gearbox failure)
Sept.	N	Gulf London	J. Porter	Cortina GT	Retired	Accident and bad handling
Nov.	I	RAC	J. Porter	Rover 2000	Retired	Engine failure
1965						
Jan.	I	Welsh	J. Porter	Cortina GT	Retired	Broken spring
Jan.	I	Monte Carlo	J. Porter	Rover 2000	6th Class 1st	

Mar.	N	Express and Star	J. Porter	Rover 2000	Retired	Diff. failure
April	I	Circuit of Ireland	J. Porter	Cortina GT	3rd	Winner: P. Hopkirk
April	I	Tulip	B. Melia	Cortina GT	Retired	Engine and electrics; first Ford works drive
May	I	Acropolis	J. Porter	Rover 2000	Retired	Accident
June	I	Scottish	J. Porter	Cortina GT	1st	
June	I	Gulf London	J. Porter	Cortina GT	1st	
July	I	Coupe des Alpes	J. Porter	Rover 2000	10th	
Nov.	I	RAC	J. Porter	Rover 2000	14th Class 2nd	
Dec.	I	Welsh	G. Robson	Lotus-Cortina	1st	First rally in Lotus-Cortina

(In 1965 Clark was RAC Rally Champion for the first time)

1966

Jan.	I	Monte Carlo	B. Melia	Lotus-Cortina	Disqualified	Lights controversey, otherwise 4th
April	I	Circuit of Ireland	J. Porter	Lotus-Cortina	Retired	Oil pump failed when leading
May	I	Shell 4000	R. Edwardes	Lotus-Cortina	3rd	
May	I	Acropolis	B. Melia	Lotus-Cortina	2nd	
June	I	Scottish	B. Melia	Lotus-Cortina	Retired	Diff. failure
June	I	Gulf-London	J. Porter	Lotus-Cortina	Retired	Diff. failure when leading
Aug.	I	Polish	B. Melia	Lotus-Cortina	4th	
Aug.	I	1000 Lakes	B. Melia	Lotus-Cortina	19th	

250

Sept.	I	Coupe des Alpes	B. Melia	Lotus-Cortina	2nd	
Nov.	I	RAC	J. Porter	Lotus-Cortina	Retired	Accident when leading
Dec.	I	Welsh	J. Porter	Lotus-Cortina	Retired	Accident
1967						
Jan.	I	Monte Carlo	J. Porter	Ford Taunus 20M	67th	22nd on scratch times before Group 2 handicap
Mar.	I	East African Safari	G. Staepelaere	Lotus-Cortina	Nowhere	Structural battering
May	I	Shell 4000	J. Peters	Lotus-Cortina Mk 2	1st	
June	I	Scottish	J. Porter	Lotus-Cortina Mk 2	1st	
June	I	Gulf London	J. Porter	Lotus-Cortina Mk 2	Retired	Broken engine oil pipe
1968						
Jan.	I	Swedish	J. Porter	Lotus-Cortina Mk 2	Retired	Driver unwell
April	I	Circuit of Ireland	J. Porter	Escort Twin-Cam	1st	First time in Escort, first win for Escort
April	I	Tulip	J. Porter	Escort Twin-Cam	1st	First big Continental win
May	I	Acropolis	J. Porter	Escort Twin-Cam	1st	
June	I	Scottish	J. Porter	Escort Twin-Cam	1st	
Sept.	I	Coupe des Alpes	J. Porter	Escort Twin-Cam	Retired	Accident. Recce with FVA 16-valve engine, not used in event

251

Nov./ Dec.	I	London- Sydney Marathon	O. Andersson	Lotus- Cortina	10th	Led all way, until engine and axle trouble on last day

1969

Mar.	I	San Remo	J. Porter	Escort Twin-Cam	10th	
April	I	Circuit of Ireland	J. Porter	Escort Twin-Cam	1st	With 1800 cc engine
May	I	Acropolis	J. Porter	Escort Twin-Cam	2nd	Winner: Toivonen's Porsche
June	I	Scottish	J. Porter	Escort Twin-Cam	Retired	Broken suspension strut
Sept.	I	Coupe des Alpes	J. Porter	Escort V-6 2.3-litre	Retired	Overheating
Oct.	I	Three Cities	J. Porter	Zodiac Mk 4	16th Class 1st	
Nov.	I	RAC	J. Porter	Escort Twin-Cam	6th	

1970

Jan.	I	Smile, Finland	C. Freud	Escort Twin-Cam	5th	
Jan.	I	Monte Carlo	J. Porter	Escort Twin-Cam	5th Class 1st	
Mar.	I	Circuit of Ireland	J. Porter	Escort RS1600	1st	First run and win for BDA 16-valve engine
May	I	London- Mexico World Cup	A. Poole	Escort 1800	Retired	Accident when not driving
June	I	Scottish	J. Porter	Escort RS1600	Retired	Engine failure when leading
Sept.	I	Jamaica 1000		Cortina GT	Retired	Navigator trouble, lost!
Oct.	I	TAP	J. Porter	Escort RS1600	Retired	Engine failure
Nov.	I	RAC	J. Porter	Escort RS1600	Retired	Half-shaft failure

252

1971						
April	I	East African Safari	G. Staepelaere	Escort Twin-Cam	Retired	Structural failure
April	N	Granite City	H. Cardno	Escort RS1600	1st	
May	I	Welsh	G. Phillips	Escort RS1600	Retired	Diff. failure
July	N	Hackle	J. Porter	Escort RS1600	1st	
Sept.	I	Ronde Cevenole		GT70	Retired	Engine failure
Sept.	N	Manx	H. Liddon	Escort RS1600	1st	
Nov.	I	RAC	J. Porter	Escort RS1600	11th	
1972						
Jan.	N	Snowman	H. Cardno	Escort RS1600	Retired	Accident
Feb.	N	Seven Dales	A. Mason	Escort RS1600	1st	
Feb.	I	Hong Kong	J. Porter	Escort RS1600	2nd	Winner: Makinen in identical car
April	N	Granite City	J. Porter	Escort RS1600	1st	
May	I	Welsh	J. Porter	Escort RS1600	1st	
June	I	Scottish	J. Porter	Escort RS1600	2nd	Winner: Mikkola in identical car
June	N	Jim Clark	J. Porter	Escort RS1600	1st	First run and win with alloy-block 2-litre engine
Sept.	N	Burmah	J. Porter	Escort RS1600	1st	
Sept.	I	Manx	J. Porter	Escort RS1600	1st	
Oct.	N	Lindisfarne	J. Porter	Escort RS1600	Retired	Wheel off

253

Oct.	N	Dukeries	J. Porter	Escort RS1600	1st	
Nov.	N	Hackle	J. Porter	Escort RS1600	1st	
Nov.	I	RAC	A. Mason	Escort RS1600	1st	

(Clark won the RAC Rally Championship in 1972)

1973

Feb.	N	Snowman	J. Porter	Escort RS1600	1st	
Feb.	N	Mintex Dales	J. Porter	Escort RS1600	1st	
April	I	East African Safari	J. Porter	Escort RS1600	Retired	Burnt out wiring, leading at half-way
April	N	Granite City	J. Porter	Escort RS1600	1st	
May	I	Welsh	J. Porter	Escort RS1600	1st	
June	I	Scottish	J. Porter	Escort RS1600	1st	
June	N	Jim Clark	A. Mason	Escort RS1600	1st	
July	I	Tour of Britain	A. Mason	Capri 3-litre	Retired	After electrics failure at Oulton Park
July	N	Hackle	J. Porter	Escort RS1600	1st	
Sept.	N	Burmah	J. Porter	Escort RS1600	1st	
Sept.	I	Manx	J. Porter	Escort RS1600	Retired	Engine failure
Sept.	N	Dukeries	J. Porter	Escort RS1600	1st	
Oct.	N	Lindisfarne	J. Porter	Escort RS1600	1st	
Nov.	I	RAC	A. Mason	Escort RS1600	2nd	Winner: Makinen in identical car

(Clark won the RAC Rally Championship in 1973)

254

1974

May	I	Welsh	J. Porter	Escort RS1600	Retired	Blown head gasket
uly	N	Jim Clark	J. Porter	Escort RS1600	1st	
uly	I	Tour of Britain	J. Porter	Escort RS2000	1st	
Aug.	N	Burmah	J. Porter	Escort RS1600	41st	Won on stages, but timing error at finish
Aug.	I	Total	A. Mason	Escort RS1600	Retired	Clutch failure
ept.	I	Manx	J. Porter	Escort RS1600	3rd	Behind two Porsches
ept.	N	Dukeries	J. Porter	Escort RS1600	Retired	Mechanic crashed regular car before start, replacement blew up
ct.	N	Lindisfarne	J. Porter	Escort RS1600	1st	
lov.	I	RAC	A. Mason	Escort RS1600	7th	From 38th after an 'off' on first day

975

eb.	N	Mintex Dales	J. Porter	Escort RS1600	Retired	Blown engine
Mar.	I	Circuit of Ireland	J. Porter	Escort RS1600	Retired	Blown engine
pril	N	Granite City	J. Porter	Escort 2 RS1800	1st	First event for Mk 2 car
lay	I	Welsh	J. Porter	Escort 2 RS1800	1st	First event with Cossack
ne	I	Scottish	J. Porter	Escort 2 RS1800	1st	
ne	I	Antibes	J. Porter	Escort 2 RS1800	Retired	Suspension failure
ly	N	Jim Clark	J. Porter	Escort 2 RS1800	Retired	Accident hit a sheep!
ug.	I	South African Total	S. Pegg	Escort 2 RS1800	1st	

255

Aug.	N	Burmah	J. Porter	Escort 2 RS1800	1st	
Sept.	I	Manx	J. Porter	Escort 2 RS1800	1st	
Oct.	I	San Remo	J. Porter	Escort 2 RS1800	Retired	Ran out of tyres
Oct.	N	Lindisfarne	J. Porter	Escort 2 RS1800	1st	
Nov.	I	RAC	A. Mason	Escort 2 RS1800	2nd	

(Clark won the RAC Rally Championship in 1975)